LETTERS FROM HEAVEN

A Devotional Guide Through Revelation

Dr. Joseph Davis

Renown

Copyright © 2024 by **Joseph Davis**

All rights reserved. No part of this publication may be reproduced, distributed, or transmitted in any form or by any means, without prior written permission.

Scripture taken from The Holy Bible, English Standard Version ® (ESV®) © 2001 by Crossway, a publishing ministry of Good News Publishers. All rights reserved. ESV Text Edition: 2016. Used by permission.

Renown Publishing
www.renownpublishing.com

Letters from Heaven / Joseph Davis
ISBN-13: 978-1-960236-14-2

CONTENTS

Foreword by Rev. Pilgrim Benham 1
Intro to the Apocalypse 3
Greetings from Patmos 11
The Voice of Resurrection Jesus 19
Our First Love 29
Faith That Conquers 39
Two Sides to Jesus 47
The False God of Compromise 55
Signs of a Dying Church 65
A Letter to Philadelphia (Not the One in Pennsylvania) 73
A Self-Reliant Church Is a Useless Church 81
A Door to Heaven 89
Sunday Mornings in Heaven 97
The Kingdom Unsealed 105
A New Song in Heaven 113
Four Horsemen of Human History 123
Why, God? How Long? 131
The Wrath of the Lamb 139
Who Can Escape? (Part One) 147
Who Can Escape? (Part Two) 155
A Moment of Silence 163
Trumpets of Judgment (Part One) 171

Trumpets of Judgment (Part Two) 179
Trumpets of Judgment (Part Three): A World Controlled by Evil
.... 187
Trumpets of Judgment (Part Four): The Bittersweet Gospel .. 195
Trumpets of Judgment (Part Five): The Story of Two Witnesses
.... 203
Trumpets of Judgment (Part Six): A New Kind of Government
.... 213
The Woman vs. the Dragon 221
The Accuser Evicted and Bound 229
Waiting in the Wilderness 237
The Beast from the Sea 245
The Number of the Beast 253
The Lamb's Faithful Followers 263
Faithful Proclamation 271
Waiting on the Harvest 279
A Song of Anticipation 287
Wickedness Is Stubborn 295
Armageddon Celebration 303
The Great Prostitute 311
Who Was, Is, and Is Not 319
Come Out of Babylon 327
A Day of Mourning 335
The Greatest Party Ever 343
The Power of His Word 353
Authority in the Millennium 361
Gathering with Gog and Magog 371
The Great White Throne 381

A New Heaven and a New Earth	389
The Perfect Church	397
You Will Be Satisfied	407
The Last Prophecy	415
Cherished Words	423
About the Author	431
Notes	435

Foreword by Rev. Pilgrim Benham

Early in his life, Martin Luther didn't think much of the book we call "Revelation." Like many believers, Luther felt its enigmatic message was too overwhelming, confusing, or even irrelevant to decode. However, after several years (and deeper study), Luther said, "As we see here in this book [of Revelation], that through and beyond all plagues, beasts, and evil angels Christ is nonetheless with his saints, and wins the final victory."[1]

My friend Joe Davis is a faithful local pastor in the same community where I have pastored for many years. He has taken the time (and the challenge!) to unpack the powerful and plain truths of this apocalyptic book—and to showcase its central and abiding message. As you begin diving into each devotional chapter, you will learn that the final book in our Bibles has little to do with unlocking the secrets of the Antichrist or the Illuminati, but everything to do with the power and presence of Christ with his people.

In our fast-paced world, it's easy to get caught up in the busyness of life and neglect our spiritual well-being. However, carving out time each day to connect with God is essential for our spiritual health. Each chapter in this devotional book takes a small passage in Revelation and unpacks it with three helpful questions:

1. What would John's readers have noticed?

2. What was Jesus telling the church?

3. What is Jesus telling us today?

This outline gives us the exegetical observation, the biblical interpretation, and the practical application of every verse in Revelation, so the reader is informed, encouraged, and inspired to know and follow Christ in the midst of difficulty.

As you embark on this journey through *Letters from Heaven*, I invite you to approach each chapter with an open heart and a willingness to listen to what Jesus is saying through the power of his Word. May this devotional guide serve as a beacon of encouragement, illuminating the path before you and leading you into deeper intimacy with our Savior, Jesus Christ. May we together experience the blessing of Revelation 1:3: "Blessed is the one who reads aloud the words of this prophecy, and blessed are those who hear, and who keep what is written in it, for the time is near."

– Rev. Pilgrim Benham

CHAPTER ONE

Intro to the Apocalypse

Revelation 1:1–3:

> *¹ The revelation of Jesus Christ, which God gave him to show to his servants the things that must soon take place. He made it known by sending his angel to his servant John, ² who bore witness to the word of God and to the testimony of Jesus Christ, even to all that he saw. ³ Blessed is the one who reads aloud the words of this prophecy, and blessed are those who hear, and who keep what is written in it, for the time is near.*

For most readers, Revelation has been not only the most intriguing book in the Bible but also the most intimidating. Even though it's talked about a lot, in many ways it's also the most neglected by individual believers. Many are even afraid to read it for themselves. As a result, what most people know about Revelation is what others have told them—or worse, what they've happened to search online.

As a result, there's perhaps more innocent misunderstanding of Revelation than of any other book in the Bible. Many Christians can't resist the urge to correlate its images with current events and world news headlines. Some try to interpret its metaphors literally, while others approach the book as if it were a sudoku puzzle, concentrating on symbology. Some use it as inspiration for doomsday preparation, a manual for surviving an inevitable future global catastrophe.

Many have used Revelation to elevate themselves, claiming special prophetic insight to unlock its "hidden" secrets. The book has been mistakenly used to divide and splinter the church based on erroneous end-times interpretations.

When John wrote Revelation, he had a purpose and a message for the church. It was never his intention to fuel fears about the end times or take us on grand symbolic rabbit trails. So, what is the purpose? What John communicated to the early church is still relevant to us: reminders to keep following and not to give up, reminders that God is in control even in a world seemingly out of control. In addition, John painted a never-before-seen picture of Jesus, reflected in Revelation 1:1–2:

> *The revelation of Jesus Christ, which God gave him to show to his servants the things that must soon take place. He made it known by sending his angel to his servant John, [2] who bore witness to the word of God and to the testimony of Jesus Christ, even to all that he saw.*

WHAT WOULD JOHN'S READERS HAVE NOTICED?

The Church Needed Hope

When he wrote Revelation, the apostle John was at an advanced age, living in exile on an isolated island called Patmos around AD 90, during a time of severe Roman persecution of the church. That brutal assault would worsen over the coming centuries, as Satan attempted to wipe out the early church before it could take hold.

In the face of this intense suffering and persecution, Jesus knew His followers desperately needed assurance directly from heaven as they tried to live faithfully and wait for His return. Revelation was intended to comfort and inspire them during this tribulation.

Revelation wasn't a prediction of some coming tribulation. It was an explanation of the tribulation and suffering *they were already experiencing*! The early church read Revelation like a series of letters from heaven, revealing details of how God has worked, is working, and will work. John brilliantly interwove links to other parts of Scripture—Old and New Testament references to Jesus' arrival and return—with details and imagery designed to inspire hope, not fear or obsession.

The Meaning Wasn't a Mystery

The metaphors and symbols John used in Revelation were not cryptic and mysterious to first-century believers. Unlike the straightforward historical narrative or instructional correspondence of most other New Testament books, John used a different genre for Revelation. Apocalyptic literature uses symbols and metaphors as codes, but John's original readers would have been familiar with his specific contemporary references. Those symbols might be tougher for us to bridge because we are separated by culture, language, and so many years, but with a little work, we can know what John was saying to early Christians and is still saying to us. As we study Revelation, it would be a mistake to read into it the modern-day correlations so many try to make.

For example, the mark of the Beast is a familiar reference we will study later. Many have tried to use it as a sign to spot the activity of a modern-day Antichrist. But John's readers knew the number 666 was Nero's name spelled in Greek letters, using numeric values assigned to them, sort of like Roman numerals. The mark of the Beast isn't about computer chips, QR codes, vaccines, or modern world leaders. It was code for the rule of Nero. Any other interpretation is more likely an example of how *not* to read Revelation and why historical context is so crucial. Revelation was providing first-century Christians with new details about Jesus to comfort, inspire, and instruct them how to live in an evil world.

WHAT WAS JESUS TELLING THE CHURCHES?

The actual name John gave his book was "apocalypse"—or, in Greek, ἀποκάλυψις (*apokalypsis*), which means "revelation" or "unveiling."[2]

Today, the word *apocalypse* conjures images of nuclear devastation or zombie horror, but it's neither. It's not the end of the world; it's pulling back the curtain. The word appears eighteen times in the New Testament, and not once is it associated with catastrophe.[3] Instead, it's always associated with revealing spiritual truth. In the context of the book of Revelation, it's an "unveiling" to John about Jesus and the spiritual realm around us. It reveals to us that the world is not as it seems, and it reveals that Jesus isn't absent when His people suffer in this world.

As we work our way through this study, we will learn that this apocalypse, this revealing, falls into these three categories:

Unveiling Jesus. Jesus revealed to John additional insights about Himself and His teachings while on earth that we won't find anywhere else in Scripture. We'll see what He told John about the Sermon on the Mount. It's as if Jesus said, "Let me reveal more about what I taught you during those three years, this time from a heavenly perspective."

Unveiling the Prophets. Jesus also gave John a heavenly perspective on Old Testament prophecies and how they were fulfilled. Revelation makes direct reference to 275 Old Testament passages, prophetic symbols, images, and colloquial phrases, laying bare several obscure, confusing concepts and exposing their true meaning. We'll discover how Revelation reveals the beautiful cyclical nature of those prophecies and how, each time those cycles occur, the pattern becomes clearer and more intense.

Unveiling how God works. Revelation discloses the details and patterns of how God has worked throughout redemptive history to preserve His elect from evil. From Adam to Noah, to Lot and his family, to the survival of the church against earthly empires, Revelation exposes the big picture of it all. It shows how God calls out His chosen, refines them, redeems them, and removes them from the encroaching flood of evil in this world. Revelation reveals how the final act of the story of redemption begins at the cross and ends with Christ's return.

Jesus also warns about the sinful patterns early churches were tempted to fall into, the same ones today's churches struggle with. That's why it's so timely for us to read and study Revelation as members of the body of Christ.

What Is Jesus Telling Us Today?

As you read this devotional guide through Revelation, what are your hopes? Do you hope all your questions about biblical prophecy will be answered? Maybe you hope you'll end up with more knowledge about Revelation than all your friends so you can be the center of attention at parties as you proclaim the secrets everyone wants to know!

Allow me to rightsize your expectations. It's natural for Christians awaiting Jesus' return to want to know how everything ends. So, of course, we turn to Revelation, hoping to find those kinds of answers there. However, we cannot allow our obsession with contemporary world issues to be the primary influence on how we read apocalyptic literature like the book of Revelation. Doing so leads to a flawed approach. Because apocalyptic revelation literature feels, sounds, and behaves differently than other biblical genres such as the Epistles, Gospels, histories, and wisdom books, we must read Revelation differently than any other book in the New Testament. A strictly literal reading of Revelation would be like trying to read poetry as a newspaper article or an instructional manual.

Revelation isn't about identifying the Antichrist or gaining clues to help us prepare for some future global catastrophe. If you are reading Revelation to understand today's current global events, to win a political argument, or to predict the future, you're not reading it the right way. If you find it merely confusing, you're not reading it the right way. But don't be intimidated! Spend some time reading Revelation. It's worth the effort. Let this devotional guide you through the difficult parts, keeping Revelation 1:3 in mind:

> *Blessed is the one who reads aloud the words of this prophecy, and blessed are those who hear, and who keep what is written in it, for the time is near.*

Understanding the true purpose behind Revelation alleviates much of the fear, confusion, and intimidation many readers experience. When we read it as an unveiling of Jesus, it becomes an encouraging, inspiring word about how to live in this world while we await His return. Revelation is a message of hope that's as urgent and vital today as it was in the first century.

What is that message of hope? No matter what happens on earth, Jesus is in control. The plans and machinations of demons and men cannot derail the work of Jesus. He has always prevailed over evil, and He always will. We will be His witnesses to the end. Revelation reveals pragmatic tools we can use to identify and respond to the ongoing battle with the forces of darkness all around us.

My prayer for this devotional is that reading Revelation will cure you from any obsession with this world and inspire you to new heights of devotion to Jesus. I pray that reading Revelation will increase your hope and anticipation for the day we finally get to meet our Jesus face-to-face.

Revelation isn't meant to decipher the latest news headlines. It's a collection of heavenly letters of hope revealing Jesus to His people. Nor is Revelation a book of mysterious images from which we should try to interpret the rest of the Bible. Rather, the Bible contains the clear teaching we can apply to the mysterious images of Revelation. From that approach, we receive three things: (1) insight as to how biblical and redemptive history is fulfilled in these end times, (2) the courage God wants for us in tribulation and persecution, and (3) inspiration from this glimpse into the glory of God and His Son.

CHAPTER TWO

Greetings from Patmos

Revelation 1:4–8:

> [4] *John to the seven churches that are in Asia:*
>
> *Grace to you and peace from him who is and who was and who is to come, and from the seven spirits who are before his throne,* [5] *and from Jesus Christ the faithful witness, the firstborn of the dead, and the ruler of kings on earth.*
>
> *To him who loves us and has freed us from our sins by his blood* [6] *and made us a kingdom, priests to his God and Father, to him be glory and dominion forever and ever. Amen.* [7] *Behold, he is coming with the clouds, and every eye will see him, even those who pierced him, and all tribes of the earth will wail on account of him. Even so. Amen.*
>
> [8] *"I am the Alpha and the Omega," says the Lord God, "who is and who was and who is to come, the Almighty."*

This passage of Scripture was written by a prisoner of Rome. He was mostly likely in his nineties and had been sentenced to exile on an isolated island with no plumbing, no electricity, no medical care, and no heating or cooling. He'd simply been left on his own to fend for himself. For someone living in such circumstances, John still had so much hope!

> *Grace to you and peace from him who is and who was and who is to come, and from the seven spirits who are before his throne, [5] and from Jesus Christ the faithful witness, the firstborn of the dead, and the ruler of kings on earth. To him who loves us and has freed us from our sins by his blood [6] and made us a kingdom, priests to his God and Father, to him be glory and dominion forever and ever. Amen. [7] Behold, he is coming with the clouds, and every eye will see him, even those who pierced him.*
>
> — ***Revelation 1:4–7***

WHAT WOULD JOHN'S READERS HAVE NOTICED?

A Priest in Prison

My wife and I once visited Fort Jefferson in Dry Tortugas National Park, an old military installation located on an island seventy miles southwest of the Florida Keys. It's a beautiful place, but hot and lacking fresh water. Men stationed there during wartime regularly suffered disease, starvation, and the ravages of ocean storms. Prisoners such as Dr. Samuel Mudd, who was convicted of conspiracy in the Lincoln assassination and imprisoned there after the American Civil War,[4] would have felt keenly the message from Dante Alighieri's *Inferno* engraved above the dungeon gate: "Whoso entereth here leaveth all hope behind." That's a good description of what the Romans intended for John's exile on Patmos.

Emperor Domitian treated John as an enemy of Rome for preaching the gospel. He sent him to Patmos with the expectation the old man would die there, all alone and in despair. Life on Patmos lacked any special privileges, proper care, and social interaction. All the other apostles had been martyred by this point, so in that sense the apostle John was indeed alone, without even access to the Scriptures and the apostolic writings. Despite this, he managed to produce a beautiful, sophisticated work, written specifically to encourage those suffering for their faith to persevere in following Jesus.

Seven

The number 7 is important culturally and historically in terms of what it represented to John's readers, especially its use in the Old Testament to indicate spiritual and physical completeness. This number of completion appears throughout the Bible, first showing up in the opening pages of Genesis and the story of the seven days of creation. John used it fifty-seven times in Revelation—three times in his greeting passage alone. First, he wrote to seven churches, which were actual congregations planted by Paul in Asia Minor (what we now call Turkey). But first-century Christians would have understood that the significance of the number 7 meant this book was also intended to be read and studied by the complete church—every congregation, everywhere, throughout the church age.

WHAT WAS JESUS TELLING THE CHURCHES?

After his personal greeting, John essentially declares, "Churches, this next greeting isn't from me. It's directly from heaven, so listen up!" This begins John's revelation of the Trinity.

The One "who is and who was and who is to come" refers directly to the name God gave Himself back in Exodus when He told Moses, "I AM WHO I AM"—or the One who has always been (Exodus 3:14). This is God's covenant name. He is the One who has no beginning and no end. He is. Unlike His creation, God the Father isn't bound by time. He created space and time and transcends them both.

Once again, when John references the seven spirits, we see the number 7 (which means completeness). The phrase "from the seven spirits" doesn't suggest seven different spirits, but one complete Spirit of God and everything that the Spirit brings when He indwells us. First-century readers would have seen the connection between these seven spirits and the description of the Spirit in Isaiah 11:2 (emphasis mine):

> And the **Spirit of the LORD** shall rest upon him, the **Spirit of wisdom** and **understanding**, the **Spirit of counsel** and **might**, the **Spirit of knowledge** and **the fear of the LORD**.

Isaiah does not explicitly mention the number 7, but his seven-fold list points to Yahweh. The Spirit of the Lord, wisdom, understanding, counsel, might, knowledge, and fear—seven qualities of the Spirit of the Lord that make one powerful Spirit!

Next, in verse 5, John offers a description of the person of Jesus. "The faithful witness" means *martyr*, a reference to Jesus' death on the cross for us. He is also "the firstborn," or the head of the church and the first to be resurrected, which Paul explained in Colossians 1:18: "And he is the head of the body, the church. He is the beginning, the firstborn from the dead, that in everything he might be preeminent." Jesus' identity as firstborn points to his role as the ruler over earthly powers, as signified in Psalm 89:27: "And I will make him the firstborn, the highest of the kings of the earth."

Verses 6 and 7 describe what Jesus has done, is doing, and will do. First, He "loves us," and so He has "freed us from our sins by His blood." He also created a kingdom of godly priests from the seven churches, thus vividly fulfilling the promise God made to Moses in Exodus 19:6: "And you shall be to me a kingdom of priests and a holy nation." Peter explains this promise even more clearly in 1 Peter 2:9: "But you are a chosen race, a royal priesthood, a holy nation, a people for his own possession, that you may proclaim the excellencies of him who called you out of darkness into his marvelous light." In Revelation 1:7, John goes on to say Jesus is coming again "with the clouds," at which point all power will be given up to Him voluntarily. Everyone will see it! Those who do evil and nations at large will "wail" and mourn their rejection of

Him. The Old Testament prophet Daniel described Jesus' return in similar terms in Daniel 7:13–14:

> I saw in the night visions, and behold, with the clouds of heaven there came one like a son of man, and he came to the Ancient of Days and was presented before him. ¹⁴ And to him was given dominion and glory and a kingdom, that all peoples, nations, and languages should serve him; his dominion is an everlasting dominion, which shall not pass away, and his kingdom one that shall not be destroyed.

This is where things get exciting! In total, John gives us seven descriptions of Jesus, stressing His completeness in every way. The last of the seven descriptions of Jesus in John's opening passage occurs in Revelation 1:8:

> "I am the Alpha and the Omega," says the Lord God, "who is and who was and who is to come, the Almighty."

The inclusion of God's covenant name in this final description reinforces the truth that Jesus is God, the timeless one. It is He who was (and who has done great things), is (and who is doing great things), and is to come (and who will do great things). He is God! Jesus declared this Himself in John 8:58 when He said, "Truly, truly, I say to you, before Abraham was, I am." This is how apocalyptic literature works. It piles descriptions up in beautifully complex literary constructions.

This brief greeting, which contains five complex Old Testament references and two New Testament references, was written by an old man left to suffer in extremely difficult circumstances. How many of us could write as beautifully in those types of conditions? The only rational explanation is that John must have had some help. There must be something more: John was given these words!

But who would have the scrolls and such comprehensive knowledge of Scripture and be able to infiltrate this Roman outpost to help John connect the dots as this greeting does? This sounds like Jesus!

WHAT IS JESUS TELLING US TODAY?

Imagine the "wow" moments of John's original readers as they caught all the Old Testament connections. Imagine them reading Revelation aloud together in community and stopping to open the Old Testament scrolls and read those connected passages aloud, too. We can see how reading this text together in community would have allowed them to experience the promise John made in Revelation 1:3: "Blessed are those who read this aloud" (my paraphrase).

This greeting from heaven, delivered through a ninety-year-old man living in harsh isolation, should affirm your faith in Scripture. The beautiful complexity of these five verses shows God didn't just inspire John to write it; He *empowered* John to write it. As we learn in 2 Peter 1:21, "No prophecy was ever produced by the will of man, but men spoke from God as they were carried along by the Holy Spirit." These words will become the foundation for our process and discipline as we study Revelation. In other words, we will use the clear Old Testament and New Testament passages, since they usually explain the imagery of Revelation.

Reflect for a few minutes on the incredible revelation (apocalypse) of Jesus in this greeting alone. If you're lacking hope or inspiration to worship Jesus, perhaps what's missing is a genuine revelation of who Jesus is. I would ask that you read this passage again, aloud, while the details you just learned are fresh. Let the beauty, complexity, and glory of God's truth penetrate your heart and bless you with renewed inspiration to worship Jesus.

CHAPTER THREE

The Voice of Resurrection Jesus

Revelation 1:9–20:

9 I, John, your brother and partner in the tribulation and the kingdom and the patient endurance that are in Jesus, was on the island called Patmos on account of the word of God and the testimony of Jesus. 10 I was in the Spirit on the Lord's day, and I heard behind me a loud voice like a trumpet 11 saying, "Write what you see in a book and send it to the seven churches, to Ephesus and to Smyrna and to Pergamum and to Thyatira and to Sardis and to Philadelphia and to Laodicea."

12 Then I turned to see the voice that was speaking to me, and on turning I saw seven golden lampstands, 13 and in the midst of the lampstands one like a son of man, clothed with a long robe and with a golden sash around his chest. 14 The hairs of his head were white, like white wool, like snow. His eyes were like a flame of fire, 15 his feet were like burnished bronze, refined in a furnace, and his voice was like the roar of many waters. 16 In his right hand he held seven stars, from his mouth came a sharp two-edged sword, and his face was like the sun shining in full strength.

17 When I saw him, I fell at his feet as though dead. But he laid his right hand on me, saying, "Fear not, I am the first *and the last, ¹⁸ and the living one. I died, and behold I am alive forevermore, and I have the keys of Death and Hades. ¹⁹ Write therefore the things that you have seen, those that are and those that are to take place after this. ²⁰ As for the mystery of the seven stars that you saw in my right hand, and the seven golden lampstands, the seven stars are the angels of the seven churches, and the seven lampstands are the seven churches."*

Often, when we think of Jesus after the resurrection, our minds go back to the first Easter morning, with the stone rolled away from the empty tomb. We recall the women relaying to the disciples that they saw angels at the tomb, but Jesus Himself was missing. We can picture Peter and John running to the tomb to see for themselves. Then, at other points, Jesus appears to His disciples. These are powerful memories from the gospel accounts—but they aren't the only descriptions of the risen Jesus. The apostle John gives us a powerful picture here in Revelation.

Maybe it's time to upgrade the image you've held of the resurrected Jesus. The description John unveils in the Revelation of Jesus—what He looks like, what He is doing right now, and what He will do—is meant to change how you see Him.

What Would John's Readers Have Noticed?

"On the Lord's Day"

When John wrote the book of Revelation, he was in exile on the island of Patmos for preaching the gospel. Yet, we read in verse 10 that he was "in the Spirit on the Lord's day." In other words, he was "in the spirit on the day of the Lord," a phrase reserved for the time when Jesus assumes His authority. It's possible this "Lord's day" was much more significant than an ordinary Sunday. I believe it could have been an anniversary of Resurrection Sunday, when Jesus defeated sin, death, and the grave. I like to think John received this message from resurrected Jesus on Easter!

The Tribulation and the Kingdom

Most of Revelation is an unveiling, from heaven's perspective, of the true spiritual nature of events that had already taken place or were unfolding at that time. Jesus connected the dots for John and for us, showing how everything fits together in God's plan for His church. Many people read the words *tribulation* and *kingdom* in Revelation as primarily prophecies of future events, but here, clearly, they're not. John described both the tribulation and the kingdom as happening concurrently with the seven churches. In other words, John, along with every follower of Jesus, has experienced both tribulation and the kingdom together, in the present tense. Jesus put it this way in John 16:33: "In the world you will have tribulation. But take heart; I have overcome the world." And in Acts 14:22, a day after being nearly stoned to death, Paul encouraged fellow disciples that "through many tribulations we must enter the kingdom of God." In fact, the Greek word for *tribulation* accurately describes our present situation.

"Patient Endurance"

John had spent three years in close proximity to Jesus. He was a witness when Jesus was glorified on the Mount of Transfiguration, and he personally spoke with Jesus on the first Easter. He saw Jesus ascend into heaven from the Mount of Olives, and he had been waiting for Jesus to return ever since. At the time he wrote Revelation, it had been roughly sixty years since John had last seen Jesus. His fellow apostles had been martyred, and he probably did not expect to see Jesus again until he passed away.

How would you feel in John's situation? Isolated? Alone? Discouraged? If anyone could have used a fresh revelation of resurrected Jesus to inspire him for "patient endurance," it was John.

But this revelation of resurrected Jesus wasn't just for him. Jesus told John to tell the seven churches—and that includes us today. Jesus taught over and over that the kingdom of God has begun, at least in part, and His disciples would suffer on account of Him. Today, we are also partners in the kingdom with the seven churches and with John, called to patient endurance in tribulation.

WHAT WAS JESUS TELLING THE CHURCHES?

While John was spending time in prayer and contemplation, he suddenly heard a loud, startling voice behind him. It was so loud, he described it in verse 10 as a "trumpet." How would you respond if you were having some devotional time and you suddenly heard a trumpet blast right behind you?

In verse 17, the voice declared Himself "the first and the last" and went on to command John to write everything down. John knew he had to record all he was about to see and hear and send it to everyone else who followed Jesus.

Turning toward this loud voice, John found himself face-to-face with the Lord Jesus, who was standing among seven lampstands and holding seven stars in His hands. Jesus was radiant, full of light and glory from the hair on His head down to His toes, and He was dressed in the robe of the high priest. Except for the stars and the lampstands, it was the same manifestation of Jesus that appears in Daniel 10:5–6:

> *I lifted up my eyes and looked, and behold, a man clothed in linen, with a belt of fine gold from Uphaz around his waist.* ⁶ *His body was like beryl, his face like the appearance of lightning, his eyes like flaming torches, his arms and legs like the gleam of burnished bronze, and the sound of his words like the sound of a multitude.*

In a traditional Jewish context, the seven lampstands were part of the furniture exclusive to the temple, which was a metaphorical representation of God dwelling among His people. Jesus standing among the lampstands (or the seven churches) indicated the church had replaced the physical temple in Jerusalem as His sanctuary and dwelling place. Jesus is present with us as the church gathers together. As the Lord said through the prophet in Ezekiel 37:27, "My dwelling place shall be with them, and I will be their God, and they shall be my people." We no longer build a temple as the dwelling place for God, because together *we* are now His sanctuary!

Both the robe and the lampstands are beautiful symbols of what resurrected Jesus is doing with His church. The high priest had a constant job: to keep the lampstands burning (see Exodus 30:2–8). Jesus is wearing a high priest's robe and sash because He is our High Priest, keeping His church—which, in Matthew 5:14, He called "the light of the world," burning bright even amid the tribulation. And Jesus explained the stars in His right hand represent the seven angels protecting His church. Do you remember another time Jesus said He held something in His hands? You might recall John 10:27–28:

> *My sheep hear my voice, and I know them, and they follow me.* [28] *I give them eternal life, and they will never perish, and no one will snatch them out of my hand.*

Even as tribulation rages, the resurrected Jesus will never let us go or allow us to be taken from Him!

This was an overwhelming experience for John, emotionally and physically. In verse 17, the apostle said he "fell at his [Jesus'] feet as though dead." Wouldn't you respond the same way? But look again at Jesus' response to John in verses 17 and 18: "But he laid his right hand on me, saying, 'Fear not, I am the first and the last, and the living one. I died, and behold I am alive forevermore, and I have the keys of Death and Hades.'"

This scripture brings me tears of joy and hope! John had a fresh encounter—a new apocalypse or unveiling—of resurrected Jesus that no one had ever seen before. Jesus, with the seven lampstands and the seven stars in His hand, is Resurrection Jesus, who conquered sin and death! It's a revelation of who He is, what He's done, what He's doing, and what He will do.

What Is Jesus Telling Us Today?

We don't physically see Jesus the way John did when God pulled back the curtain for a moment. That unveiling was temporary but meaningful because the same Jesus is alive—resurrected and glorified—and with you right now! He holds you in His hand, the same as all His sheep.

Whatever troubles you are going through, Jesus' message for you is, "Do not fear tribulation. Keep going and don't give up, because I have conquered death! I am with you and will keep you in My hand, burning bright. No one can take you from Me!"

Resurrected Jesus hasn't just conquered death and hell; He is also the Great Shepherd, calling to us with His voice. Right now, He stands among His people (the seven lampstands) and holds us in His hands (the seven stars). This revelation of resurrected Jesus is to reassure you that you have nothing to fear. Death could not hold Him, and if you are in Christ, death cannot hold you. And yes, we are currently all partners in this tribulation, but we're also partners in His kingdom right here, right now.

There are times we all need to hear this word, to experience a new revelation of resurrected Jesus. It may not be a trumpet blast right behind us or an audible voice, but as with John, the voice of the Spirit of Jesus often seems to call us when He knows we need Him most.

Have you experienced moments like this? When the voice of resurrected Jesus calls to you and suddenly you see Him in a fresh way? For some, His voice calls you during recovery from addiction. For others, the voice of resurrected Jesus calls you amid a battle with depression or anxiety. Maybe His voice is calling you during a time of loss or grief. He also calls people who are confronted and broken over their own sin. The voice of resurrected Jesus may be calling you because you've become distracted, careless, or apathetic—disinterested in walking in step with the kingdom of God.

One day, we'll all see for ourselves this Jesus of the Resurrection, whom John saw that day on Patmos. I imagine, like John, we will fall stunned at the feet of Jesus. Until then, each of us must persevere and listen for His voice. If you know

Him, you'll hear Him and turn to Him. What is His Spirit saying to you today?

LETTERS FROM HEAVEN

CHAPTER FOUR

Our First Love

Revelation 2:1–7:

> ¹ *"To the angel of the church in Ephesus write: 'The words of him who holds the seven stars in his right hand, who walks among the seven golden lampstands.*
>
> ² *"'I know your works, your toil and your patient endurance, and how you cannot bear with those who are evil, but have tested those who call themselves apostles and are not, and found them to be false.* ³ *I know you are enduring patiently and bearing up for my name's sake, and you have not grown weary.* ⁴ *But I have this against you, that you have abandoned the love you had at first.* ⁵ *Remember therefore from where you have fallen; repent, and do the works you did at first. If not, I will come to you and remove your lampstand from its place, unless you repent.* ⁶ *Yet this you have: you hate the works of the Nicolaitans, which I also hate.* ⁷ *He who has an ear, let him hear what the Spirit says to the churches. To the one who conquers I will grant to eat of the tree of life, which is in the paradise of God.'"*

For nearly six years, our church met for worship in a comedy club, our children's ministry met in an adjoining office building, and our weekly outreach ministries met in a strip mall. This gave us an opportunity to love people more than a building or an organization. We had to be mobile, organic, biblical, and generous.

Our humble beginnings were a blessing. They helped us find and maintain our first love: to serve hurting people in our community through love, generosity, and truth. Here is a question all of us in the body of Christ should ask ourselves: If my church closed its doors, how would my community feel? Would my neighbors notice my church's absence?

This chapter in Revelation begins a section of letters from Jesus to seven churches. He personalized each letter to address what the churches were doing well and where they were failing. All of them are relevant for every church.

What Would John's Readers Have Noticed?

"Ephesus Community Church"

Of the seven churches, Ephesus was located closest to Patmos. The believers there would have been the first to receive the book of Revelation. They would have been responsible not only for reading and teaching Revelation for the first time but also for carefully copying it and circulating it to the next church. Like us, these churches would have noticed the symbolism of the number 7, since there were, after all, more than seven churches in the area—the church in Colossae, for example. But these letters weren't intended merely for the seven churches any more than the letters to Corinth were exclusively for the Corinthians. The symbolic 7 exhorts us all to be overcomers in this world.

At one time, the city of Ephesus had been the most powerful commercial hub in the region. The church there was affluent as well, enjoying influence and prestige among the seven churches. Ephesus was also a cultural melting pot for pagan rituals, particularly as it was home to the Temple of Artemis and other temples known for their orgiastic celebrations, including feasts of meat offered to idols. The culture had succeeded in making immorality a spiritual quality to be desired and admired. It was very similar to the culture we find ourselves in today, a culture that glorifies things that are antithetical to the teachings of Jesus.

They Were Biblical

Even though Ephesus was a mecca for false teachers, this church stood strong against them. Jesus affirmed their commitment to orthodox teaching at both the beginning and the end of His letter to them. The church in Ephesus was faithful, maintaining "patient endurance," even while other churches compromised their beliefs and assimilated to their surrounding cultures. Today, many contemporary churches face the same temptation to compromise obedience to Jesus in an effort to gain society's approval.

That wasn't the case with Ephesus. For centuries, they were a driving force in proclaiming and maintaining apostolic teaching. In this letter, Jesus referenced a certain heretical group, the Nicolaitans, and commended the church for despising their false teachings and standing up to them.

Nikolaitas (Νικολαΐτης)

The name Nikolaitas (Νικολαΐτης) comprises two Greek words: *nikē*, meaning "to conquer or destroy," and *laos*, or "people."[5] The epithet may even refer to some of the same false teachers mentioned in letters written by John, Peter, and Paul. This is the Greek version of the Hebrew word *Balaam* seen throughout the Old Testament, which also means "destroyer of people."[6]

Balaam was a false prophet who sought to destroy Israel from within by corrupting their sexual and moral values. Nicolaitans were guilty of trying to do the same thing to the early church. They corrupted God's people by enticing them to accept and even participate in pagan rituals that included substance abuse and almost any type of sexual immorality imaginable. They succeeded in branding anything sensual as worship.

WHAT WAS JESUS TELLING THIS CHURCH?

Losing Their First Love

During His ministry, Jesus established the two following foundational teachings. First, in John 21:17, He warned Peter of a failing priesthood:

> *He said to him the third time, "Simon, son of John, do you love me?" Peter was grieved because he said to him the third time, "Do you love me?" and he said to him, "Lord, you know everything; you know that I love you." Jesus said to him, "Feed my sheep."*

And in Matthew 22:37–39, Jesus had this to say to the Pharisaic lawyer who asked about the great commandment in the Law:

> *You shall love the Lord your God with all your heart and with all your soul and with all your mind. ³⁸ This is the great and first commandment. ³⁹ And a second is like it: You shall love your neighbor as yourself.*

Despite their love for truth, the Ephesians had left their first love. They forgot the greatest commandment. Jesus essentially told them, "You've been faithful to stand against false teachers who destroy lives, but you've lost balance. You allowed the honorable love of protecting truth to turn you into judgmental, unloving people. You have become a church that loves theology more than humble service."

It's true that they courageously stood against the Nicolaitans, even while being persecuted and shunned for their stand. However, they forgot about the royal priesthood in the process. They forgot to love the people.

"I Will Remove Your Lampstand"

Jesus warned the Ephesians, "If you don't repent and return to that first love, I will remove your lampstand."

Imagine being one of the Ephesian church elders, reading this letter directly from Jesus, who has accused them of having forgotten how to be a light on a hill.

But doesn't Jesus hold the stars in His hands? Isn't He among the lampstands? Didn't He say that He will never leave us nor forsake us? Why would he remove their lampstand? What Jesus was saying to the church in Ephesus was that He would remove their status as one the seven churches and replace them with another one. It didn't mean the people had lost their faith or salvation. It was a warning to the church itself: if you don't shine, your lampstand will be removed and given to a new group of people. It's the same warning God gave Israel time and again. It's a corporate warning, not a personal one. Sadly, it was a warning that proved true: the church in Ephesus disappeared within a few centuries of Jesus' words.

There's also a clever play on words embedded in Christ's warning in verse 7 that is easy to overlook, which ties in with the origin of the word "Nicolaitans":

> *He who has an ear [His individual sheep who hear his voice and follow Him], let him hear what the Spirit says to the churches. To the one who conquers I will grant to eat of the tree of life, which is in the paradise of God.*

In verse 6, Jesus said He hates the *Nike*-laitans (destroyers or overcomers of people), but in this verse, He says, if we ni-kaō (overcome or conquer) by keeping our first love, He will reward us![7]

WHAT IS JESUS TELLING US TODAY?

First Love

Could a church be one hundred percent committed to the gospel and still lose its first love? For the American church, standing up to groups who have taken on the modern-day role of these first-century Nicolaitans isn't as treacherous as it was for the Ephesians. It doesn't require all that much courage, apart from a willingness to be mocked on social media. But we can easily fall into the same trap as Ephesus, as our world tries to infiltrate and pollute what the church believes. Churches must steward God's truth faithfully, but there's a delicate balance to maintain as we also seek to live out the new commandment Jesus gave us in John 13:34–35:

> *A new commandment I give to you, that you love one another: just as I have loved you, you also are to love one another. ³⁵ By this all people will know that you are my disciples, if you have love for one another.*

The church is a gathering of saints, chosen and transformed by Jesus, empowered with qualities given by the Spirit dwelling within us, including faith, virtue, knowledge, self-control, stability, reverence, brotherly affection, humble love, and service. Notice how God designed all these qualities to empower us, His royal priesthood, to patiently and humbly serve people while we proclaim the truth?

Every church struggles with these duties from time to time, so we need frequent reminders. Sadly, there are many churches like Ephesus that are faithful theologically but have lost their first love. They might still value truth, but they have become unwilling to get their hands dirty when it comes to loving people where they are. They have metaphorically closed their doors to outsiders and have become impotent as it relates to impacting lives. Where there is no love, there is also no light, even if the organization is teeming with talented leaders and people, resources, and facilities. Other things become more important than loving and serving neighbors. The people remain in Christ, but the institutions themselves are no longer lampstands. They have forgotten what Jesus urged in Matthew 5:16:

> *In the same way, let your light shine before others, so that they may see your good works and give glory to your Father who is in heaven.*

What happens when church buildings or programs become more important than people in the neighborhood? What happens when churches are more passionate about preserving the truth than they are about loving people? What if churches become successful organizations in earthly terms but become too inwardly focused in the process? What happens when they become less generous and open to others who need God's love and truth? What if people can no longer tell we are His disciples by our love? How tragic it would be if Jesus had to remove the lampstand of your church and give it to someone else! Let us pray to our heavenly Father for protection for our churches from this sin, and may we keep our hearts focused on our first love.

LETTERS FROM HEAVEN

CHAPTER FIVE

Faith That Conquers

Revelation 2:8–11:

> [8] "And to the angel of the church in Smyrna write: 'The words of the first and the last, who died and came to life.
>
> [9] "'I know your tribulation and your poverty (but you are rich) and the slander of those who say that they are Jews and are not, but are a synagogue of Satan. [10] Do not fear what you are about to suffer. Behold, the devil is about to throw some of you into prison, that you may be tested, and for ten days you will have tribulation. Be faithful unto death, and I will give you the crown of life. [11] He who has an ear, let him hear what the Spirit says to the churches. The one who conquers will not be hurt by the second death.'"

Have you ever wondered if you would have what it takes to stand up under real persecution? Have you ever imagined being forced to choose between your faith and your life, or between your faith and your family's or friends' lives?

Thankfully, for most Americans today, this scenario is hypothetical. That's what makes this passage of Revelation so difficult to teach. It's much easier to warn about sin in the church because we can all relate to that! But Jesus doesn't do that in His letter to Smyrna. Instead, he warns that persecution is real and comes in many forms.

What Would John's Readers Have Noticed?

Suffering in Smyrna

By this time in the first century, adherence to the imperial cult of Rome had reached a new high (or low, depending on your perspective). Under Emperor Domitian, who was in power as John wrote Revelation, loyal citizens were expected to pay respects to the emperor through practices such as making sacrifices and offerings to him as a living god—something both Jews and Christians would have found abhorrent.[8]

Prior to Domitian's reign, the Roman Empire had often adopted a policy of religious tolerance, as long as the practices of their subjects didn't threaten imperial power or stability. This meant the Jews were generally exempt from imperial cult requirements. And since Romans had difficulty distinguishing early Christians from Jews—seeing the movement as an offshoot of Judaism—Christians had some ability to exercise their faith. But as the century wore on, animosity between Jews and their conquerors led to a series of revolts against Rome, culminating in the brutal siege of Jerusalem in AD 70. This started a new era of intense Roman persecution of Jews, which also had a spillover effect for Christians and their freedom to worship.

The empire saw anyone who refused to participate in the imperial cult as seditious—especially Christians, whose religion was new and considered socially disruptive. As early as the reign of Nero (AD 54 to 68), citizens caught worshiping other deities risked financial ruin, prison, or possibly death, depending on the whims of local authorities. John would later warn Christians of "the mark of the beast" in reference to this very real danger, which we'll investigate later in this book.

Smyrna was a city in Asia Minor known for its loyalty to Rome and the imperial cult. Early in the century, the city won the honor of erecting a temple built to worship the emperor and the *genius* (or divine spirit) of the Senate. Its inhabitants took the cult of Caesar seriously.

Resentment for Christians

During His earthly ministry, Jesus predicted the siege of Jerusalem and warned his followers to flee the city when they saw signs of invading Roman forces approaching. This prophecy became a central component of gospel preaching from AD 33 until the stunning moment it all came true in AD 70.

By heeding those warnings and leaving Jerusalem for other cities along the Mediterranean, most Christians escaped the slaughter many Jews suffered. The fulfillment of Jesus' prediction was seen by many as affirmation of the gospel's authenticity. After Jerusalem's destruction, the story became core to the teachings of the early church, and as it was repeated, it gave the gospel credibility as it spread.

Of course, constantly hearing this story of how followers of Jesus had escaped the carnage by fleeing Jerusalem did not improve Jewish sentiment toward Christians. They resented Jewish followers of Jesus who, in their view, had abandoned the fight against evil. They questioned how Christians could say they worship the one true God without remaining loyal to Israel.

Meanwhile, many members of synagogues in Smyrna became apostate to avoid persecution, and they resented Christians who refused to do the same. In their view, if they had to compromise their worship of God to survive, then Christians should, too. They became known as "accusers" of Christians. Satan's name also means "accuser," which is why Jesus called opponents of Christianity "synagogues of Satan"—or "synagogues of accusers."

Worshiping in Fear

Smyrna was not the only Roman region to put its boot on the neck of believers. Churches in other regions faced similar pressures, and to one degree or another, many gave in. They compromised theology, morality, and even their liturgy of worship by mingling them with the immoral sensual practices conducted in Roman pagan temples.

As a result, many of these churches had been infiltrated by false teachers and others who weren't really believers. In fact, in many regions, it became difficult to tell the church apart from the rest of society.

But the believers in Smyrna were different. True faith inspired and empowered them to stand firm against this persecution. Any gathering of Christians in Smyrna could be broken up by Roman soldiers, so when they went to church, it could well be the last time they ever met. In Hebrews 11:35–38, we learn they were, among other things, mocked, imprisoned, flogged, tortured, stoned, and sawn in two.

WHAT WAS JESUS TELLING THIS CHURCH?

This letter from heaven to the church in Smyrna is distinct from the letters to the other churches because it doesn't contain any rebuke or correction. Instead, Jesus affirmed the church's faithfulness and warned that their suffering would worsen. Jesus specifically cautioned them that the devil would put them in prison for ten days. There are many interpretations offered for what these ten days mean. For example, Daniel and his friends were tested for ten days in a story that reminds us that suffering persecution is greater than worshiping idols (see Daniel 1:11–16). Looking at the ten days in context, however, suggests this is also a prediction from Jesus about ten distinct periods when Rome would attack Christianity with special vehemence:

AD 54–68. Persecution under Nero, during which Peter and Paul were executed

AD 81–96. Domitian reigned and exiled John to Patmos

AD 104–117. Persecution under Trajan

AD 161–180. Persecution under Marcus Aurelius, during which Polycarp, Bishop of Smyrna, was martyred

AD 200–211. Persecution under Septimius Severus

AD 235–237. Persecution under Maximinus Thrax

AD 249–251. Persecution under Decius

AD 257–260. Persecution under Valerian

AD 270–275. Persecution under Aurelian

AD 303–313. Persecution under Diocletian, possibly the most severe period

These decrees came like waves, but they were not surprising to early Christians because Jesus had warned His disciples of this very thing in Matthew 24:9–10:

> *Then they will deliver you up to tribulation and put you to death, and you will be hated by all nations for my name's sake.* [10] *And then many will fall away and betray one another and hate one another.*

The church in Smyrna refused to worship Caesar but, at the same time, lived in obedience to every other Roman law. This was the command Peter gave them in his first letter, to live in submission to Rome except for the worship of Caesar. The church in Smyrna wasn't perfect—yet, even with a sea of paganism around them, they remained faithful.

Jesus promised them their faith would persevere and, though they might die, they would "not be hurt by the second death," the eternal judgment for anyone not listed in the Book of Life. This isn't just encouragement for Smyrna but also a promise for all believers. Smyrna would persevere, no matter what might happen, because Jesus held the seven stars in His hands.

Jesus had no criticisms for the church in Smyrna. So, why would God allow them to face that level of persecution? They were being tested so the testimony of their faithfulness could inspire other churches throughout church history, even today. Their faithfulness in the face of severe persecution revealed them to be what a church of people with divine faith should look like. Smyrna passed the test because they had ears to hear the voice of the Great Shepherd and they followed His word.

WHAT IS JESUS TELLING US TODAY?

The warning of the second death comes with a bright side—the hope of being an overcomer! Just look at John's words in 1 John 5:4–5:

> *Everyone who has been born of God overcomes the world. And this is the victory that has overcome the world—our faith.* [5] *Who is it that overcomes the world except the one who believes that Jesus is the Son of God?*

Who gets the credit for the faithfulness of the first-century believers in Smyrna? Likewise, where should the credit go for the faithfulness of contemporary Christians in places like China or Iran who resist the same type of persecution? Are they just special, super-spiritual people? No, they're no different than you or me. It is sovereign Jesus who gets the credit. John began this letter saying, "The words of the first and the last, who died and came to life." In that respect, the letter to the church in Smyrna is also a letter to us.

If you have an ear that hears the Great Shepherd's voice, listen well to this letter. Its promises are for you. Our faith will be completed by Jesus on the day He returns. Fear not—the faithful cannot be hurt by the second death! The enemy, the great accuser, cannot get you. Even if you are persecuted for ten days, you have been sealed in Jesus' hands, and evil is powerless to pry you out of them. That is why this verse in Paul's letter to Jude became one of the most important creeds of the early church (Jude 1:24–25):

> *Now to him who is able to keep you from stumbling and to present you blameless before the presence of his glory with great joy, 25 to the only God, our Savior, through Jesus Christ our Lord, be glory, majesty, dominion, and authority, before all time and now and forever. Amen.*

If you want to overcome the second death, this is where it happens—in the mighty grip of the hands of the First and the Last.

CHAPTER SIX

Two Sides to Jesus

Revelation 2:12–17:

> ¹² *"And to the angel of the church in Pergamum write: 'The words of him who has the sharp two-edged sword.*
>
> ¹³ *"'I know where you dwell, where Satan's throne is. Yet you hold fast my name, and you did not deny my faith even in the days of Antipas my faithful witness, who was killed among you, where Satan dwells.* ¹⁴ *But I have a few things against you: you have some there who hold the teaching of Balaam, who taught Balak to put a stumbling block before the sons of Israel, so that they might eat food sacrificed to idols and practice sexual immorality.* ¹⁵ *So also you have some who hold the teaching of the Nicolaitans.* ¹⁶ *Therefore repent. If not, I will come to you soon and war against them with the sword of my mouth.* ¹⁷ *He who has an ear, let him hear what the Spirit says to the churches. To the one who conquers I will give some of the hidden manna, and I will give him a white stone, with a new name written on the stone that no one knows except the one who receives it.'"*

Imagine this letter to the church in Pergamos (the modern Greek form of Pergamum) being read in earshot of those who had actually compromised the gospel. Jesus called their city the place where Satan has his throne.

Now, imagine this letter being written to your church today in your city: "Repent, or I will war against you." Would that get your attention?

So far in this chapter of Revelation, Jesus has introduced Himself to the church in Ephesus as the one who holds the seven stars and stands among the seven lampstands. He has told Smyrna He is the first and the last, the one who died and rose again, the sovereign over the faithful. But He tells the church in Pergamos He has a two-edged sword in His mouth, and He's not afraid to use it.

We often forget there are two sides to Jesus. Yes, He's the Great Shepherd who holds the church in His hand, and He will never leave nor let go of His people. But he is also the Jesus who wields a two-edged sword.

WHAT WOULD JOHN'S READERS HAVE NOTICED?

Where Satan Dwells

Pergamos was the regional capital of the Roman province of Asia (a part of Asia Minor under Roman control) and a regional center for Roman political power.[9] It also became a pagan hotspot, a sort of pagan Jerusalem with temples built to the most popular Greco-Roman gods—Zeus, Dionysus, Athena, and Asklepios[10]. People worshiped in these temples to gain political connections, financial power, prestige, and even promises of healing. These false religions collaborated, under Satan's control, against the gospel and Judaism.

Syncretism

The Roman Empire didn't demand its subjects to abandon their religious beliefs. People could worship whomever and however they wanted, as long as they worshipped Caesar first. Because of this, many religions adapted their beliefs to Roman culture in a process called *syncretism*. In other words, they adopted aspects of Caesar worship and the Roman religion into whatever they already believed. This practice of syncretism was not only a political expectation, but it had also become a cultural virtue and was seen as a way to unite the diverse populations throughout the empire!

Syncretism was celebrated. Many Romans considered it a sacred duty, practically an unwritten law if you wanted to remain in good standing with society. Anyone who refused could become the target of an extremely aggressive and destructive cancel culture. If you desired to achieve financial success and power, or merely to get along, you were expected to accept and even participate in the idolatrous temple practices through syncretism.

Pagan "Christians"

Christians and Jews were expected to syncretize, too. Anyone who desired success in any area of life attended the temple feasts. False teachers insisted it was the church's duty to syncretize so they could exercise influence on society. This included abandoning Jesus' teachings about there being eternal consequences for living an immoral lifestyle.

Many believers in Pergamos had chosen to fuse their faith with pagan feasts and orgies. Today, some churches and individuals, in an effort to appeal to more people, preach a more tolerant gospel that leaves out the "two-edged sword" part of who Jesus is.

WHAT WAS JESUS TELLING THIS CHURCH?

Jesus began by affirming those in Pergamos who had not compromised their faith, even under threat of severe persecution. He even commended Antipas, a beloved elder in the church who had been martyred because he refused to syncretize his faith with pagan cults. Imagine how his family must have felt when his name was mentioned by Jesus in a letter to that church!

But then Jesus unleashed a scathing rebuke to those in the church who had adopted the teachings of the Nicolaitans and of Balaam—those who had embraced syncretism. This was the same group of false teachers Jesus warned the church in Ephesus about—false teachers who were convincing Christians to syncretize. Unlike the believers in Ephesus, many in Pergamos listened to them and enthusiastically embraced the pagan rituals in these temples, participating in worship services that included things like substance abuse and orgies.

The earthly payoff for them was rich! It provided lucrative business opportunities and wide cultural acceptance.

Jesus, the Lamb of God, commanded them to repent or He would come and "make war" against them. This isn't a gentle fatherly rebuke of His children. This is "two-edged sword" Jesus threatening judgment. They might have been afraid of Rome's swords, but they didn't want Jesus to come with His sword, the word of His judgment.

Then, to the faithful in Pergamos who overcome, Jesus promised the manna, the stone, and a new name. These references might seem cryptic to us two thousand years later, but the first-century church knew exactly what these symbols were supposed to represent.

Hidden manna. The hidden manna is "hidden salvation," meaning salvation given exclusively to God's chosen, which no one can take from His hands. It's only for those who have ears to hear. Consider Jesus' words in John 6:49–51:

> *Your fathers ate the manna in the wilderness, and they died. [50] This is the bread that comes down from heaven, so that one may eat of it and not die. [51] I am the living bread that came down from heaven. If anyone eats of this bread, he will live forever. And the bread that I will give for the life of the world is my flesh.*

White stone. In first-century sporting events, the victor's prize would often include a valuable white stone.[11] It also provided admission to the champions' feast. We can think of the white stone Jesus described as an "overcomer's ticket" into the great marriage feast in heaven.

New name. That white stone of victory was usually personalized with the victor's name so no one else could claim the reward. Jesus said each faithful person gets his or her own white stone with a "new name" inscribed on it—a new heavenly identity.

God has always been in the business of giving people new identities: Jacob became Israel, Abram became Abraham, and Simon became Peter. Several times, the prophet Isaiah mentioned God's chosen being called by their new names. It's one of the glorious benefits of our redemption and transformation! Maybe these are the names written in the Book of Life? Old things have passed away and all things have become new, including us, who are thankful for a fresh start with God.

The promises here are personal and intimate—but so is the threat of judgment.

WHAT IS JESUS TELLING US TODAY?

Jesus addressed two groups of people in His letter to the Pergamos church. In Matthew 13:30, He said of these groups, "Let both grow together until the harvest, and at harvest time I will tell the reapers, 'Gather the weeds first and bind them in bundles to be burned, but gather the wheat into my barn.'"

All Christian communities have both wheat and weeds—those who are authentic and those who are imposters.

Sometimes a church becomes so full of weeds, it's hard to tell the difference between the church and the world around them. That's what happened in Pergamos, and it's why Jesus wrote what he did to them.

Jesus drew a very clear line: He's the only way to the Father. That message cannot be blended with lies. Paul wrote in Hebrews 4:12–13:

> *For the word of God is living and active, sharper than any two-edged sword.... ¹³ And no creature is hidden from his sight, but all are naked and exposed to the eyes of him to whom we must give account.*

We must never be ashamed of the gospel. It's the power for our salvation against evil and the wrath we all deserve. Syncretizing with the world isn't a strategy for growth; it's a compromise of what makes the church strong. When churches preach the gospel and leave out either "two-edged sword" Jesus or "no one comes to the Father but through me" Jesus, that gospel message is counterfeit and impotent. It no longer has the power to transform or save in the way John described in 1 John 5:4–5:

> *For everyone who has been born of God overcomes the world. And this is the victory that has overcome the world—our faith. ⁵ Who is it that overcomes the world except the one who believes that Jesus is the Son of God?*

Sooner or later, Jesus will encounter everyone, either as a friend or as a judge. If you have the faith that overcomes the world, you will be given the exclusive hidden bread of life. You will receive the victor's stone with a secret name etched on it, a new identity given to you by Jesus. If you are nervous, wondering which Jesus you will meet, I believe this is evidence you have been given the gift of faith, the ability to recognize not only how scary two-edged sword Jesus is but also how precious Savior Jesus is! Your desire for the hidden things demonstrates you have ears to hear.

And because you have been given faith to overcome, this letter isn't a warning from Jesus but a personal message of comfort. Your reading of Revelation today is a blessing, and it should give you cause for rejoicing!

CHAPTER SEVEN

The False God of Compromise

Revelation 2:18–29:

> [18] "And to the angel of the church in Thyatira write: 'The words of the Son of God, who has eyes like a flame of fire, and whose feet are like burnished bronze.
>
> [19] "'I know your works, your love and faith and service and patient endurance, and that your latter works exceed the first. [20] But I have this against you, that you tolerate that woman Jezebel, who calls herself a prophetess and is teaching and seducing my servants to practice sexual immorality and to eat food sacrificed to idols. [21] I gave her time to repent, but she refuses to repent of her sexual immorality. [22] Behold, I will throw her onto a sickbed, and those who commit adultery with her I will throw into great tribulation, unless they repent of her works, [23] and I will strike her children dead. And all the churches will know that I am he who searches mind and heart, and I will give to each of you according to your works. [24] But to the rest of you in Thyatira, who do not hold this teaching, who have not learned what some call the deep things of Satan, to you I say, I do not lay on you any other burden. [25] Only hold fast what you have until I come. [26] The one who conquers and who keeps my works until the end, to him I will give authority over the nations, [27] and he will rule them with a rod

of iron, as when earthen pots are broken in pieces, even as I myself have received authority from my Father. ²⁸ And I will give him the morning star. ²⁹ He who has an ear, let him hear what the Spirit says to the churches.'"

It's human nature to desire a community that embraces your values and enhances your opportunities for success or happiness. It's natural to desire a world that will protect the things that are most important to you, like family and faith. That's why people of all faiths, philosophies, and backgrounds have passionate opinions for what society should look like. It's one of the reasons people often move to new communities, change jobs, choose new churches, and so forth.

The gift of faith will always inspire true followers of Jesus to desire a community and a culture that embrace the values of the kingdom of God. Sadly, thousands of years of human history tell us the world isn't interested in our opinions—and it won't be until Jesus returns. Until then, this world will constantly pressure us to compromise our lives and beliefs in exchange for acceptance.

So, what does Jesus want us to do until He returns?

WHAT WOULD JOHN'S READERS HAVE NOTICED?

Thyatira, the Guild City

Thyatira was a manufacturing hub in Asia Minor, in the Roman Empire. It was dominated politically and culturally by trade guilds—people grouped by their specific occupation, including leatherworkers, silversmiths, blacksmiths, and weavers. These guilds were not unlike trade unions, but they were more influential and of greater social importance. Lydia, who became an early follower of Jesus, would have been part of a guild for purple goods dyers in Thyatira before moving to Philippi, as we learn in Acts 16:14–15:

> *One who heard us was a woman named Lydia, from the city of Thyatira, a seller of purple goods, who was a worshiper of God. The Lord opened her heart to pay attention to what was said by Paul. [15] And she was baptized, and her household as well.*

Guild Temples

Membership in the guild that corresponded to a trade was mandatory if a worker wanted to be successful. In return, the guild protected its members and their interests financially, culturally, and politically. While this type of guild was critical to survival in the first century, it also had a sinister side. Each guild developed its own exclusive pagan rituals and feasts, which often included orgies and rampant drunkenness.

Attendance at these guild feasts was mandatory for all members. If Christians refused to participate, they could be shunned by society, and their businesses could be destroyed.

Jezebel

Jesus mentions by name an influential false prophetess who encouraged Christians to integrate into the guilds. Just as Jesus linked the Nicolaitans by name to Balaam in the Old Testament, He linked this woman to an evil Old Testament queen of Israel. Jezebel was the wife of King Ahab, the most idolatrous, immoral king in Israel's history (see 1 Kings 18).

In this passage in Revelation, *Jezebel* was either a pseudonym for an actual prophetess spreading false teachings or the false teaching itself. She is representative of the Gnostics John wrote about in 1 John: "Everyone who makes a practice of sinning also practices lawlessness; sin is lawlessness" (1 John 3:4). These Gnostics espoused an ancient, pagan feminism that seduced Christians into immoral guild feasts, which included temple prostitutes. They insisted that Jesus would want them to do this as part of the Great Commission. But they didn't stop there: they also taught that women should avoid marriage and childbearing. Jesus called these teachings the "deep things of Satan." While only "some" followed the Nicolaitans in Pergamos, it seems the majority of Thyatira had been corrupted by these false doctrines.

This Jezebel had convinced Christians in the city to be comfortable with idolatry and immorality. As a result, they had fully compromised their theology and sexual morality. How could true Christians fall for this? Maybe they weren't Christians after all. Maybe they never had ears to hear.

WHAT WAS JESUS TELLING THIS CHURCH?

Christians in Thyatira were known for their love, mercy, and compassion for others—the very qualities the church in Ephesus seemed to have in short supply. They fed the poor and cared for widows and orphans. Jesus affirmed their goodness toward their neighbors. He commended their ministry of love and service, which hadn't faded. In fact, their ministry of love and service had grown. It was their first love, and unlike in Ephesus, they had not lost their first love.

Yet, He rebuked Thyatira for embracing Jezebel's immorality instead of resisting false teachers like Ephesus did. We can see how both churches faced opposition and both failed in different ways.

The pagan guilds' grip on society must have been very discouraging for those who remained faithful, perhaps to the point of causing them to question their faithfulness. But Jesus made it clear His church cannot compromise by participating in the pagan guild feasts. He warned Jezebel and "her children" (followers) via apostolic letters and visits, and He gave them time to repent. But they never did, so He promised to judge them with sickness. We can deduce that this illness was a deadly contagious epidemic among the participants in those guild feasts.

This may seem harsh, but Jesus was actually safeguarding His church by ensuring the deep things of Satan didn't ensnare them. Jesus showed Himself to be a loving shepherd who protects His flock from things we might not be able to resist on our own. As a shepherd slays a bear or wolf, Jesus intervenes against evil to preserve those who have ears to hear His voice.

Fortunately, there was a faithful remnant in Thyatira who withstood Jezebel's influence. Jesus said He has no other burden or command for the remnant than to keep doing what they're doing—loving others and remaining faithful to Him. How we all long to hear such encouragement from Jesus! Have you ever found yourself in a place where a pep talk from Jesus was something you desperately needed to hear? Well . . . here it is!

The faithful in Thyatira likely desired to change how the guilds were run, to make them fairer and more righteous. Yet, Jesus didn't tell them they would successfully change their culture. Instead, He told them they would have to endure it until the day He returns to set things right. On that day, He promises the faithful will rule with the Son of God. I'm reminded of God's words in Psalm 2:7–9:

> *I will tell of the decree: The* Lord *said to me, "You are my Son; today I have begotten you. ⁸ Ask of me, and I will make the nations your heritage, and the ends of the earth your possession. ⁹ You shall break them with a rod of iron and dash them in pieces like a potter's vessel."*

Jesus didn't promise His followers in Thyatira that they would be able to transform the guilds into righteous organizations but that their faith would enable them to endure the power and temptation of the guilds. As we're reminded in 1 John 5:4–5, the faithful will overcome the world.

Jesus described Himself as the Son of God, with eyes like a burning fire and feet like bronze. In each letter, He used one of those descriptions. When He returns, He'll judge the guilds, and together, the faithful will become a new, righteous guild. He will become our "morning star," our true King, and this world will finally become everything we who have ears to hear have hoped for.

WHAT IS JESUS TELLING US TODAY?

We have been given no other burden from Jesus but to remain faithful in a hostile world until the Son of God returns. So, why do we insist on carrying burdens and obsessions we don't need?

First, we must never compromise the gospel in an attempt to make it more appealing to the world. There's no power in a false gospel. But the enemy will use other pressures from this world's "guilds" to squeeze us into what he desires us to be. The "guilds" we face are social pressures to blend our faith. They can easily become idols.

Just as the church in Thyatira blended faith with membership in the guilds, too many Christians are blending their faith with their politics, both on the left and the right. Too many Christians have become more obsessed with activism than with the responsibilities given to us when Jesus made us His royal priests. Too many Christians are more obsessed with winning culture wars than with loving others. Too many Christians feel destined, even entitled, to political power and cultural influence in America.

Imagine a world in which Christians are in charge of governments and society. Would you cheer that? Let me break the news to you. Jesus says that will *never* happen until *He* returns as King of kings. Why would we even think we could fulfill the promises of Psalm 2:7–9 without the Son of God personally leading the way?

Until then, we cannot compromise the royal priesthood. These present-day political guilds are not part of that priesthood, and they never will be. They cannot be reformed as some hope for. Instead, we must follow the counsel of Hebrews 12:14–16:

> *Strive for peace with everyone, and for the holiness without which no one will see the Lord.* [15] *See to it . . . that no "root of bitterness" springs up and causes trouble, and by it many become defiled;* [16] *that no one is sexually immoral or unholy . . .*

Jesus and His apostles *never* commanded the church to establish a political power base, an earthly guild of our own. The fact is, until Jesus returns, there is no such thing as a utopia. We can and should participate in the political process, but followers of Jesus can't transform lives and love people by gaining political power. We can only do that by remaining faithful to the gospel.

Has Jesus given us the burden of taking over the world's guilds? No. Christians are called to one burden, which this letter identifies: love and faithfulness.

Patient endurance without compromise, loving others, and proclaiming the gospel won't be easy. It might cost you your business, friends, and reputation, but you'll overcome when Jesus returns to purify the world. The promise Jesus makes to the faithful is an eternal kingdom of heaven when He returns to set everything right.

CHAPTER EIGHT

Signs of a Dying Church

Revelation 3:1–6:

> [1] *"And to the angel of the church in Sardis write: 'The words of him who has the seven spirits of God and the seven stars.*
>
> *"'I know your works. You have the reputation of being alive, but you are dead.* [2] *Wake up, and strengthen what remains and is about to die, for I have not found your works complete in the sight of my God.* [3] *Remember, then, what you received and heard. Keep it, and repent. If you will not wake up, I will come like a thief, and you will not know at what hour I will come against you.* [4] *Yet you have still a few names in Sardis, people who have not soiled their garments, and they will walk with me in white, for they are worthy.* [5] *The one who conquers will be clothed thus in white garments, and I will never blot his name out of the book of life. I will confess his name before my Father and before his angels.* [6] *He who has an ear, let him hear what the Spirit says to the churches.'"*

What if your church received a letter from Jesus saying, "Your church is dying! Repent and return to the gospel, or be judged!" Does your church show signs of life, like joyfully caring for one another, enthusiastically worshiping, doing good works, and reaching out to the surrounding community?

No church is perfect, but is yours alive? Can it stay that way?

And what does a dying church look like? Declining attendance? A lack of money? Lots of conflict? A church can measure well in those categories, and even be well regarded by the community, but that doesn't mean it's alive.

What Would John's Readers Have Noticed?

A Dying City

Sardis had been a major power center, serving as either a primary or regional capital for various empires. It remained a wealthy and prestigious military stronghold for centuries. The world saw it as an unconquerable city.

Over time, Sardis became complacent, allowing invaders to conquer it twice. The city's power and influence waned, leading to its deterioration. It still held an immense amount of wealth, but it lacked a thriving industry like the ones in Thyatira and Ephesus. The population aged, and economic mobility declined. Sardis was described as a peaceful city, but that wasn't a compliment. It was peaceful because its dreams had died.

The Dead Church

Today, we have archeological proof for why the church in Sardis died. Just like the city, the church, too, was living off its reputation of past glory, but it had become impotent. On the outside, the church looked alive, yet Jesus deemed it dead. They had become experts at blending into the culture rather than being a lampstand for truth within it. They had abandoned the offensive parts of the gospel, including an emphasis on salvation through Jesus alone and the need for repentance.

While other nearby churches suffered persecution, the church in Sardis lived at peace with the culture. To do that in the first century, a church had to embrace syncretism, meaning worshiping Caesar and blending pagan practices into their worship. Sardis was so successful at syncretism, it lost its mooring and became a fake church, a dead church—certainly beautiful on the outside but rotting and decomposing on the inside. It had become just like Jesus' description of Jerusalem's religious elite in Matthew 23:27–28:

> *Woe to you, scribes and Pharisees, hypocrites! For you are like whitewashed tombs, which outwardly appear beautiful, but within are full of dead people's bones and all uncleanness. 28 So you also outwardly appear righteous to others, but within you are full of hypocrisy and lawlessness.*

WHAT WAS JESUS TELLING THIS CHURCH?

Jesus introduced Himself to the Sardian church as the one who holds the seven spirits in His hand. We learned in an earlier chapter that Isaiah 11:2 identifies what these seven spirits represent:

> *And the Spirit of the LORD shall rest upon him, the Spirit of wisdom and understanding, the Spirit of counsel and might, the Spirit of knowledge and the fear of the LORD.*

Jesus holds the fullness of the Holy Spirit in His hands and directs it to His church for His purposes. Why did He introduce Himself to the church in Sardis in this way? It's a clue to why this church was dead: it was no longer empowered by the Holy Spirit. Jesus didn't affirm any good works. He merely said, "You have the reputation of being alive, but you are dead."

How does that happen? How can a church full of people with ears to hear no longer have the Holy Spirit? They can't. Jesus said their works were incomplete, and that's why Sardis was a dead church. In Philippians 1:6, Paul told the church in Philippi he was confident that "he who began a good work in you will bring it to completion at the day of Jesus Christ."

How could Paul be so confident? Because Jesus taught us in Luke 24:49 that it is He who completes those works—through the Holy Spirit, which He holds in His hands:

> *I am sending the promise of my Father upon you. But stay in the city until you are clothed with power from on high.*

No church can take credit for its good works, because they're a result of the Holy Spirit, as Ephesians 2:8–9 says: "For by grace you have been saved through faith. And this is not your own doing; it is the gift of God, not a result of works, so that no one may boast." When a church is full of people who say they believe but demonstrate no works, it's a sign Jesus has not sent the Spirit. That was the church of Sardis. Its members didn't have the Holy Spirit.

Following Jesus must be more than just a verbal expression. The Spirit will ensure that following Jesus is a continual journey. When Jesus calls His sheep, they *will* follow His voice, and He sends the Holy Spirit to empower them to good works. Because the church in Sardis lacked ears to hear the Shepherd's voice, they lacked the power to produce good works.

Jesus warned Sardis they had only a glowing ember of life left. They needed to return to His gospel and repent or else His judgment would come.

Then Jesus went on to describe Sardis as a church full of people with soiled garments, reminiscent of Isaiah 64:6: "We have all become like one who is unclean, and all our righteous deeds are like a polluted garment." It's a foul image, but Jesus said there was a handful of Christians in Sardis who were still clothed in the pure white garments of the faithful. They had more than a legacy of faithfulness; they had ears to hear and were empowered by the seven spirits. Their faith displayed virtue, knowledge, reverence, self-control, stability, and love.

The ones in Sardis with the faith that conquers (*nikaō*) could still hear His voice, and they followed Jesus.[12] They would never have their names removed from the Book of Life. It's a beautiful affirmation that those with ears to hear the Shepherd's voice will never fall away.

WHAT IS JESUS TELLING US TODAY?

Jesus told the church in Sardis, "You have the reputation of being alive, yet you are dead." What if He were to write a letter declaring your church beautiful on the outside but a rotting corpse on the inside? The church might look beautiful and appear to be thriving—with regard to money, facilities, and attendance numbers—but its works would be incomplete.

How can we spot a church like that when it looks great on the outside? Dead churches might have more passion for political activism than for proclaiming the gospel. Dead churches might put liturgy ahead of seeking out hurting people and loving them where they're at. Dead churches tend to be better at branding or marketing than they are at preaching, teaching, loving, and serving. Dead churches can look more like a club than a fellowship of believers.

Another telltale sign of dead churches is that they abandon the offensive parts of the gospel—salvation by faith in Jesus alone, for instance—and replace them with many alternatives, invoking Jesus only when it's convenient or expedient.

However, when a church is passionate and active in the royal priesthood, you know Jesus has sent the seven spirits He holds in His hands, like God told us in Ezekiel 37:14: "And I will put my Spirit within you, and you shall live."

Healthy churches have many things in common. They're full of people who battle complacency by responding to the call to fresh biblical Kingdom work and by walking closer with Jesus. They love their communities while boldly proclaiming the gospel message, even if the world is offended. They're innovative and surprisingly generous, acknowledging that everything belongs to Jesus anyway.

Most importantly, a healthy church never tries to change or adapt the gospel, knowing it's the power of salvation. It's by the gospel that Jesus sends the Spirit in His hand into the hearts of those with ears to hear. Because we are filled with that Spirit, we have the assurance shared in 1 John 5 that we will overcome and we will *not* have our names removed from the Book of Life.

CHAPTER NINE

A Letter to Philadelphia (Not the One in Pennsylvania)

Revelation 3:7–13:

7 "And to the angel of the church in Philadelphia write: 'The words of the holy one, the true one, who has the key of David, who opens and no one will shut, who shuts and no one opens.

8 "'I know your works. Behold, I have set before you an open door, which no one is able to shut. I know that you have but little power, and yet you have kept my word and have not denied my name. 9 Behold, I will make those of the synagogue of Satan who say that they are Jews and are not, but lie—behold, I will make them come and bow down before your feet, and they will learn that I have loved you. 10 Because you have kept my word about patient endurance, I will keep you from the hour of trial that is coming on the whole world, to try those who dwell on the earth. 11 I am coming soon. Hold fast what you have, so that no one may seize your crown. 12 The one who conquers, I will make him a pillar in the temple of my God. Never shall he go out of it, and I will write on him the name of my God, and the name of the city of my God, the new Jerusalem, which comes down from my God out of heaven, and my own new name.

> *¹³ He who has an ear, let him hear what the Spirit says to the churches.'"*

Our culture inevitably influences how we observe life. Christians in the United States tend to interpret Scripture strictly from an American perspective. Sometimes that's okay, but it often doesn't serve us well. We can easily slip into flawed interpretations, missing out on a much bigger story than our nation's short history.

Today's passage requires us to exchange our earthly citizenship for our heavenly one. To help with this, we will examine the Old Testament in one hand and John's letter in the other.

What Would John's Readers Have Noticed?

Philadelphia

Philadelphia was established around 189 BC as a Greek outpost for the expansion of Hellenistic influence and culture into Asia Minor. The Greek ruler who founded it was close to his brother, so he called it the "city of brotherly love." It became a major trade hub and also contributed to the spread of *koine* Greek as the common written language, which was perfect for legal documents and personal letters. The New Testament was originally recorded using this form of Greek.

The city's location on a plain near the mountains provided it with rich soil that was great for agriculture, but Philadelphia was all but destroyed in AD 17 when a massive earthquake ravaged the region (also affecting Sardis and Pergamos). The Roman emperor Tiberius granted them a significant financial boon and tax reprieve to aid rebuilding, and, for some time after that, they renamed themselves "New Caesarea" in his honor.[13]

Pressured, Persecuted, and Powerless

The faithful little church started by Paul in Philadelphia was the antithesis to the one in Sardis. Its poverty-stricken members lived under constant threat of death and scrutiny from resentful Jews and a culture of syncretism. The Jewish synagogues there embraced Caesar worship. And because Rome associated Christianity with Judaism, many Jews felt the so-called stubborn Christians who refused to embrace syncretism were putting Jewish synagogues at risk of retribution from Rome by association.

The synagogues, in the name of authority they believed was given from God, persecuted the church relentlessly. Christians were targeted economically and physically with banishment and even death. It is plausible they even faced the threat of spies inside the church who might turn in followers of Jesus to the authorities. In this letter, Jesus calls those among the synagogues who targeted the church in Philadelphia "the synagogue of Satan"—his second use of this phrase in Revelation.

If Jesus' followers in Philadelphia had simply agreed to worship Caesar, their suffering would have ended, but the faithful refused! Their faithfulness cost them dearly; they had "little power." Contrast this with the American church, which in some quarters seems obsessed with gathering political influence and power.

WHAT WAS JESUS TELLING THIS CHURCH?

In Isaiah 22:22–23, God speaks these words through the prophet:

> *I will place on his shoulder the key of the house of David. He shall open, and none shall shut; he shall shut, and none shall open.* ²³ *And I will fasten him like a peg in a secure place, and he will become a throne of honor to his father's house.*

The historical context of this Old Testament prophecy was the Assyrian invasion of Israel and Jerusalem (2 Chronicles 32:1–23). Shebna, a steward of King Hezekiah, was full of pride and considered himself firmly rooted in his position as the king's representative. But he betrayed the Kingdom of Israel by collaborating with Assyria for the invasion. In Isaiah 22:15–25, God demoted Shebna and gave the position to Eliakim, awarding him the "keys to the kingdom of David." Eliakim held the position of the highest gatekeeper, with authority to grant or deny access to the house of David according to his own judgment. Once he opened the door, no one had the power to close it.

This replacement of the unfaithful Shebna with the faithful Eliakim is what Jesus revealed to the church in Philadelphia. Ultimately, this authority to grant or deny access to the King would rest on the Messiah's shoulders. So, here, Jesus declared Himself the holy one, with the keys to open and shut all doors to the kingdom of God. He decides who gets in.

Through this beautiful Old Testament metaphor, Jesus was declaring the transition of spiritual authority from Israel to His church. Though the synagogues in Philadelphia had shut their doors to the church, Jesus said He had given His followers the keys to the real door. He is the way, the truth, and the life. He essentially told the church, "You may have little power now, but they'll have no power to close or open My doors. You have that power now. If they want to come to Me, they will have to go through you—through your preaching and the sacraments."

Jesus promised this faithful church they would be spared the "hour of trial" soon coming. This does not refer to today's popular tribulation theology. Many people teach that Jesus has promised to rapture His church before a devastating seven-year period of global suffering. But that theology is flawed. Jesus *never* promised to spare His church from tribulation; instead, He said His followers will always suffer in this world on account of Him. He also told them in Matthew 24 that when the great tribulation comes, they should flee to the mountains:

> ¹⁶ *Then let those who are in Judea flee to the mountains. . . .* ²¹ *For then there will be great tribulation, such as has not been from the beginning of the world until now, no, and never will be. . . .* ²⁵ *See, I have told you beforehand.*

It's clear the church at Philadelphia, along with Smyrna, was already in tribulation. In the first chapter of Revelation, John referred to himself as a "partner in the tribulation" with them. The trial will be before Jesus on the day of the Lord, and the faithful who overcome will be spared the day of judgment because they have already been declared righteous.

In addition to keys and doors, the imagery of pillars also appears in the Old Testament. Notice this part of Solomon's design for the temple in 2 Chronicles 3:17:

> *He set up the pillars in front of the temple, one on the south, the other on the north; that on the south he called Jachin, and that on the north Boaz.*

Pillars weren't merely decorative architecture; they were designed as prominent, immovable components of a structure. When Solomon built the temple, he named its two main pillars Jachin ("the LORD establishes") and Boaz ("the LORD strengthens"). Though the synagogues of Satan had kicked the Christians out of Philadelphia, Jesus said He would make His followers immovable pillars in His new temple. First-century believers would have understood this to be a heavenly temple, not an earthly one. Jesus promised to *establish* them and *strengthen* them; in other words, He offered them eternal security.

Also, remember how the city of Philadelphia took the name of Caesar to honor Tiberius? Well, Jesus one-upped the emperor. He said the church will bear the name of His new city and the name of God. His identity will be forever tied to His church, and He is the Holy One with the power to do it. The church in Philadelphia had His authority, identity, security, and status as God's chosen people!

WHAT IS JESUS TELLING US TODAY?

Are we guilty of what I like to call "Revelation narcissism" when we study biblical prophecy? Let me explain.

Christians in Philadelphia endured real tribulation. There are churches in the world today that endure this type of persecution and still remain faithful. But it can be hard for Christians in present-day North America to relate.

We must be wary of approaching Scripture with a victim mentality or looking to affirm political and cultural expectations. Instead, we should read Revelation as citizens of something much bigger—the kingdom of God. Jesus hasn't promised to give us the keys to power in America. This letter to the faithful, suffering church in Philadelphia is a reminder of our responsibility and privilege as holders of the keys, keepers of the door, and bearers of the name of Jesus and His new city, which He's been building since His resurrection. Jesus affirmed this responsibility and privilege in Matthew 16:18–19:

> *"On this rock [immovable like a pillar] I will build my church, and the gates of hell shall not prevail against it. ¹⁹ I will give you the keys of the kingdom of heaven, and whatever you bind [shut] on earth shall be bound in heaven, and whatever you loose [open] on earth shall be loosed in heaven."*

Nations will come and go, but the kingdom of God endures, and evil won't prevail against it. God has made His church an immovable pillar in His spiritual temple, and He will keep it faithful no matter the circumstances. Our responsibility is to the kingdom of heaven above any other nation.

Jesus has entrusted us with the keys to His heavenly kingdom—to doors no one else can open or close. We children of God no longer go by our own names; we carry His name. We are reminded to put our identity in the kingdom of heaven, as the new representatives of the King of kings, before our personal and national identities. Jesus assures us in Revelation 3:20, "If anyone hears my voice and opens the door, I will come in to him and eat with him, and he with me."

Let's use the key Jesus has given us to enter through our new door and celebrate our Kingdom identity!

CHAPTER TEN

A Self-Reliant Church Is a Useless Church

Revelation 3:14–22:

14 "And to the angel of the church in Laodicea write: 'The words of the Amen, the faithful and true witness, the beginning of God's creation.

15 "'I know your works: you are neither cold nor hot. Would that you were either cold or hot! 16 So, because you are lukewarm, and neither hot nor cold, I will spit you out of my mouth. 17 For you say, I am rich, I have prospered, and I need nothing, not realizing that you are wretched, pitiable, poor, blind, and naked. 18 I counsel you to buy from me gold refined by fire, so that you may be rich, and white garments so that you may clothe yourself and the shame of your nakedness may not be seen, and salve to anoint your eyes, so that you may see. 19 Those whom I love, I reprove and discipline, so be zealous and repent. 20 Behold, I stand at the door and knock. If anyone hears my voice and opens the door, I will come in to him and eat with him, and he with me. 21 The one who conquers, I will grant him to sit with me on my throne, as I also conquered and sat down with my Father on his throne. 22 He who has an ear, let him hear what the Spirit says to the churches.'"

Not too long ago, our young church plant was becoming a little complacent. Attendance was up, and giving was strong. Our core ministries were growing. We had just started preaching through the Gospel of Mark. It seemed we had it all handled.

Then the COVID-19 pandemic hit. We couldn't meet in person, and as a result, some regular attenders left the church. Money got tight. Profound grief hit us, more than once, as we lost beloved members of our congregation. Those years taught us our church cannot be self-reliant. We need to cling to Jesus each day.

What Would John's Readers Have Noticed?

A City and a Church with Everything

Laodicea was a big, powerful city. To start with, it was a wealthy financial center, like New York or London, and boasted a high-end clothing industry as well. It was also famous for medicinal ointments and salves, the most renowned being a treatment for eye ailments.

In short, Laodicea didn't need anything from anyone. Remember how Tiberius Caesar gave a tax reprieve and funds to rebuild Philadelphia after a massive earthquake? Laodicea also experienced an earthquake in AD 60, but it turned down aid from Rome because it had enough people, power, and money to rebuild and preserve its identity on its own.

Don't Drink the Water

Despite its seeming self-reliance, Laodicea was in short supply of water. Because of rapid growth, water had to be imported from two sources: Hierapolis (six miles north), which had hot water springs famous for healing, and Colossae (ten miles east), famed for its cold, clean mountain water. Laodicea built impressive underground aqueducts from both sources to replenish its water supply.

But by the time the water arrived at the city, it was neither hot nor cold—it was lukewarm. The Hierapolis water had lost its healing properties, and the water from Colossae had lost its purity. Modern archeology has shown that Laodicea's ancient pipes were corroded with minerals, so the transported water was not only remarkably useless but also contaminated and repulsive.

The Last Church

By the time Jesus got to the church in Laodicea, He had written to six churches, clearly preparing them for what they would hear in the rest of Revelation. He rebuked four of them for apostasy, false teaching, immorality, apathy, and failing to love others, yet He also affirmed them in some way. Jesus had only good things to say to Smyrna and Philadelphia, the two smallest and poorest churches, which remained faithful even during their suffering.

Yet, Jesus gave no affirmation of any kind to the church in Laodicea. Like the city, the church had lots of money, people, influence, and power. They believed their material possessions gave them spiritual advantages—but they couldn't have been more wrong.

WHAT WAS JESUS TELLING THIS CHURCH?

Jesus' greeting in this letter provides clues to the core of Laodicea's spiritual sickness: their rejection of His supremacy. He is "the Amen," the origin and essence of everything that is true—an attribute they didn't embrace. He is "the Faithful," the author and perfector of faith and of all who remain faithful—a quality they didn't possess. And He is "the Beginning of God's creation," the catalyst of creation power—a truth they had forgotten.

This description is one of the strongest theological statements in Scripture about the power and authority of Jesus. He is so loving and so powerful, no real church would ever imagine trying to live or function without Him!

But Laodicea had tried. Paul warned against this attitude in Colossians 1:15–16:

> *He is the image of the invisible God, the firstborn of all creation.* ¹⁶ *For by him all things were created, in heaven and on earth, visible and invisible, whether thrones or dominions or rulers or authorities—all things were created through him and for him.*

The church in Colossae had rejected the deity of Jesus, and that heresy spread to Laodicea. In fact, Paul instructed the Colossians to forward his letter to Laodicea!

Faithful churches can disagree on things like spiritual gifts, liturgy, and prophecy, but the preeminent deity of Jesus is nonnegotiable. When a church is no longer fully reliant upon the mercy, grace, power, and authority of Jesus, it's simply not a church anymore.

The church at Laodicea had become self-reliant because of their material wealth and success, and they couldn't see how truly desperate they were. Jesus linked His warning to them with Hosea 12:8–9, when God rebuked Israel for the same thing:

> *[You have] said, "Ah, but I am rich; I have found wealth for myself; in all my labors they cannot find in me iniquity or sin." ⁹ I am the Lord your God; . . . I will again make you dwell in tents.*

Jesus told Laodicea, "You think you're successful, but really, you're wretched, pitiful, poor, and naked. Your eyes are blind. You need a salve like the ones you sell, but for your spirits, so you can see the truth of who you really are. You need to be poor in spirit and let go of things you love more than Me."

Further, Jesus told the church in Laodicea that they needed to stop being like lukewarm water. Hot or cold water would do, so long as they weren't tepid! Jesus' desire to spit out lukewarm water wasn't His way of comparing emotional states to water temperature; His message wasn't that the church needed to be "on fire for Jesus." The analogy of the Laodicean water was about the church being useless for the Kingdom. Just as the lukewarm city water was toxic, the church in that city made Jesus sick. They weren't like the useful healing hot springs of Hierapolis or the refreshingly cold streams of Colossae. He wanted to spit them out!

But there was one speck of hope in this letter: Jesus said He corrects those He loves and commands them to repent. Jesus loves His church enough to tell us the truth, even if it's hard or scary to hear. Jesus said He was knocking at their door, promising to reward them if they just let Him in.

Many preachers like to use verse 20 as an evangelistic knock. But Jesus was inviting the church, not merely individuals, to open the door and enjoy fellowship with Him. His invitation was directed at the whole church—to let Jesus back into their community.

WHAT IS JESUS TELLING US TODAY?

Could your church ever forget how much it needs Jesus? Would it answer if He were to knock and desire to come in and be with you?

When a church starts to forget how desperately it needs Jesus, it becomes useless for the kingdom of God. The church in Laodicea became rich, self-reliant, and comfortable, which made them useless. They forgot how much they needed Jesus, and they stopped relying on Him for all a church needs to be faithful.

Money comes and goes. Buildings can deteriorate and fall. But these uncertainties should make us grateful, because Jesus uses them to remind us of an important truth: your church is fully reliant on Him.

Your church and mine desperately need Jesus. His authority, supremacy, presence, and fellowship should be central to everything we do. Not only are we not self-sufficient, but we're also hanging by a thread daily, clinging desperately to Jesus. Why? Because, unlike the church in Laodicea, which said, "We are rich," we have been given eyes to see our spiritual poverty and our overwhelming need for Him.

John 14:23 describes what we want our church to be—a place where Jesus is always in our midst, as He says:

> *"If anyone loves me, he will keep my word, and my Father will love him, and we will come to him and make our home with him."*

The moment we think we are rich and have all we need, we shut our door to Jesus, as if we don't really need Him. But not letting Jesus into the midst of everything we do is crazy! We know He is indispensable. Spiritual humility is essential for our health. We may have some fears about the future, but do you know what a church should fear the most? That it will forget how much it needs Jesus and, in doing so, become like useless, lukewarm, contaminated city water.

Our churches need Jesus deep in our midst, every step of the way. We may not know what the future holds, but when Jesus knocks, we must always let Him in.

CHAPTER ELEVEN

A Door to Heaven

Revelation 4:1–5:

> *¹ After this I looked, and behold, a door standing open in heaven! And the first voice, which I had heard speaking to me like a trumpet, said, "Come up here, and I will show you what must take place after this." ² At once I was in the Spirit, and behold, a throne stood in heaven, with one seated on the throne. ³ And he who sat there had the appearance of jasper and carnelian, and around the throne was a rainbow that had the appearance of an emerald. ⁴ Around the throne were twenty-four thrones, and seated on the thrones were twenty-four elders, clothed in white garments, with golden crowns on their heads. ⁵ From the throne came flashes of lightning, and rumblings and peals of thunder, and before the throne were burning seven torches of fire, which are the seven spirits of God...*

When our church found a new home, we celebrated with a grand opening. But what exactly did we mean by a *grand opening*? What does that phrase mean to you?

In the case of GraceLife, we were celebrating an accomplishment, but it was more than that. A building is just bricks and mortar, after all. We were really celebrating the new door of ministry Jesus had opened for us: future opportunities in our new neighborhood to be a lampstand and to preach the gospel, which we know is the power of God for salvation.

And that leads us to the first grand opening of the church—the other side of the door Jesus has opened for us, where we find His mercy, grace, majesty, and glory. This is the theme of Revelation 4:1–5. It's intended to be an epilogue to the letters Jesus prompted John to write to the seven churches.

WHAT WOULD JOHN'S READERS HAVE NOTICED?

"After This"

Some people believe this passage, along with the rest of Revelation, should be interpreted primarily as an unfulfilled foretelling of future events. But that approach robs us of the incredible inspiration and encouragement it gives to all churches, including your own. Better to see this passage, and most of Revelation, as a perspective on the whole history of redemption—past, present, and future. It's much more than prophecy; it's a door into a higher spiritual dimension, as real as the one we inhabit. It's *already*, *right now*, and *not yet* all at once!

When John wrote "after this," he was referring to those seven letters Jesus told him to write to the seven churches. Although John transcribed them nearly 1,900 years ago, the content Jesus included in those letters transcends time. Jesus was preparing the churches for what they would hear next, as well as how to understand and interpret it.

"Isaiah Was Here"

Surely, you've seen where someone has scribbled on a wall to memorialize his or her presence there, only to be followed by others. That's essentially what we see in this passage. As far as Scripture tells us, John was the fourth human to experience the heavenly throne room. Each biblical description of the throne room provides more details than the previous, with John's being the most vivid—a critical clue for how to read Revelation. This structure teaches us that the Bible is an epic story of the progress of redemption throughout human history.

The first recorded person to experience the throne room was Moses when he received the Ten Commandments from God, beginning in Exodus 19:16:

> *On the morning of the third day there were thunders and lightnings and a thick cloud on the mountain and a very loud trumpet blast, so that all the people in the camp trembled.*

The second was Isaiah, when God commissioned him to be a prophet, in Isaiah 6:1:

> *In the year that King Uzziah died I saw the Lord sitting upon a throne, high and lifted up; and the train of his robe filled the temple.*

And the third was Ezekiel, when he was a prophet to Israel during the Babylonian captivity, in Ezekiel 1:1:

> *In the thirtieth year, in the fourth month, on the fifth day of the month, as I was among the exiles by the Chebar canal, the heavens were opened, and I saw visions of God.*

This history informs us Revelation isn't describing some distant future but, rather, that which always has been, is now, and always will be.

WHAT WAS JESUS TELLING THE CHURCHES?

The foundations of Revelation 4 are revealed in the promises given to the churches in the first three chapters. As John describes what He saw in the throne room, the promises in the seven letters form a central theme. The first link to those letters is the door Jesus spoke about in Revelation 3:8 to the believers in Philadelphia:

> *I know your works. Behold, I have set before you an open door, which no one is able to shut. I know that you have but little power, and yet you have kept my word and have not denied my name.*

We previously discovered this open door is a reference to a prophecy back in Isaiah 22:22:

> *And I will place on his shoulder the key of the house of David. He shall open, and none shall shut; and he shall shut, and none shall open.*

This prophecy reveals Jesus' promise to give to His faithful the key to the open door, which is the preaching of the gospel—a powerful privilege and responsibility for His followers.

John then describes that same voice like a trumpet that beckoned him in Revelation 1: "Come with me and see what happens next." Suddenly, he was "in the Spirit," meaning, even though his body was still in exile on a prison island, his consciousness was in another dimension with Jesus. John depicts the brilliance of the one sitting upon the throne, shining like precious stones and surrounded by a rainbow. The rainbow made another key appearance in Genesis 9:12–13, when God used it as a sign to comfort His people after the flood:

> *This is the sign of the covenant I make between me and you and every living creature with you, for all future generations:* [13] *I have set my bow in the cloud, and it shall be a sign of the covenant between me and the earth.*

This rainbow around the throne represents Jesus' nature as a covenant keeper, the ultimate promise keeper. The rainbow is also an apt metaphor for heaven itself. Even though we can see a rainbow's light and marvel at it, we can't touch it or arrive at it. It's a great picture of what heaven is for us right now!

Surrounding the throne are twenty-four smaller thrones, on which elders dressed in white robes are seated. Remember, in His letter to Sardis, Jesus said He would replace the soiled garments of the faithful with white robes. The elders in white robes are ruling with God, which was a promise in Revelation

2:26. The elders represent the twelve tribes of Israel and the twelve apostles. When we study Revelation 21, we will learn how numbers rooted in 12, such as these twenty-four elders, represent God's chosen throughout human history—those with ears to hear the voice of the Great Shepherd and follow Him. In other words, all of these people seated around the throne are intended to be metaphors for the church!

Once again, we see the Holy Spirit, represented by the seven spirits John mentioned in Revelation 1. The Spirit caused thunder and lightning around the throne, like what Moses experienced on Mount Sinai. This thunder and lightning, which we'll see referenced again later, is more evidence that this place was already, is right now, and is not yet. It's the same throne room Ezekiel, Isaiah, and Moses saw, except John's visit also details the white robes, the twenty-four thrones with the elders, and those promises Jesus made in the letters to the churches.

What Is Jesus Telling Us Today?

What's on the other side of the door is a mystery—a mystery nobody can resist. Anyone would love to open that door, but Jesus has entrusted only His followers with the keys, so we can show the world the glorious mystery.

We don't often reflect on the throne of God. It's hard to think beyond the dimensions of the time and space we live in; we're literal prisoners to the moment. But this open door is a timeless place of goodness, majesty, glory, grace, and promises kept! It's the natural hope of every human heart. The scene John saw of the *already*, the *right now*, and the *not yet* is at the core of what inspires those of us who belong to Jesus. In fact, without the throne room, church would be a complete waste of time. We would have nothing to aspire to. There would be no need to desire redemption or receive grace. There would be nothing but hopeless obsession with all the broken promises of the world's leaders and flawed economic systems. There would be no reason to hope and wait for the return of Jesus, who alone has the authority to set all things right.

But there really is a throne room, which already was and is right now but is not yet. We can celebrate that grand opening each day, including right now! We know through the power of preaching the gospel that Jesus has made a door to heaven on earth for us. Why do you think Jesus said repeatedly that the kingdom of heaven is now—not in the skies, or in the future, but here and now? As He told His followers in Hebrews 12:18–24,

> *For you have not come to what may be touched, a blazing fire and darkness and gloom and a tempest [19] and the sound of a trumpet and a voice whose words made the hearers beg that no further messages be spoken to them. [20] For they could not endure the order that was given, "If even a beast touches the mountain, it shall be stoned." [21] Indeed, so terrifying was the sight that Moses said, "I tremble with fear." [22] But you have come to Mount Zion and to the city of the living God, the heavenly Jerusalem, and to innumerable angels in festal gathering, [23] and to the assembly of the firstborn who are enrolled in heaven, and to God, the judge of all, and to the spirits of the righteous*

made perfect, ²⁴ and to Jesus, the mediator of a new covenant, and to the sprinkled blood that speaks a better word than the blood of Abel.

Jesus also assured us of our access to the throne room in Matthew 18:18–20:

> Truly, I say to you, whatever you bind [close] on earth shall be bound [closed] in heaven, and whatever you loose [open] on earth shall be loosed [opened] in heaven. ¹⁹ Again I say to you, if two of you agree on earth about anything they ask, it will be done for them by my Father in heaven. ²⁰ For where two or three are gathered in my name, there am I among them.

CHAPTER TWELVE

Sunday Mornings in Heaven

Revelation 4:6–11:

> *6 . . . and before the throne there was as it were a sea of glass, like crystal.*
>
> *And around the throne, on each side of the throne, are four living creatures, full of eyes in front and behind: 7 the first living creature like a lion, the second living creature like an ox, the third living creature with the face of a man, and the fourth living creature like an eagle in flight. 8 And the four living creatures, each of them with six wings, are full of eyes all around and within, and day and night they never cease to say, "Holy, holy, holy, is the Lord God Almighty, who was and is and is to come!"*
>
> *9 And whenever the living creatures give glory and honor and thanks to him who is seated on the throne, who lives forever and ever, 10 the twenty-four elders fall down before him who is seated on the throne and worship him who lives forever and ever. They cast their crowns before the throne, saying, 11 "Worthy are you, our Lord and God, to receive glory and honor and power, for you created all things, and by your will they existed and were created."*

Have you ever had a worship experience so powerful you sensed something unusual? Perhaps it was a greater awareness of God's presence. What makes these moments happen? And how can we experience them more often?

Worshiping together has always been an important benefit of gathering in Christian community, from the first century until today. Throughout history, those who follow Jesus have put great effort, thought, and resources into corporate worship. When we gather together, Jesus promises to open a door to heaven we can enter with Him. This passage from Revelation shows us what it looks and sounds like, right now, in the throne room.

WHAT WOULD JOHN'S READERS HAVE NOTICED?

Exposed by God's Glory

There was a frustrating recurring problem throughout the Old Testament: people wanted to gather before God to worship Him but were prevented by their own limitations. The exchange between Moses and God in Exodus 33:18–20 describes the spiritual barrier sin had erected between God and His chosen followers. Moses's request to see God's glory was met with this response from the Lord: "you cannot see my face, for man cannot see me and live."

There's a reason for sinners to hesitate before entering the presence of the glory of God: it could kill them! In Numbers

17:12–13, it's clear God's people were keenly aware of this consequence:

> And the people of Israel said to Moses, "Behold, we perish, we are undone, we are all undone. ¹³ Everyone who comes near, who comes near to the tabernacle of the Lord, shall die. Are we all to perish?"

Isaiah Transformed

This is why we need redemption, mercy, grace, and forgiveness. Isaiah 6:2–7 provides a great historical example of someone who saw this same scene and knew he wasn't ready for it:

> Above him stood the seraphim. Each had six wings: with two he covered his face, with two he covered his feet, and with two he flew. ³ And one called to another and said: "Holy, holy, holy is the Lord of hosts; the whole earth is full of his glory!" . . . ⁵ And I said: "Woe is me! For I am lost; for I am a man of unclean lips, and I dwell in the midst of a people of unclean lips; for my eyes have seen the King, the Lord of hosts!" ⁶ Then one of the seraphim flew to me, having in his hand a burning coal he had taken with tongs from the altar. ⁷ And he touched my mouth and said: "Behold, this has touched your lips; your guilt is taken away, and your sin atoned for."

Isaiah's sinfulness and frailty was exposed in the throne room. Experiencing the glory of God drove him to desperation, but he didn't say, "Let me get back to you, God." Instead, he declared, "Woe is me. I have been exposed, disrobed!" Yet, at that point, God cleansed and forgave Isaiah.

And He has done the same thing for us through Jesus! God has now removed the barriers between Him and His people so we can come near His glory together.

WHAT WAS JESUS TELLING THE CHURCHES?

The sea of glass is the least understood image in this passage. Here's my view: The book of Hebrews described the tabernacle God instructed Israel to build as an earthly copy of the heavenly throne room. According to these instructions, a large tub of water called a laver was to be placed before the entrance to the holy of holies for cleansing. I think the sea of glass represents a fixed barrier to the throne, uncrossable for the unredeemed, but also a vast source of cleansing, such as the Old Testament priests used.

As for the "four living creatures," they are better described as "ones who live" or "living ones." Ezekiel saw the same "living ones" in chapters 1 and 10 of his book and called them *cherubim*. John described them as having eyes all around. In Proverbs 15:3 and 2 Chronicles 16:9, eyes are associated with knowledge and wisdom.

These awesome "living ones" see everything happening and keep God's throne in constant focus. John uses the same likeness of animals Ezekiel did to describe certain attributes of these angels. The Old Testament uses the lion as a symbol of authority, the ox for strength and faithful service, man for wisdom, and the eagle for airborne power and speed. The beings around the throne embody all these attributes! They're fierce angels, not the fat little cherubs from Greek mythology we see in Valentine's Day advertising. The real cherubim (or seraphim) have greater access to and understanding of the glory of God than any other creation. They never stop declaring God's unchangeable nature: He was, is, and is to come.

But they don't worship alone. The twenty-four people in white robes on smaller thrones around God, who represent us, respond in a way the angels cannot, because the angels haven't experienced grace, love, and mercy. This worship was, is, and will continue nonstop. When believers on the earth gather in community to worship, it happens there, too. In those places and moments, heaven and earth overlap!

What Is Jesus Telling Us Today?

Too often, Christianity in America elevates individualism above community in our connection to Jesus. It has become primarily about "me and Jesus." We make personal quiet time and prayer higher priorities than gathering in community. This mindset was foreign to the first-century church.

Worshiping God in solitude is wonderful, but it will never compare to worshiping God in community. Just ask the angels in heaven. Of course, personal time with God is vital. It helps us cope with the burdens of surviving in this world. But worship in heaven is not done in isolation. Followers of Jesus should never be so arrogant to think they could give God the glory He deserves without their community around them. Read this next sentence carefully. Solitude with God is made powerful by first worshiping in community, not the other way around!

When we gather in community, Jesus is by our side. It's not our devotional life or our prayer time that prepares us for worship; it's Jesus Himself, along with our community. Revelation helps us see the privileges Jesus reserves for those who gather to worship Him, which He described in Matthew 18:18–20:

> *Whatever you bind on earth shall be bound in heaven, and whatever you loose on earth shall be loosed in heaven. [19] . . . if two of you agree on earth about anything they ask, it will be done for them by my Father in heaven. [20] For where two or three are gathered in my name, there am I among them.*

Gathering in community is the highest expression of following Jesus in this life, outside of dying for our faith. Humility before the throne, combined with community, is how we experience these glorious moments together. Like Isaiah, the cherubim and seraphim, and the twenty-four elders in white robes, we acknowledge the undeniable majesty and glory of God. When we gather in community and Jesus takes us through the door to heaven, all we can say is, "Woe is me, I've been exposed!" We become part of the *already*, the *right now*, and the *not yet*—a spiritual community fully prepared to declare God's glory. Let's enjoy the door Jesus has opened for us into heaven by following the elders' example in verses 10 and 11:

> *They cast their crowns before the throne, saying, [11] "Worthy are you, our Lord and God, to receive glory and honor*

and power, for you created all things, and by your will they existed and were created."

Any glory, fulfillment, joy, or reward is like a crown for our personal achievement. But as this passage says, we willingly throw them down before the glory of the Lord, who created us and gave us all these talents and blessings. Praise God!

CHAPTER THIRTEEN

The Kingdom Unsealed

Revelation 5:1–7:

> *¹ Then I saw in the right hand of him who was seated on the throne a scroll written within and on the back, sealed with seven seals. ² And I saw a mighty angel proclaiming with a loud voice, "Who is worthy to open the scroll and break its seals?" ³ And no one in heaven or on earth or under the earth was able to open the scroll or to look into it, ⁴ and I began to weep loudly because no one was found worthy to open the scroll or to look into it. ⁵ And one of the elders said to me, "Weep no more; behold, the Lion of the tribe of Judah, the Root of David, has conquered, so that he can open the scroll and its seven seals."*
>
> *⁶ And between the throne and the four living creatures and among the elders I saw a Lamb standing, as though it had been slain, with seven horns and with seven eyes, which are the seven spirits of God sent out into all the earth. ⁷ And he went and took the scroll from the right hand of him who was seated on the throne.*

What does the phrase "end of times" mean to you? Does it cause you anxiety? Excitement? Fear? Do you associate it with headlines about the possible coming of the Antichrist?

Does it make you want to hunker down in preparation for an onslaught of darkness?

So far, Revelation has been about what has happened already, right now, but not yet in complete fullness. What if I told you the "end of times" is actually the glorious, joyful *right now* part of Revelation? This book is intended to provide comfort, not doom or images of a nightmarish end-times scenario. After all, we know evil is here already. Instead, Revelation is about revealing how God will fulfill His plan for redemption and the relentless expansion of His kingdom here on earth! It lays bare the troubling mystery of our conflict between good and evil, which nobody could really have understood until it was written.

What Would John's Readers Have Noticed?

Scrolls and Seals

In the ancient world, important covenants or documents were written on scrolls and then rolled up, tied, and secured with a personalized wax seal. For typical documents, the contract was written on the smooth inner side of the scroll with no details on the outside. But when a document was special, scribes would write a summary on the outside describing the contents of the scroll, including the parties involved, the benefits, and sometimes dire warnings. The appearance would typically include beautiful calligraphy and decorative seals and ribbons meant to stand out. Multiple seals were indicators of elevated importance, communicating severe consequences for unworthy parties attempting to break them.

The Sealed Scroll

The scroll John describes in chapter 5 has writing inside and out, and its seven seals are meant to indicate it is the ultimate heavenly document. As we'll learn later, this scroll was God's covenant between His chosen people and His kingdom, containing His plan of salvation. But John wasn't the first human to see this vital scroll. It had appeared to Ezekiel, in Ezekiel 2:9–10:

> *And when I looked, behold, a hand was stretched out to me, and behold, a scroll was in it.* [10] *And he spread it before me. And it had writing on the front and on the back, and there were written on it words of lamentation and mourning and woe.*

The prophet Isaiah likewise described the scroll of God's covenant, in Isaiah 29:11–12:

> *And the vision of all this has become to you like the words of a scroll that is sealed. When men give it to one who can read, saying, "Read this," he says, "I cannot, for it is sealed."* [12] *And when they give the book to one who cannot read, saying, "Read this," he says, "I cannot read."*

It's understandable why Ezekiel and Isaiah would be troubled by such an important scroll. In Ezekiel's case, words of "mourning and woe" are written on the outside, and Isaiah found the scroll unreadable. Daniel, too, was troubled by visions that were sealed, possibly in this very scroll, in verses 8:26–27 of his book:

> "The vision... that has been told is true, but seal up the vision, for it refers to many days from now." [27] And I, Daniel, was overcome and lay sick for some days. Then I rose and went about the king's business, but I was appalled by the vision and did not understand it."

All four men—Ezekiel, Daniel, Isaiah, and John—were distraught by the scroll because they couldn't understand why evil coincided with good. The outside of the scroll heralded lamentation, mourning, and woe, and though the inside promised redemption, they couldn't open the scroll to see how it would be accomplished. Why does God allow evil and suffering to flourish? The prophets couldn't understand the whole scope of the plan of redemption in their time, but we can.

WHAT WAS JESUS TELLING THE CHURCHES?

This passage in Revelation can't be understood without the book of Daniel. The prophet described the end times in Daniel 12:1–4 and 12:8–10:

> *"There shall be a time of trouble, such as never has been since there was a nation till that time. But at that time your people shall be delivered, everyone whose name shall be found written in the book [scroll].* ² *And many of those who sleep in the dust of the earth shall awake, some to everlasting life, some to shame and everlasting contempt.* ³ *And those who are wise shall shine like the brightness of the sky above; and those who turn many to righteousness, like the stars forever and ever.* ⁴ *But you, Daniel, shut up the words and seal the book, until the time of the end. Many shall run to and fro, and knowledge shall increase."* . . .
>
> ⁸ *I heard, but I did not understand. Then I said, "O my lord, what shall be the outcome of these things?"* ⁹ *He said, "Go your way, Daniel, for the words are shut up and sealed until the time of the end.* ¹⁰ *Many shall purify themselves and make themselves white and be refined, but the wicked shall act wickedly. And none of the wicked shall understand, but those who are wise shall understand."*

When I read that, I hear Jesus' words in Matthew 11:15: "He who has ears to hear, let him hear." This scroll contained God's covenant with His people, His plan of redemption for them from beginning to end, which was initiated by Jesus' incarnation, something He taught repeatedly. The scroll held all the hopes and promises for those who overcome—hope for the *already, right now,* and *not yet*. It's true that the outside depicted suffering and evil, but the inside offered something better, though it had not yet been revealed. We can see clearly now that Daniel prophesied how God would use the church in a world of evil six hundred years later. This vision troubled Daniel so much because it pointed to something he couldn't understand: the kingdom of God. God told him, "Seal it up, Daniel. Now's not the time for all to be revealed."

This is why John was full of sorrow—because there seemed to be no one in heaven to open the redemption scroll. But then one of the elders said in verse 5, "Weep no more; behold, the Lion of the tribe of Judah, the Root of David, has conquered, so that he can open the scroll and its seven seals." These are descriptions of the Messiah taken from Genesis 49, where He appeared as the Lion of Judah, and Isaiah 53:7, where He was described as a Lamb led to slaughter.

This slain lamb appeared with seven horns, seven eyes, and the seven spirits of God. Horns were a common symbol of strength, authority, and divinity in the ancient Near East, and the more horns, the more power the bearer had.[14] So, the seven horns represent Jesus' supreme power and authority to open the seven seals, while the seven eyes are a metaphor for His complete wisdom and knowledge. And the seven spirits, as we have seen previously, represent the fullness of the Spirit of God. The one who looked like a slain Lamb, and who had all authority (horns) and knowledge (eyes and Spirit), took the scroll to open it. This was Jesus, the one who possesses all authority and yet laid down His life.

WHAT IS JESUS TELLING US TODAY?

When Jesus unsealed His Father's plans for the kingdom of God, evil was powerless to stop it. I can understand why Ezekiel, Isaiah, Daniel, and John were all so distraught with the sealed-up scroll. Until it was unsealed, the kingdom of God couldn't arrive; it couldn't start. But when the time was right, Jesus came to open the seals. And, because He did, we now have the benefit of experiencing all those things that frustrated Daniel by remaining out of reach.

Yes, evil still seems to run rampant, but the kingdom of God is *now*. Jesus launched the kingdom, and it's still expanding as God redeems His chosen. The Lion of Judah, the root of Jesse, the slain Lamb of God, approaches the Father and says, "Here, give Me the scroll, the covenant, Your full plan of redemption. I'll take it from here. I'll fulfill it—in the fullness of time, I'll unite heaven and earth." What a beautiful description of the end times! By contrast, many Christians interpret "end times" as a global political crisis and think our job is to stop the advancement of evil.

God told Daniel to "shut up the words and seal the book, until the time of the end." The opening of the scroll is now possible because we are in the last days, the end times. The cross of Jesus changed everything, and the opening of the scroll marks that moment. We can now reveal what had been sealed, that which caused Daniel to be appalled to the point of illness. We must learn what it means to live in the reality of the unstoppable kingdom of God, which Jesus has unsealed and unleashed. If Christians can grasp what truly happened the moment Jesus broke these seals, it will transform how we see and live in this world. And yes, the outside of that scroll describes the suffering, but the inside promises the glorious ending, as Paul summed up well in 2 Corinthians 4:8–9 and 4:15:

> *We are afflicted in every way, but not crushed; perplexed, but not driven to despair; [9] persecuted, but not forsaken; struck down, but not destroyed.... [15] For it is all for your*

sake, so that as grace extends to more and more people it may increase thanksgiving, to the glory of God.

We have all experienced moments when evil seems to be advancing unabated as it inflicts loss and death on the world. The tribulation is here and now—but so is the kingdom! They exist side by side, just as Jesus described in His parable of the wheat and the weeds! In fact, the kingdom is winning. This is the end of times, the ever-expanding kingdom of God. We aren't called to hunker down; we are on the move. And even though it may not feel like it sometimes, evil's days on this earth are numbered!

CHAPTER FOURTEEN

A New Song in Heaven

Revelation 5:8–14:

> [8] And when he had taken the scroll, the four living creatures and the twenty-four elders fell down before the Lamb, each holding a harp, and golden bowls full of incense, which are the prayers of the saints. [9] And they sang a new song, saying, "Worthy are you to take the scroll and to open its seals, for you were slain, and by your blood you ransomed people for God from every tribe and language and people and nation, [10] and you have made them a kingdom and priests to our God, and they shall reign on the earth."
>
> [11] Then I looked, and I heard around the throne and the living creatures and the elders the voice of many angels, numbering myriads of myriads and thousands of thousands, [12] saying with a loud voice, "Worthy is the Lamb who was slain, to receive power and wealth and wisdom and might and honor and glory and blessing!"
>
> [13] And I heard every creature in heaven and on earth and under the earth and in the sea, and all that is in them, saying, "To him who sits on the throne and to the Lamb be blessing and honor and glory and might forever and ever!"

> [14] And the four living creatures said, "Amen!" and the elders fell down and worshiped.

Music is a huge part of what most Christians do on Sunday mornings. Each week, churches expend much time and effort—not to mention budget—on worshiping through music. Why do we believe it's so important to have skilled musicians and high-quality sound, lights, and production? From an earthly perspective, it can sure seem like a waste of money, but Scripture suggests otherwise.

What Would John's Readers Have Noticed?

Old Testament Worship

We see several components of heavenly worship in this passage: harps, songs, prayers, and crowds of worshipers. Throughout the Old Testament, these were important parts of worship for God's people. Harps and strings helped initiate worship and gather people for prophecy, which meant not only predictions but also other relevant declarations of God's word. In 2 Kings 3:15–16, the prophet Elisha had a musician play before sharing prophecy:

> "But now bring me a musician." And when the musician played, the hand of the Lord came upon him. [16] And he said, "Thus says the Lord, . . ."

Think of how King David—a warrior, a man's man, but also a poet and a singer—made sure to accompany praise and prophecy with music. The writer of 1 Chronicles 25:1–3 described how David organized the musicians for worship services:

> *David and the chiefs of the service also set apart for the service ... [those] who prophesied with lyres, with harps, and with cymbals. ... ³ [And those] who prophesied with the lyre in thanksgiving and praise to the LORD.*

Incense

Incense was also used in the Old Testament as part of an offering to prepare people to approach God. This specific incense was called the "daily offering," a morning and evening temple ritual described in Exodus 30:7–9:

> *And Aaron shall burn fragrant incense on it. Every morning when he dresses the lamps he shall burn it, ⁸ and when Aaron sets up the lamps at twilight, he shall burn it, a regular incense offering before the LORD throughout your generations. ⁹ You shall not offer unauthorized incense on it, or a burnt offering, or a grain offering, and you shall not pour a drink offering on it.*

New Songs

The biblical term *new song* used in Revelation 5:9 doesn't just mean something that's never been heard before; it means something inspired by a new act of God's salvation. Throughout Scripture, the phrase describes a spontaneous artistic response to acts or words of God, those special gifts from the Lord marking an intersection of heaven and earth. The Bible contains numerous examples of people singing a new song in response to God's accomplishments: Moses, when God led Israel out of Egypt in Exodus 15; David, when God delivered him from danger in Psalm 18; Asaph, when the temple construction was completed in 2 Chronicles 5:13; Hezekiah, when God allowed him to repair the Temple in 2 Chronicles 29:27; and Mary, when God fulfilled His promise she would bear a son as a virgin in Luke 1:46–55.

WHAT WAS JESUS TELLING THE CHURCHES?

Worship begins with the twenty-four elders leading all those who represent God's chosen redeemed throughout history. Look closely at what the Lord tells Moses in Exodus 19:6:

> "'And you shall be to me a kingdom of priests and a holy nation.'"

The idea that God's people should be a kingdom of priests is fulfilled here in Revelation 5:10 and is a repeat of Revelation 1:6. The bowls of incense form a beautiful picture of this *kingdom of priests* in action. Once you understand the meaning of these bowls, the rest of the passage falls into place. Numbers 16:40 emphasized the role of priests in burning incense:

> *No outsider, who is not of the descendants of Aaron, should draw near to burn incense before the LORD, lest he become like Korah and his company.*

Who are Aaron's descendants? They are the priesthood of proclamation, integrity, and industry. Recall the Exodus passage above about the evening offering. Psalm 141:2 was a prophecy of this offering being replaced by the prayers of the redeemed because they fully satisfy the Lord:

> *Let my prayer be counted as incense before you, and the lifting up of my hands as the evening sacrifice.*

Jesus' followers lead the worship in heaven and on earth with a new song, celebrating what only the redeemed can fully appreciate! Our new song is a declaration to all creation of what the Lamb did for us when He opened the scroll. Psalm 33:3–4 described this song:

> *Sing to him a new song; play skillfully on the strings, with loud shouts. ⁴ For the word of the LORD is upright, and all his work is done in faithfulness.*

God doesn't intend for these new songs to be solos, either. Throughout Scripture, God calls His redeemed to worship together in large gatherings, like in 1 Chronicles 16:23–24:

> *Sing to the LORD, all the earth! Tell of his salvation from day to day. ²⁴ Declare his glory among the nations, his marvelous works among all the peoples!*

And in Psalm 102:21–22:

> *That they may declare in Zion the name of the LORD, and in Jerusalem his praise, ²² when peoples gather together, and kingdoms, to worship the LORD.*

Because the Lamb who opened the scroll has made us a kingdom of priests, all creation can sing our song "from the end of the earth," as Isaiah 42:10 described it:

> *Sing to the LORD a new song, his praise from the end of the earth, you who go down to the sea, and all that fills it.*

The scope of this worship reverberates as our new song reaches the expanse, touching "myriads of myriads and thousands of thousands" (Revelation 5:11). *Myriad* derives from the Greek word *myrioi*, which means "ten thousand."[15] So, in other words, John saw an immense number, because the response of all creation, including angels and every living being in heaven and on earth, is to join in our new song.

Notice in Revelation 4:10 that the elders fell and worshiped God on the throne, but now in this passage, they worship "the Lamb who was slain." What has occurred? The Lamb opened the scroll and took His place with the Father on the throne. This is Jesus stepping into the authority of His role as our high priest after having offered Himself for our sins as the Lamb, as Hebrews 10:11–12 describes:

> *Every priest stands daily at his service, offering repeatedly the same sacrifices, which can never take away sins. 12 But*

when Christ had offered for all time a single sacrifice for sins, he sat down at the right hand of God.

WHAT IS JESUS TELLING US TODAY?

God has designated His church to lead worship in all heaven and earth—another reason we should always cherish time together in community. Revelation 5:8–14 describes worship in heaven led by the redeemed, a kingdom of priests that includes you and me. For everyone with ears to hear, Jesus opening the scroll changed the reason for worship from awe and sacrifice to joy and celebration. Our worship of the Lamb of God is so compelling, so powerful, all heaven and earth cannot help but follow our lead.

Why? Because we the redeemed, the royal priesthood, understand redemption more than anyone in heaven or on earth. The order of worship we have seen in this passage from Revelation—music, a new song, the proclaiming of truth, and multitudes—is organic. It's a pattern we instinctively follow today in response to Jesus' love for us and what He did on the cross, as Ephesians 5:2 explains when it says, "as Christ loved us and gave himself up for us, a fragrant offering and sacrifice to God."

Our worship is a satisfying experience, not just for us but for God, too—and the whole world sees it, according to Paul in 2 Corinthians 2:15:

> *For we are the aroma of Christ to God among those who are being saved and among those who are perishing.*

This is further evidence of how Jesus' sacrifice on the cross and His opening the scroll made everything new. We don't gather on Sunday mornings just for us. Heaven and earth eagerly await our new song to the King! Paul elaborated on this point in Romans 8:19–23, 26:

> *For the creation waits with eager longing for the revealing of the sons of God.* [20] *For the creation was subjected to futility, not willingly, but . . . in hope* [21] *that the creation itself will be set free from its bondage to corruption and obtain the freedom of the glory of the children of God.* [22] *For we know that the whole creation has been groaning together in the pains of childbirth until now.* [23] *And not only the creation, but we ourselves . . . groan inwardly as we wait eagerly for adoption as sons, the redemption of our bodies. . . .* [26] *Likewise the Spirit helps us in our weakness. For we do not know what to pray for as we ought, but the Spirit himself intercedes for us with groanings too deep for words.*

Many people are tempted to worship creation itself, but creation is longing for us to worship its Creator. Does this responsibility intimidate you? Don't worry—the Spirit is interceding to help us when we meet together to worship God and encourage one another in love, the way Hebrews 10:24–25 describes:

> *Let us consider how to stir up one another to love and good works,* [25] *not neglecting to meet together, as is the habit of some, but encouraging one another, and all the more as you see the Day drawing near.*

Our prayers fill the earth even as evil still runs rampant. How frustrated the forces of darkness must feel, constantly overcome by the sweet fragrance from the prayers of God's redeemed, because the Lamb opened that scroll! Constantly smelling our prayers, hearing the strum of our strings, and hearing the words of our new song must be like nails on a chalkboard to Satan and his forces of darkness. How relieved they must be when we neglect our community worship!

But to our Father, it's a fully satisfying sacrifice of praise from the holy nation of priests the Lamb has created. And when we worship together in community, we are part of this same scene John described, which is still happening right now in heaven.

CHAPTER FIFTEEN

Four Horsemen of Human History

Revelation 6:1–8.

1 Now I watched when the Lamb opened one of the seven seals, and I heard one of the four living creatures say with a voice like thunder, "Come!" 2 And I looked, and behold, a white horse! And its rider had a bow, and a crown was given to him, and he came out conquering, and to conquer.

3 When he opened the second seal, I heard the second living creature say, "Come!" 4 And out came another horse, bright red. Its rider was permitted to take peace from the earth, so that people should slay one another, and he was given a great sword.

5 When he opened the third seal, I heard the third living creature say, "Come!" And I looked, and behold, a black horse! And its rider had a pair of scales in his hand. 6 And I heard what seemed to be a voice in the midst of the four living creatures, saying, "A quart of wheat for a denarius, and three quarts of barley for a denarius, and do not harm the oil and wine!"

7 When he opened the fourth seal, I heard the voice of the fourth living creature say, "Come!" 8 And I looked, and behold, a pale horse! And its rider's name was Death, and Hades followed him. And they were given authority over a fourth of the earth, to kill with sword and with famine and with pestilence and by wild beasts of the earth.

Many people like to say we are living in crazy times because our current age is filled with anxiety, economic strife, disease, political conflict, and more. But are these times really so crazy? Are they that different from the rest of human history? Not even close. Many people suffer from what I call "apocalyptic narcissism," thinking we endure unique turmoil in our day. Previous generations have endured so-called crazy times, most of them far crazier than ours. For thousands of years, human thirst for political, economic, cultural, and military conquest has caused suffering, pain, and death.

How do we reconcile living by faith, as part of the kingdom of God, in a world like this? How can we place hope in the One who has opened the scroll of redemption when so much of humanity is permitted to act this way?

What Would John's Readers Have Noticed?

Scary Horses

Many see these first four seals as future prophecy, part of a terrible seven-year tribulation to come. But that's a flawed interpretation, one that robs Jesus' followers of the ability to fully understand why the world is the way it is. A proper interpretation of the first four seals requires us to examine the words of the prophet Zechariah. In Zechariah 6:1–8, he saw four chariots pulled by horses the same colors as the ones John saw: red, black, white, and pale.

Horsemen from Heaven

Zechariah described these chariots as "winds from heaven," meaning they were sent by the Spirit of God. In verse 7, he wrote, "When the strong horses came out, they were impatient to go and patrol the earth. And [the angel] said, 'Go, patrol the earth.' So they patrolled the earth." Why are these horsemen eager to patrol the earth? Are they bloodthirsty? Do they just love wreaking havoc? No, they're eager to preserve God's people because they carry His judgment on Israel's enemies.

"Already"

After the four horses departed, Zechariah saw what direction only the black, white, and pale horses took. He didn't provide much detail other than the result, which he recorded in Zechariah 6:8:

> Then [the angel] cried to me, "Behold, those who go toward the north country have set my Spirit at rest in the north country."

We know these horsemen have been patrolling the earth long before John wrote about them. For example, in Zechariah's time, the Persians conquered Babylon in 539 BC and then allowed exiled Jews to return to Jerusalem to begin building the Second Temple. But what exactly are these horsemen?

WHAT WAS JESUS TELLING THE CHURCHES?

John's vision of the heavenly horsemen matched Zechariah's, but as we have already seen, John's vision provides greater detail. He described their appearance as resulting from Jesus opening the scroll—which He did slowly, in His timing, to execute God's plan of redemption.

Kings and emperors frequently rode into battle on a white horse, projecting themselves as champions, as chosen ones (or messiahs), with wisdom and power to bring lasting peace and justice. This pursuit of conquest in all venues of life is part of the judgment for sin.

The peace taken by the rider of the red horse is the inevitable result of the conquering rider of the white horse. The thirst for conquest drives earthly conflicts. Since the fall, beginning with Cain and Abel, man has risen against man, and nation against nation. The image of red represents the blood of war that always accompanies the thirst for conquest.

The black horse's rider brings famine, destruction, and suffering—the inevitable results of nation rising against nation in war. John described food shortages, massive inflation, and the exploitation of the conquered: the price of wheat for a single meal inflated to a full day's wages for a Roman soldier. Barley, which was normally reserved for livestock, became the cheaper but more unpleasant alternative to wheat for a family.

War always disrupts production. John's readers in Asia Minor would have understood this effect because they imported wheat. But what can we make of the line about "the oil and wine" in verse 6? It's about the exploitation of those conquered. As major providers of oil and wine to the empire, residents of Asia Minor were ordered by Rome not to disrupt those supply lines—even if Rome failed to pay.

The fourth seal released the pale horse and its rider—Death and Hades, which are proper names for death and the grave. The Greek word *chloros* used here for the color of the pale horse indicates the sickly green color of rotting flesh.[16] This rider has the power to kill a quarter of the world's population—more a description of consequences than an exact number.

Altogether, these horsemen summarize human history's cycle of conquest, followed by war, suffering, disease, and death. We saw Jesus describe this cycle to His disciples in Matthew 24:4–8 as a sign of the approaching end times:

> *And Jesus answered them, "See that no one leads you astray. [5] For many will come in my name, saying, 'I am the Christ,' and they will lead many astray. [6] You will hear of wars and rumors of wars. See that you are not alarmed, for this must take place, but the end is not yet. [7] For nation will rise against nation, and kingdom against kingdom, and there will be famines and earthquakes in various places. [8] All these are but the beginning of the birth pains."*

Those who "will lead many astray" are the antichrists John warned about in 1 John 2:13-22 and 2 John 1:7—those who believe they are chosen to bring peace and prosperity to the world through conquest and who see themselves as worthy of Christ's crown and white horse. By contrast, the four horsemen represent God's judgment for His enemies. They expose and weed out darkness for the purpose of advancing His plan of redemption. Some Christians die because of these horsemen, but not spiritually. The horsemen don't always follow in perfect order either, but they are acts of judgment feeding off one another. This passage explains how God's plan for the kingdoms of this world and the kingdom of God overlap. The scroll contained His ordained plan of redemption, carried out by the Lamb who opened it.

WHAT IS JESUS TELLING US TODAY?

Any student of history knows how often men on white horses have ridden in with promises they cannot keep, kicking off cycles of war, famine, and death. Since the fall of man, the world has seen only brief moments of false peace in between these four patrolling horsemen. Yet, somehow, even God's chosen are tempted to put hope in worldly leaders, just as Jesus cautioned against in Matthew 24:24:

> *For false christs [who believe they have been chosen by God for great things] and false prophets [who claim to speak truth] will arise and perform great signs and wonders, so as to lead astray, if possible, even the elect.*

After seven thousand years of recorded human history, you'd think we would have learned, but only those with ears to hear actually do. Try to think of judgment not as punishment but as a process of separation, as Paul explained in Romans 1:18:

> *For the wrath of God is revealed from heaven against all ungodliness and unrighteousness of men.*

These four horsemen are part of Jesus' plan of redemption, a repeated cycle of judgment. As He plants seeds of wheat, evil plants its weeds among them. In Matthew 3:12, Jesus said this of Himself:

> *"His winnowing fork is in his hand, and he will clear his threshing floor and gather his wheat into the barn, but the chaff he will burn with unquenchable fire."*

And in Matthew 13:30, Jesus explained how the Lamb waits patiently as His harvest grows:

> *"Let both grow together until the harvest, and at harvest time I will tell the reapers, 'Gather the weeds first and bind them in bundles to be burned, but gather the wheat into my barn.'"*

Then, Christ allows the horsemen to patrol the earth and do their job. They're intended to be a reminder, a sign to the redeemed that our Jesus is advancing His kingdom! Jesus' words in Matthew 10:34 and 10:39 sound ominous, but they should offer us comfort:

> *Do not think that I have come to bring peace to the earth. I have not come to bring peace, but a sword.... ³⁹ Whoever finds his life will lose it, and whoever loses his life for my sake will find it.*

These verses are comforting because the sword is in *His* hands! By contrast, it's a fool's errand to place our hope in any man riding a white horse and making promises of peace and prosperity. Jesus says placing hope in this world may provide moments of false peace, but it will all end with the pale horse: death.

When we see the impact of these horsemen in the headlines, they should remind us that only Jesus is worthy of our hope. He calls His chosen, those who hear His voice, to salvation. Yes, there may be suffering as He separates the weeds from His harvest, but He is in control. He is perfectly executing His plan for our redemption—so keep your hope in Him!

CHAPTER SIXTEEN

Why, God? How Long?

Revelation 6:9–11:

> ⁹ When he opened the fifth seal, I saw under the altar the souls of those who had been slain for the word of God and for the witness they had borne. ¹⁰ They cried out with a loud voice, "O Sovereign Lord, holy and true, how long before you will judge and avenge our blood on those who dwell on the earth?" ¹¹ Then they were each given a white robe and told to rest a little longer, until the number of their fellow servants and their brothers should be complete, who were to be killed as they themselves had been.

Have you ever been frustrated with God, wondering why He would allow His children to suffer at the hands of evil in this world? I'm not talking about suffering because of our own choices, which isn't true suffering but a matter of consequences. I'm talking about paying a price for identifying with Jesus, the gospel, and the kingdom of God. More than ninety thousand Christians worldwide are killed each year because of their faith![17]

Paul says we can experience joy in the midst of suffering, especially when it's because of the gospel. This is one of those scriptural truths to which we may say *amen* but from which we secretly hope to be spared. Why can't we just expect blessings to flow when we follow Jesus? What is a proper response to real persecution? Why doesn't Jesus come back and take care of evil?

What Would John's Readers Have Noticed?

The Golden Altar

The temple in Jerusalem had two altars. The first was the golden altar, upon which bowls of incense were burned. It was an earthly copy of the heavenly altar of prayer John described in this passage. The golden bowls of incense are the prayers of the saints. Hebrews 9:24 indicates the presence of earthly copies of heavenly things:

> *For Christ has entered, not into holy places made with hands, which are copies of the true things, but into heaven itself, now to appear in the presence of God on our behalf.*

The Bronze Altar

The second altar, made of bronze, was also an earthly replica in the temple. Animal sacrifices were performed on this bronze altar, and under it was a trough through which the blood of the animals would run off into a receptacle to be burned away. Hebrews 9:22 explained the purpose of this altar:

> *Indeed, under the law almost everything is purified with blood, and without the shedding of blood there is no forgiveness of sins.*

This altar would have been the first thing anyone who entered the gate of the temple would see, standing as a reminder of how desperately we need to be made righteous if we are to dwell with God. A perfect sacrifice must be offered to make us righteous so we can receive a white robe. The bronze altar, with the blood of atonement gathering below, was an unmistakable image of redemption and its price.

The bronze altar was also a symbol to remind Israel of God's promise to send a savior, a defender, a deliverer. And it represented the future defeat of evil—the moment the fate of this war between good and evil would be decided. The prophet Isaiah described this victory of Christ over the evil oppressing the earth in Isaiah 19:19–20:

> *In that day there will be an altar to the* Lord *in the midst of the land of Egypt . . .* [20] *It will be a sign and a witness to the* Lord *of hosts in the land of Egypt. When they cry to the* Lord *because of oppressors, he will send them a savior and defender, and deliver them.*

WHAT WAS JESUS TELLING THE CHURCHES?

Let's return to the four horsemen for a moment. They were unstoppable forces sent by Jesus when He opened the first four seals of the scroll, eager to complete the separation of the wheat from the weeds. They have patrolled the earth from the days of Cain and Abel until now; evil has been powerless to stop them.

Evil has only one possible counterattack against the kingdom of God: to attack those who have been redeemed. Jesus told us this would happen when the Kingdom first began. In Matthew 24:9, He warned His followers, "Then they will deliver you up to tribulation and put you to death, and you will be hated by all nations for my name's sake."

The martyrs under the heavenly bronze altar expressed frustration. How long would they have to wait for justice? Maybe you have felt the same way, wondering why God seems to allow evil to win. Consider the master's response in this parable from Matthew 13:27–30:

> The servants of the master of the house came and said to him, "Master, did you not sow good seed in your field? How then does it have weeds?" [28] He said to them, "An enemy has done this." So the servants said to him, "Then do you want us to go and gather them?" [29] But he said, "No, lest in gathering the weeds you root up the wheat along with them. [30] Let both grow together until the harvest [rest a little longer, until the number of their fellow servants and their brothers should be complete], and at harvest time I will tell the reapers, 'Gather the weeds first and bind them in bundles to be burned, but gather the wheat into my barn.'"

So, we understand that the voices under the altar come from those who died for the cause and who are wondering aloud, "How long, Jesus, until our sacrifices and deaths are vindicated?" This is the fifth seal: evil's war against the church after the resurrection of Jesus.

WHAT IS JESUS TELLING US TODAY?

Many times throughout Scripture, God's people ask, "How long?" Even His followers don't realize how often they get angry with Him, questioning His purpose and His goodness. At points, we feel the urge to remind Him that evil needs to be judged.

The questions "Why, God?" and "How long?" can be asked from different perspectives. Some refuse to believe in a God who allows suffering to happen. They aren't atheists, but they're angry with Him. They say God is callous or negligent. Others assume God provides earthly blessings and prosperity as a reward for their faith. But it's a mistake to assume God is obligated to do so. When they question God about their perceived suffering, it shows ignorance regarding the plan of redemption. Neither perspective inspires motivation to prioritize living for God's kingdom. Both are rooted in selfishness, putting higher value on comfort and safety than on the kingdom of God.

A third group asks the question "How long?" from the realization we're in a battle with evil until Jesus returns. We're not gluttons for suffering, but we understand it's part of the reality of following Jesus in this world. Ephesians 6:12 describes the church in battle:

> *For we do not wrestle against flesh and blood, but against the rulers, against the authorities, against the cosmic powers over this present darkness, against the spiritual forces of evil in heavenly places.*

The smallest inconvenience or slightest opposition often makes us neglect our Kingdom responsibilities. Earthly goals such as work, culture, and money derail us from being living sacrifices. Most of us will never be martyrs for the gospel. Frankly, we give in to much less than the threat of death.

Evil hates the redeemed, but this passage in Revelation promises that hatred will not hinder God's plan of redemption. Once He finishes redeeming those He has called, Jesus *is* coming. He will set things right. On that day, we will no longer wrestle against the forces of darkness. We will take our part in the church's total victory. Until then, we are called to endure the battle, as the kingdom of God grows up among the weeds. That way, as Paul wrote in Philippians 3:10–11,

> *[We] may know him and the power of his resurrection, and may share his sufferings, becoming like him in his death, ¹¹ that by any means possible [we] may attain the resurrection from the dead.*

The plan of redemption is a far-reaching, long-lasting phase in a war that began long before we were born. For the sake of those yet to be redeemed, we are called and equipped to endure this final stage of the war, just as those who came before us have. If you are a child of God, you have benefited from the past endurance of the faithful church in battle. This idea of expecting suffering may seem counterintuitive, but it is the miracle of joy, a supernatural satisfaction with the presence of God over anything else. It's a privilege to be a part of the church in battle, awaiting Jesus to complete his victorious plan of redemption.

One day, when Jesus opens the last seal, this final stage of the war we are in will end in glorious fashion. Until then, we work, we worship, we pray, we sacrifice, and we persevere for the kingdom, for this world is not our home!

CHAPTER SEVENTEEN

The Wrath of the Lamb

Revelation 6:12–17:

> [12] When he opened the sixth seal, I looked, and behold, there was a great earthquake, and the sun became black as sackcloth, the full moon became like blood, [13] and the stars of the sky fell to the earth as the fig tree sheds its winter fruit when shaken by a gale. [14] The sky vanished like a scroll that is being rolled up, and every mountain and island was removed from its place. [15] Then the kings of the earth and the great ones and the generals and the rich and the powerful, and everyone, slave and free, hid themselves in the caves and among the rocks of the mountains, [16] calling to the mountains and rocks, "Fall on us and hide us from the face of him who is seated on the throne, and from the wrath of the Lamb, [17] for the great day of their wrath has come, and who can stand?"

Jesus represents mercy, grace, and forgiveness for those of us who trust in Him. Yet, there is another side of Jesus that can make Him seem just as frightening as He is comforting. Many of us can be uncomfortable with the idea that Jesus isn't *only* the gentle Lamb of God. But maybe the passages of Scripture describing the wrath of God aren't intended to be scary at all. What if the wrath of the Lamb is intended to provide affirmation for believers?

What Would John's Readers Have Noticed?

Symbols of Judgment

For seventeen centuries of church history, the first five seals were understood to be the unfolding of the entire plan of redemption. Then, in 1830, dispensationalism appeared on the theological scene. English preacher John Darby popularized this theological theory, which mistakenly identifies those five seals as future events.

Dispensationalism erroneously teaches that before Jesus opens the first seals, He will come to "rapture" His church out of this world, followed by a seven-year period of global tribulation from which the church will be spared. This five-seal interpretation appealed to the American church because it countered the growing popularity of theological liberalism, which denied the literal return of Christ. Dispensationalism became a well-intentioned rallying cry against that theology.

Heavenly Signs

Old Testament prophets often used earthquakes, falling stars, and all sorts of cosmic upheaval as symbols of judgment. These metaphors are found in Isaiah, Jeremiah,

Ezekiel, Nahum, Zephaniah, Joel, Malachi, Hosea, and Haggai. Isaiah 13:9–11 is just one example of when God's prophets used hyperbolic, metaphorical imagery to warn of dramatic changes in the world order:

> *Behold, the day of the* LORD *comes, cruel, with wrath and fierce anger... ¹⁰ For the stars of the heavens and their constellations will not give their light; the sun will be dark at its rising, and the moon will not shed its light. ¹¹ I will punish the world for its evil, and the wicked for their iniquity; I will put an end to the pomp of the arrogant, and lay low the pompous pride of the ruthless.*

This passage was an oracle warning of Babylon's downfall. When Persia conquered Babylon, the sun didn't literally go dark and the mountains didn't move, but Babylon was wiped out. These acts of judgment on empires always mark major points in Jesus' plan of redemption. In Revelation 6, John did just that by using familiar Old Testament prophetic metaphors to call attention to the final change in the world order.

Traumatic Moments

Ancient empires dominated the known world for hundreds of years at a time. Therefore, transitions from one regime to the next would be traumatic. When new empires rose to power, they brought with them different cultural ideals and values, creating massive disruptions to the way of life. This unrest often led to great suffering for those who found themselves caught in the transition. It could feel like the end of the world.

The Gospels describe earthquakes and darkness when Jesus died on the cross. These signs marked a catastrophic blow to the forces of evil. It was a flip of the theological calendar, initiating the last days, in which the church would take over until the day of the Lord. So, we the church are living in and experiencing the countdown to the final judgment of evil.

WHAT WAS JESUS TELLING THE CHURCHES?

Jesus described the day of the Lord in Matthew 24:29–30: "Immediately after the tribulation of those days the sun will be darkened, and the moon will not give its light, and the stars will fall from heaven, and the powers of the heavens will be shaken. Then will appear in heaven the sign of the Son of Man, and then all the tribes of the earth will mourn, and they will see the Son of Man coming on the clouds of heaven with power and great glory."

The prophet Joel described it as "a day of darkness" accompanied by earthquakes (Joel 2:2). The heavens will tremble. The earth will be wreathed in blood, fire, and smoke. Hebrews 10:30–31 depicted God's "fearful" judgment:

> *For we know him who said, "Vengeance is mine; I will repay." And again, "The Lord will judge his people."* [31] *It is a fearful thing to fall into the hands of the living God.*

This is what the martyrs under the altar have been longing for: the vindication of the righteous through the wrath of the Lamb. Meanwhile, as Paul observed in 1 Thessalonians 5:3, people who hope in worldly assurances of peace and safety will be sorely disappointed:

> *While people are saying, "There is peace and security," then sudden destruction will come upon them as labor pains come upon a pregnant woman, and they will not escape.*

"Peace and security" is often the slogan of powerful leaders who vow to put the world at ease. However, human history tells us those promises are temporary at best, forever elusive at worst, and rarely, if ever, rooted in God's wisdom. On the day of the Lord, when evil and darkness are dealt with once and for all, God will show the world order that the true path to peace and safety starts with the wrath of the Lamb poured out as just judgment against evil.

As with all acts of God's judgment throughout history, an intended blessing for the righteous goes along with it—a day of redemption. Notice, in Matthew 24:31, He also sends out His angels to collect God's chosen from the earth and throughout history:

> *"He will send out his angels with a loud trumpet call, and they will gather his elect from the four winds, from one end of heaven to the other."*

The day of the Lord, when Jesus vanquishes evil, is the same day as the resurrection Paul described in 1 Thessalonians 4:14–17. It is the day we will meet Jesus in the air, when the dead shall arise with new bodies and those of us still alive will be changed *after* the dead. This is the day He will gather His harvest. As Jesus said in Matthew 13:30, "Let both grow together until the harvest, and at harvest time I will tell the reapers, 'Gather the weeds first and bind them in bundles to be burned, but gather the wheat into my barn.'"

WHAT IS JESUS TELLING US TODAY?

To fully appreciate the joy of redemption, we must also acknowledge the day of the Lord and the horror of facing the wrath of the Lamb. This might appear like an attempt to scare people into following Jesus, to elicit an emotional response of confession and repentance. But we know John wrote Revelation not to scare non-Christians but to be a blessing and encouragement to those who follow Jesus.

People fear many things in life, especially those things that could bring massive, painful change. But most of the world, as Jesus Himself explained in Matthew 13:14–15, does *not* fear His return:

> *Indeed, in their case the prophecy of Isaiah is fulfilled that says:* "*You will indeed hear but never understand, and you will indeed see but never perceive.*" [15] *For this people's heart has grown dull, and with their ears they can barely hear, and their eyes they have closed, lest they should see with their eyes and hear with their ears and understand with their heart and turn, and I would heal them.*

As John portrayed in Revelation 6:16, most people would rather call out for the rocks to bury them than to acknowledge the Lamb of God. This persistent willingness not only to reject God but to hate Him is the natural state of man. Without the gift of faith, people will live obliviously to the very thing they should fear most: the coming wrath of the Lamb. Sadly, for those who refuse to put their hope in Jesus, that day will be a surprise, and not a good one. As a result, their only hope for this life is earthly stability and peace, which, of course, is never more than a temporary illusion.

If you understand the reality that one day the Lamb will come to judge, you recognize two things: how scary the two-edged sword Jesus wields is, but also what a precious Savior Jesus is. The fact that you have apprehension about facing the wrath of the Lamb is itself evidence you have been given ears to hear. Why? Because as Scripture says, the fear of the Lord is the beginning of wisdom, knowledge, understanding!

In 1 Thessalonians 5:4–6, Paul encouraged Jesus' followers to allow their fear of the Lord to make them hopeful and alert as they await the day of the Lord:

> *But you are not in darkness, brothers, for that day to surprise you like a thief. ⁵ For you are all children of light, children of the day. We are not of the night or of the darkness. ⁶ So then let us not sleep, as others do, but let us keep awake and be sober.*

Child of God, your understanding of that day is proof God has already spared you from wrath and has called you to life.

CHAPTER EIGHTEEN

Who Can Escape? (Part One)

Revelation 7:1–8:

> [1] *After this I saw four angels standing at the four corners of the earth, holding back the four winds of the earth, that no wind might blow on earth or sea or against any tree.* [2] *Then I saw another angel ascending from the rising of the sun, with the seal of the living God, and he called with a loud voice to the four angels who had been given power to harm earth and sea,* [3] *saying, "Do not harm the earth or the sea or the trees, until we have sealed the servants of our God on their foreheads."* [4] *And I heard the number of the sealed, 144,000, sealed from every tribe of the sons of Israel:*
>
> [5] *12,000 from the tribe of Judah were sealed, 12,000 from the tribe of Reuben, 12,000 from the tribe of Gad,* [6] *12,000 from the tribe of Asher, 12,000 from the tribe of Naphtali, 12,000 from the tribe of Manasseh,* [7] *12,000 from the tribe of Simeon, 12,000 from the tribe of Levi, 12,000 from the tribe of Issachar,* [8] *12,000 from the tribe of Zebulun, 12,000 from the tribe of Joseph, 12,000 from the tribe of Benjamin were sealed.*

Can you recall a time when, as a child, you did something wrong that you just knew would draw the ire of your parents or another authority figure? I'm guessing one of your first thoughts was, "What can I do to escape their judgment?" Now, as an adult, perhaps you've found yourself asking a similar question: "Who can possibly escape the judgment of a righteous God?" Revelation 7:1–8 answers this question by explaining, "Well, as it turns out, *this* group escapes judgment."

The Holy Spirit prompts us to specific actions, words, or choices we otherwise wouldn't engage in. Sometimes, He provides experiential moments through prayer, prompting, and guidance. Perspectives differ on the frequency, manifestation, and purpose of these moments, but there is broad agreement among followers of Jesus that the Holy Spirit is active among His people. But there is something else the Holy Spirit does for every Christian—the first, most critical act for our survival: He marks us with a seal that gives us the ability to escape judgment.

What Would John's Readers Have Noticed?

Winds, Seals, and Tribes

The Old Testament has many references to the four winds of the earth. We aren't talking about gentle breezes but stormy gales. These are metaphors for the inevitable, inescapable judgment and destruction that will come for the unredeemed from all sides, as told in Jeremiah 49:36:

> *I will bring upon Elam the four winds from the four quarters of heaven. And I will scatter them to all those winds, and there shall be no nation to which those driven out of Elam shall not come.*

Seals of Ownership

In the ancient world, seals and marks designated something or someone as belonging to an individual, tribe, or kingdom. Though sometimes a seal could be a shameful reminder of punishment or guilt, seals often brought pride, belonging, and privilege, as in Ezekiel 9:4–6:

> *The Lord said to him, "Pass through the city, through Jerusalem, and put a mark on the foreheads of the men who sigh and groan over all the abominations that are committed in it. ⁵... Your eye shall not spare, and you shall show no pity. ⁶... But touch no one on whom is the mark [seal]."*

The Old Testament contains many symbolic, spiritual references to the seal of God, which sets His people apart from the world. These seals represent God's sovereign hand keeping His promise between Him and His people.

Twelve Tribes

The twelve tribes of Israel are listed in several places throughout the Old Testament, usually after significant events, to mark a transition or to signal the start of a new era. We find the tribes listed in Genesis, Exodus, and Numbers, revealing growth or regression, consequences of rebellion, and name changes. The names of the tribes, and even their order, were intentional and significant. In the same way, John's list in Revelation is unique yet similar to other lists found in the Bible.

What Was Jesus Telling the Churches?

Revelation 7 isn't a catalog of chronological events. It's an answer to the question asked in Revelation 6 by those facing the Lamb's wrath: "Who can escape the judgment of the Lamb? It's coming from every corner of the world!" The answer is, "Yes, this judgment is coming; yes, this judgment is inescapable. But it's not for you."

The four angels who bring judgment are told to stand down until God has finished marking and sealing His people, because they are *not* to be touched. This is foreshadowed by Passover, when the angel struck down the firstborn male of every Egyptian house but passed over the homes of the Hebrews who had the visible seal of the blood of a lamb over the doorposts, as Moses explained in Exodus 12:23:

> *For the* Lord *will pass through to strike the Egyptians, and when he sees the blood on the lintel and on the two doorposts, the* Lord *will pass over the door and will not allow the destroyer to enter your houses to strike you.*

The list of Israelite tribes in Revelation 7:5–8 differs from any other biblical list of the twelve tribes. For instance, why was Dan left out? Why was Joseph listed even though it wasn't one of the original tribes? Why were Joseph's sons listed as separate tribes? And why were tribes born from Jacob's gentile concubines listed? We encounter many idiosyncrasies like this as we read through Revelation—and that's okay. It doesn't shroud the purpose of the passage.

In the Old Testament, the tribes were made up of Jews, but in the New Testament, the church is grafted in and made part of the tribes. As Paul made clear in Romans 9:8, "it is not the children of the flesh who are the children of God, but the children of the promise are counted as offspring." And he confirms this point in Galatians 3:28–29:

> *There is neither Jew nor Greek, there is neither slave nor free, there is no male and female, for you are all one in Christ Jesus. ²⁹ And if you are Christ's, then you are Abraham's offspring, heirs according to promise.*

The number 144,000 is not intended to be a literal number as much as a symbol of the completeness of the sealed. Remember, the book of Numbers in the Old Testament was part of the Pentateuch, the sacred books of Moses. Not so important to us, maybe, but it was very important to the formation of Israel, God's people who were to fulfill their spiritual destiny by invading the land of Canaan.

The Bible frequently uses numerical symbolism. For example, Jesus said to forgive others not just seven times but seventy times seven times. But we know He didn't mean we are to keep a running tally and forgive exactly 490 times. He was showing the extent and extravagance of complete forgiveness.

Revelation 21 describes the church, the Bride of Christ, as a city called New Jerusalem, with twelve gates named after the twelve tribes and with twelve foundation stones named after the apostles. The number 1,000 is often used as a multiplier to describe God's people in Revelation. We have an example of that here with the twelve by twelve sealed: 12 x 12 x 1,000 = 144,000. This number is a symbolic way of describing the multiplication of God's Kingdom as the Holy Spirit marks God's chosen throughout the story of redemption.

John said he saw this group here on earth. I believe they represent all of God's sealed and chosen people throughout the Old and New Testaments and at any given moment throughout human history who are fighting in this battle between good and evil. The 144,000 symbolizes the first half of the answer to the question asked in Revelation 6:17: "Who can stand?" There are two groups. First, there's the 144,000, representing what I call the "church in battle," the redeemed on the earth. The other group is the rest of the redeemed who are with the Lord in the heavenly realm. I call them the "church in victory."

WHAT IS JESUS TELLING US TODAY?

Why does Jesus delay judgment of evil in the world? He delays because of His love for His chosen who are not

Who Can Escape? (Part One)

yet sealed by the Holy Spirit. We learn in Nahum 1:3 that "the LORD is slow to anger and great in power, [but] the LORD will by no means clear the guilty." The martyrs ask, "How long?" The answer is, "until all the redeemed are sealed," as Peter wrote in 2 Peter 3:9:

> *The Lord is not slow to fulfill his promise as some count slowness, but is patient toward you, not wishing that any should perish, but that all [of the sealed] should reach repentance.*

But who can stand against the wrath of the Lamb? In the next verse (3:10), Peter declared, "But the day of the Lord will come like a thief, and then the heavens will pass away with a roar, and the heavenly bodies [stars] will be burned up and dissolved, and the earth and the works that are done on it will be exposed." The first part of the answer to "who can stand?" is *us*—right now, today—because Jesus is waiting on the Spirit to seal all believers throughout redemptive history before He brings judgment. As the sealed on earth leave for heaven, the Spirit is already working to seal the next crop of wheat that is being born again.

As the Holy Spirit seals us on earth, He makes us all children of the promise, part of the twelve tribes. Paul assured his readers in Ephesians 1:13, "You also, when you heard the word of truth, the gospel of your salvation, and believed in him, were sealed with the promised Holy Spirit." In 2 Corinthians 1:21–22, he explained, "It is God who establishes us with you in Christ, and has anointed us, and who has also put his seal on us and given us his Spirit in our hearts as a guarantee." And he wrote in 2 Timothy 2:19, "But God's firm foundation stands, bearing this seal: 'The Lord knows those who are his.'"

The Holy Spirit calls God's chosen, seals God's chosen, and protects God's chosen from the wrath of God. If you are a follower of Jesus, you bear a seal that has been made visible in the spiritual realm. It's so clear that not only do the angels of judgment at the four corners of the earth see it, but the forces of evil do, too. The forces of darkness may be able to cause us suffering in this tribulation we endure, but they cannot remove your seal!

I believe the Spirit enables us to know intuitively, theologically, and experientially that we are among this 144,000 and also the multitude that cannot be numbered. When the sealed read this passage, we know the voice of the Lamb. We don't fear the wrath of the Lamb, and because we're sealed, we live in anticipation of it as we continue to preach the gospel.

CHAPTER NINETEEN

Who Can Escape? (Part Two)

Revelation 7:9–17:

⁹ After this I looked, and behold, a great multitude that no one could number, from every nation, from all tribes and peoples and languages, standing before the throne and before the Lamb, clothed in white robes, with palm branches in their hands, ¹⁰ and crying out with a loud voice, "Salvation belongs to our God who sits on the throne, and to the Lamb!" ¹¹ And all the angels were standing around the throne and around the elders and the four living creatures, and they fell on their faces before the throne and worshiped God, ¹² saying, "Amen! Blessing and glory and wisdom and thanksgiving and honor and power and might be to our God forever and ever! Amen."

¹³ Then one of the elders addressed me, saying, "Who are these, clothed in white robes, and from where have they come?" ¹⁴ I said to him, "Sir, you know." And he said to me, "These are the ones coming out of the great tribulation. They have washed their robes and made them white in the blood of the Lamb.

¹⁵ "Therefore they are before the throne of God, and serve him day and night in his temple; and he who sits on the throne will shelter them with his presence. ¹⁶ They shall

> hunger no more, neither thirst anymore; the sun shall not strike them, nor any scorching heat. ¹⁷ For the Lamb in the midst of the throne will be their shepherd, and he will guide them to springs of living water, and God will wipe away every tear from their eyes."

As a Christian, do you ever lament the direction this world is heading? Do you ever get frustrated when it seems like evil constantly wins? Injustice is rampant. Society seems depraved. People naturally desire to celebrate some type of victory over their perception of evil, which is why they obsess over politics, culture wars, and social movements.

But Christians don't need to hope in these things. We know there is only one way evil will be defeated. Revelation was written to encourage Christians to look to Jesus. Yes, we wrestle with evil daily, but there's a great day coming, and even when life seems as far removed from heaven as it can get, evidence of God's advancing kingdom is everywhere.

What Would John's Readers Have Noticed?

Hopeful in Tribulation

In the first century, palm branches were used to celebrate military victory. We see this in a different way when Jesus entered Jerusalem. The crowd praised Him as the one they hoped would defeat Rome and restore Israel's sovereignty. They were so eager to celebrate victory, but their vision of victory was too small. Jesus had something greater in mind.

A week later, this same crowd cheered for His crucifixion, which, ironically, was the moment ultimate victory over evil was accomplished.

Faithful in Tribulation

The church was in the heat of intense tribulation and persecution from Rome when Paul wrote in 2 Corinthians 4:8–9, "We are afflicted in every way, but not crushed; perplexed, but not driven to despair; persecuted, but not forsaken; struck down, but not destroyed."

When John wrote Revelation, things had worsened. The church was powerless politically and culturally to defend itself. The only power the church had was the power of the gospel and the ability to love the unloved and excluded.

Living in that kind of hopeless tribulation creates a desperation for justice. You can understand the first-century church's deep longing for Jesus to return in victory. I believe their tribulation helped them understand better than us that worldly solutions are nothing more than empty, unfulfillable promises.

That's why Peter taught the church in his first letter to stop obsessing over the evils of Rome and to focus on the kingdom of God instead. As a result, they understood that the day of Christ's return will bring the greatest victory ever.

WHAT WAS JESUS TELLING THE CHURCHES?

In Genesis 32:12, Jacob remembered God's covenant with Abraham: "I will surely do you good, and make your offspring as the sand of the sea, which cannot be numbered for multitude."

Consider the similarity in the language used in God's promise to Abraham and John's description of the church in victory. The crowd around the throne is too large for anyone to count. There are people in this multitude from every nation. In Galatians 3:28–29, Paul described the church like this:

> *There is neither Jew nor Greek, there is neither slave nor free, there is no male and female, for you are all one in Christ Jesus.* ²⁹ *And if you are Christ's, then you are Abraham's offspring, heirs according to promise.*

People from every tribe, nation, and language assemble to celebrate one Lord and one victory. This multitude is the complete fulfillment of the promise to Abraham.

How does John describe the church in victory? They are celebrating—with the symbol of palm branches—that great ultimate victory. It's a spontaneous expression of glory and honor to the Lamb of God, who has fulfilled the scroll of redemption. They are celebrating the end of the war between good and evil. The Lamb of God has conquered sin and death! He has rescued his people! It's all so

Who Can Escape? (Part Two)

stunning. They fall on their faces, declaring utter amazement at the whole epic story of redemption.

Amid the celebration, one of the elders asked John an interesting question: "Who are these clothed in white? Where are they from?" John answered, "Sir, you know." This wording is reminiscent of God's question in Ezekiel 37:3, as well as the prophet's response:

> And he said to me, "Son of man, can these bones live?" And I answered, "O Lord GOD, you know."

Asking a question with an obvious answer was a common device in Jewish literature, especially the Hebrew Bible. It was often used to set up an important dramatic teaching moment. Imagine John's state of mind—maybe with a massive smile, or tears of joy, his answer is, "Sir, you know!"

Do you remember the question the martyrs under the altar asked during the opening of the fifth seal? They cried out, "How long?" A different question was asked by the unredeemed facing the wrath of the Lamb: "Who can escape?" And now, a third question: "Who are these, John? Where did they come from?" All three questions are answered the same way: These people in white robes are us, the redeemed, celebrating the Lamb's great victory.

WHAT IS JESUS TELLING US TODAY?

It may not always feel like it, but in our battle against evil, the church is not losing. We are waiting. The prophet Jeremiah spoke of God's promise to redeem His people in Jeremiah 32:37–38:

> *I will gather them from all countries. . . . I will bring them back to this place, and I will make them dwell in safety. ³⁸ And they shall be my people, and I will be their God.*

There's evidence for our hope in this victory everywhere, plain to see, if we aren't blinded by our obsession with this world. The website Billionbibles.com conservatively estimates the number of underground Christians in China as of 2018 at 147 million[18]. And this figure doesn't include professing Christians in the state-controlled church. That's a massive number, but it's just a snapshot of one country and doesn't account for what God is doing in so many other places.

The kingdom of God isn't hanging on by a thread. It's steamrolling toward this scene in Revelation. The multitude in this scene will be the culmination and celebration of the Holy Spirit's ultimate and completed work—the sealing of all God's chosen throughout all of history. This victory celebration reveals the precious relationship between the Lord and His church. God the Father is shepherding and sheltering His redeemed, guiding them to living water. It's a celebration in which hunger and thirst and scorching heat (biblical symbols of tribulation) are no more. In Romans 8:30, Paul described the advancing kingdom of God:

> *Those whom he predestined he also called, and those whom he called he also justified, and those whom he justified he also glorified.*

Until that day, we are called to endure the tribulation, the suffering, and the pain of fighting evil, by persevering and proclaiming the gospel. No doubt, this tribulation can be painful and discouraging. All of us have experienced in some way the heartbreak that comes from living alongside evil. No matter who wins the next election or how the latest iteration of the culture wars unfolds, no matter our circumstances, we will shed tears along the way. But Jesus offers His encouragement in John 16:33:

> *I have said these things to you, that in me you may have peace. In the world you will have tribulation. But take heart; I have overcome the world.*

The tears Jesus will wipe away represent all our hurt and pain caused by our struggles and losses. This is the existence every human craves—for all those things to be wiped away. Even atheists want this. Sadly, no one in this world promising peace and safety can ever deliver. Only Jesus can.

Until then, we recognize we are just a small sliver, a part of something so much bigger than our town or state or country.

We, along with millions of brothers and sisters, faithfully wait for the Spirit to seal the rest of God's chosen.

CHAPTER TWENTY

A Moment of Silence

Revelation 8:1–5:

> *¹ When the Lamb opened the seventh seal, there was silence in heaven for about half an hour. ² Then I saw the seven angels who stand before God, and seven trumpets were given to them. ³ And another angel came and stood at the altar with a golden censer, and he was given much incense to offer with the prayers of all the saints on the golden altar before the throne, ⁴ and the smoke of the incense, with the prayers of the saints, rose before God from the hand of the angel. ⁵ Then the angel took the censer and filled it with fire from the altar and threw it on the earth, and there were peals of thunder, rumblings, flashes of lightning, and an earthquake.*

Why do humans pray? It's a fascinating human behavior, a spiritual discipline practiced across the world in many different religious traditions. Prayer is the easiest thing a follower of Jesus can do. Yet, despite how many Christians claim to pray, it's very easy to misunderstand the purpose of prayer. Strangely, it's also very easy to neglect, even abuse.

What do you pray for most often? Healing for friends and family seems to occupy a large percentage of our heavenly requests. Do you ever wonder if God likes or hears your prayers? Do you ever worry you're not praying the right way? Are there things you should be praying for but don't?

What Would John's Readers Have Noticed?

Silence, Incense, Fire, and Trumpets

There are no wasted words or phrases in Revelation. John used many clear links to the Old Testament, which aid our interpretation of it. By tracing these links to the Old Testament, we can begin to make sense of the symbolism in Revelation, which might at first seem obscure and bizarre.

Silence Before God

Silence is a metaphor for warning throughout the Old Testament, like a precursor to God's judgment. A stark transition from noise to silence demands your attention—stop what you're doing, look and listen to what's happening. In Zephaniah 1:7, the prophet warns the people of Judah:

> *Be silent before the Lord GOD! For the day of the LORD is near; the LORD has prepared a sacrifice and consecrated his guests.*

In Revelation 8, the continual praise in heaven stops for "about half an hour" as all attention is turned to the opening of the seventh seal. There is something so fascinating, so riveting about this seal that everything stops—except for one thing.

Incense Offering

In chapter 14, we examined Revelation 5:8, which illustrated that the prayers of the saints are like incense in heaven:

> *When he had taken the scroll, the four living creatures and the twenty-four elders fell down before the Lamb, each holding a harp, and golden bowls [censers] full of incense, which are the prayers of the saints.*

We learned this incense offering was also a temple ritual in Exodus, performed twice daily, every evening and morning. The censers, or golden incense bowls, mentioned in these verses were vessels used to burn the incense. In Leviticus 16:12, God provided instructions to Moses for how Aaron should enter the Holy Place on the Day of Atonement:

> *He shall take a censer full of coals of fire from the altar before the LORD, and two handfuls of sweet incense beaten small, and he shall bring it inside the veil.*

Old Testament worshippers of Yahweh understood the symbol of the incense offering as prayers to God. King David demonstrated this understanding in Psalm 141:2:

> *Let my prayer be counted as incense before you, and the lifting up of my hands as the evening sacrifice!*

Trumpets

The trumpet used in Judaic rituals is a *shofar*, an instrument made from the twisting horn of a ram that produces a distinctive piercing sound when blown. In the ancient Mediterranean world, there were no sirens, explosions, or fireworks, so nothing else was as loud as one of these trumpet blasts! The Old Testament writers depicted trumpets as attention-grabbing announcements of God's impending judgment against enemy nations on behalf of His people. Joshua and the Israelites circled Jericho, and with the blast of trumpets and the shouts of the people, God turned the city walls to rubble. Or consider the prophet Joel's exhortation in Joel 2:1 (emphasis mine):

> *Blow a trumpet in Zion;* **sound an alarm** *on my holy mountain! Let all the inhabitants of the land tremble, for the* **day of the Lord** *is coming; it is near.*

WHAT WAS JESUS TELLING THE CHURCHES?

After Jesus opened the seventh seal, revealing the entire history of the plan of redemption, there was dramatic silence for a symbolic half hour. What was everyone focused on during that time?

Just as in Revelation 4, this passage reminds us how precious the redeemed are to God. There's something intimate and comforting in how all of heaven's attention turns to these seven angels and the prayers of the saints. And not just for a brief moment. It's the moment in redemptive history when God has chosen to answer all our prayers.

Centuries of pleading for justice, rising as incense, have captured God's attention. This silence displays the special love and connection between Him and us—His holy priesthood, the church. In the silence, the seven angels line up with the seven trumpets, setting up the next cycle in Revelation.

While the six seals are a wide-angle shot of the history of redemption and judgment from the perspective of the redeemed, the seventh seal provides a wide-angle shot of that same judgment, but this time from the perspective of those who are being judged. As verse 5 describes, "Then the angel took the censer and filled it with fire from the altar and threw it on the earth, and there were peals of thunder, rumblings, flashes of lightning, and an earthquake."

It's important to remember that *Revelation is not chronological but cyclical*. We will see this exact description of thunder, lightning, earthquakes, and hail twice more in Revelation—at the blowing of the seventh trumpet (11:19) and at the pouring out of the seventh bowl of judgment (16:18–21). All three represent the day of the Lord.

Who are the seven angels holding seven trumpets? Our first clue is lifted straight from the battle of Jericho, particularly this description in Joshua 6:4–5:

> *"Seven priests shall bear seven trumpets of rams' horns before the ark. On the seventh day you shall march around the city seven times, and the priests shall blow the trumpets.* ⁵*... and the wall of the city will fall down flat, and the people shall go up, everyone straight before him."*

For our second clue, we must return to Revelation 1:20, which indicates that "the seven stars are the angels of the seven churches."

The third clue is those "prayers of the saints," the burning incense in the golden bowl (censer) with its aroma filling the throne room. These clues point to the church's pleading for Jesus to return.

An angel took the censer, which holds coals that ignite the incense (prayers), and flung it to the earth. Recall how the martyrs associated with the fifth seal had pleaded, "How long, oh Lord?" This is God answering, "Now."

WHAT IS JESUS TELLING US TODAY?

The forces of evil hate the sweet aroma of our prayers. It reminds them that judgment day is coming. But our heavenly Dad loves our prayers. In fact, they are one of His favorite things around the throne room. Our prayers for the judgment of evil throughout human history are His first wave of attack in the final battle.

Typically, we pray for many things, mostly for our own benefit or for those we love. God can and does answer those prayers, and it's so wonderful and comforting when our Father hears them. But maybe they aren't even the best prayers we can offer. The greatest answer to prayer will be the day when Jesus vindicates His reputation, judges evil, and gathers us to be with Him forever. When Jesus instructed his followers how they should pray in Matthew 6:7–13, he began with the following guidance in verses 7 and 8:

> *When you pray, do not heap up empty phrases as the Gentiles do, for they think that they will be heard for their many words. ⁸ Do not be like them, for your Father knows what you need before you ask him.*

If God knows what we want or need before we even ask, perhaps these personal prayers shouldn't be our first priority. I know I can and should pray for those things, but they tend to be an overwhelming majority of my prayers. Perhaps they shouldn't be.

Starting in verse 9, Jesus reinforced His instructions with a model we know as the Lord's Prayer: "Pray then like this: 'Our Father in heaven, hallowed be [holy is] your name.'" Isn't this what the multitude around the throne declares over and over?

Jesus continued His model prayer: "Your kingdom come, your will be done, on earth as it is in heaven." This isn't a magical, liturgical salutation rule. It should be the first priority of our prayers to God. *Jesus, please judge evil! Redeem us! Open the final seal of that redemption scroll. Make this place just like your throne room. Bring heaven to earth.*

The Lord's Prayer concludes:

> Give us this day our daily bread, [12] and forgive us our debts, as we also have forgiven our debtors. [13] And lead us not into temptation, but deliver us from evil.

Lord, we trust you for what we need to get through this day. We know it all comes from you anyway. We know we don't deserve forgiveness. Please remind us of this whenever we sit in judgment of someone else.

Praying like this is an acknowledgment that everything we have belongs to God and that we trust Him for what we need. It also acknowledges that the most important things we can receive in this life are humility and forgiveness.

Jesus urged us in Matthew 6:33 to "seek first the kingdom of God and his righteousness." Do you have the courage to pray that way? Do you even have the desire to pray that way? I believe Revelation is providing us with a priority order for our prayers: "All right, God, I want my loved ones, church, and work to be blessed, but I would rather You come back today, judge evil, and gather us to be with You forever." Today, offer up a sweet-smelling prayer asking Jesus to return.

CHAPTER TWENTY-ONE

Trumpets of Judgment (Part One)

Revelation 8:6–13:

> *6 Now the seven angels who had the seven trumpets prepared to blow them.*
>
> *7 The first angel blew his trumpet, and there followed hail and fire, mixed with blood, and these were thrown upon the earth. And a third of the earth was burned up, and a third of the trees were burned up, and all green grass was burned up.*
>
> *8 The second angel blew his trumpet, and something like a great mountain, burning with fire, was thrown into the sea, and a third of the sea became blood. 9 A third of the living creatures in the sea died, and a third of the ships were destroyed.*
>
> *10 The third angel blew his trumpet, and a great star fell from heaven, blazing like a torch, and it fell on a third of the rivers and on the springs of water. 11 The name of the star is Wormwood. A third of the waters became wormwood, and many people died from the water, because it had been made bitter.*
>
> *12 The fourth angel blew his trumpet, and a third of the sun was struck, and a third of the moon, and a third of the*

> stars, so that a third of their light might be darkened, and a third of the day might be kept from shining, and likewise a third of the night.
>
> ¹³ Then I looked, and I heard an eagle crying with a loud voice as it flew directly overhead, "Woe, woe, woe to those who dwell on the earth, at the blasts of the other trumpets that the three angels are about to blow!"

In 2021, I had the incredible opportunity to cheer for my favorite childhood team, the Tampa Bay Buccaneers, in the Super Bowl. I was there in person, in our hometown stadium, as we defeated the Kansas City Chiefs. I was so thrilled with what I had just witnessed, I wanted more! On the way home from the game, I turned on the radio to hear expert commentary. When I got home late that night, I watched the whole game again on TV. I was desperate for detailed close-up views of plays I'd cheered from far off in the stands while present.

That's how we should see these cycles of judgments in Revelation. At first, they give us a wide shot from far away, and then we get a zoomed-in, up-close view. John gives us new angles and different perspectives. We've already seen the seven trumpets come out of the seventh seal. Later, seven bowls will emerge from the seven trumpets. John employs a Jewish literary device used within apocalyptic literature: describing the same events but from an alternate view.

What Would John's Readers Have Noticed?

"Trumpets" in Egypt

John's vision has a very clear connection to Exodus, in which God unleashed ten plagues upon Egypt. John's Jewish Christian readers would have immediately made this connection, but it requires some work for us to uncover what they would have seen right away. This is why historical context is critical. For example, if the first-century church were to read the message "Tom Brady is the GOAT" (which we know stands for the Greatest Of All Time), their question might be, "Why is this Tom considered the GOAT, the sacrificial scapegoat animal?" Their historical context would hinder their full understanding.

The plagues in Egypt were a simple warning to Pharaoh: let Israel leave slavery in Egypt or you and your nation will face judgment. The plagues didn't just punish him; they were specially designed to directly challenge the legitimacy of the revered Egyptian gods one by one. However, as horrific as the plagues were, they weren't complete judgment, only partial, providing Pharoah and his people the opportunity to repent.

Pharaoh refused God's demands until the tenth plague, at which point he finally let Israel go. However, once the Israelites had left, he immediately tried to recapture them. Why would he backtrack? You would think obedience should have been the only rational response after witnessing God's power. To us, Pharaoh appears stubborn and foolish to go against God, but he was desperate to keep the Jewish slave labor that had become so crucial to Egypt's economic and military success. Like humanity without Jesus today, all he had was the world's temporary benefits, and he just couldn't let them go.

John's first-century readers were no strangers to the brutalities of life under Roman occupation. Like the Egyptian plagues, these symbols in historical context would immediately connect to Roman military tactics. When Roman legions invaded, they torched everything, and the smoke could become so thick it would block the sun. They crippled any military response and disrupted the economy by destroying supplies and killing livestock. But they also kept some spoils. You might recall one of the four horsemen shouting, "Do not harm the oil and the wine!" After this, the people who survived the invasion became wholly reliant on Rome.

What Was Jesus Telling the Churches?

These seven trumpets announce the same judgment described in the seven seals but from a new angle and with different details. Remember, the seals are comforting, reassuring symbols to God's chosen, reminders that redemption is being carried out. But the trumpets are loud and frightening, inspiring fear and hopelessness in the unredeemed.

The plagues in Egypt were literal, yet here in Revelation, they're used as cosmic symbols, another common device in Jewish apocalyptic literature. For example, if a third of the sun really were to darken, you might think the summer weather in Florida would turn nice and cool, but in reality, Earth would become uninhabitable.

We should take this same symbolic approach when considering the star called Wormwood. The word itself is given to a woody shrub with a bitter aromatic taste, the application of which we see in Jeremiah 9:15: "Therefore thus says the LORD of hosts, the God of Israel: Behold, I will feed this people with bitter food, and give them poisonous water to drink." The bitter food and poisonous water are metaphors for the spiritual consequences of sin on the heart and on the world, as is Wormwood. In other words, resentment, disappointment, and anger are also part of God's judgment.

Have you ever felt bitter toward someone but were so powerless to fight back that you were forced to eat that bitterness? This is at the heart of Pharoah's refusal to repent. It's why some people resent the gospel. The call to repent is not met with obedience, or even ambivalence, but with raised fists of rage and rebellion.

But woe to those who are still on the earth when the other three trumpets blow! The first four were warning shots. These same warnings to repent, obey, and taste the grace and mercy Jesus offers are also active today. Like Egypt, the contemporary world cannot see the sovereign hand of God preparing the earth for a great exodus of His people. Why did God send plagues in Egypt? For the same reason He allows cycles of judgment on the world today: He is calling out His redeemed and preparing the land for the deliverance of God's people to a promised place.

What Is Jesus Telling Us Today?

The gospel is the only escape from an evil world trapped in an endless cycle of destruction, bitterness, and disobedience. The world believes if it can try harder, be smarter, and become unified, then peace will reign. Humanity has always believed peace, prosperity, and unity are attainable with the right wisdom, government, economic system, or philosophy. But underlying the wisdom of this world is one goal: to stop these unrelenting cycles of judgment.

That's the end goal of any worldly ideology. Man attempts to strike the right balance of freedom, power, greed, and moralism, but ultimately, all ideologies will fail, leaving behind disappointment and bitterness. Humanity's infection by depravity renders us incapable of redeeming this world on our own. Each generation has a "new" idea for how society can find the answer to inequity and injustice: "The world has never tried this! At least not the way it should." Except that, according to Ecclesiastes 1:9, it *has* already tried:

> *What has been is what will be, and what has been done is what will be done, and there is nothing new under the sun.*

Society responds, "But if we did it the right way this time, it would work!" No, it wouldn't. How vain and empty is the hope that perhaps in our lifetime, or our children's lifetime, humanity will create the world we've dreamed of? Classical Greek tragedies understood the despair of this endless cycle, but they had no answer. The book of Ecclesiastes does, however. See the writer's admonition in Ecclesiastes 7:10:

> *Say not, "Why were the former days better than these?" For it is not from wisdom that you ask this.*

Without God, nostalgia for the past is just as foolish as hope in some future wisdom. We see this tension play out today in the constant tug-of-war between traditionalism and progressivism. Maybe you long for the so-called good old days. Pharaoh did, too. He wanted to go back to the days when life was great for him, his family, and his kingdom. But as Jeremiah 8:9 teaches, this is a futile, selfish hope:

> *The wise men shall be put to shame; they shall be dismayed and taken; behold, they have rejected the word of the Lord, so what wisdom is in them?*

Just as the plagues exposed the Egyptian gods as futile figureheads, these trumpets remind us of the futility of hoping in human wisdom. Many become angry at God as they grapple with the question, "If God is real, why would He allow *this*?" This bitterness is part of the cycle of judgment. After thousands of years, why can't humanity see the rational, logical truth? Revolution isn't the answer; redemption is. But, like Pharaoh, the world is unable to see this undeniable cycle of failures as a warning to abandon hope in this world, its politicians, its governments, its promises, its materialism. They fail to see the only true solution is faith in Jesus, belief in the gospel, and repentance.

But those of us who have ears to hear and eyes to see can read Revelation and understand what God is doing. By God's grace, these cyclical judgments don't leave us hopeless and bitter but hopeful, longing and waiting for our deliverance. We can share in the assurance of Hebrews 13:14: "For here we have no lasting city, but we seek the city that is to come."

The seven trumpets remind followers of Christ about the inevitable ineffectiveness and cyclical failure of man's wisdom. They also remind us that we should have a different perspective. God is preparing us for something far beyond this life. Our hope is in the day of the Lord, when we will be delivered from this feckless Egypt and into the promised land. Ask Jesus for the discernment to see the futility of this world's greatest hopes and for the patience to endure until He returns.

CHAPTER TWENTY-TWO

Trumpets of Judgment (Part Two)

Revelation 9:1–12:

> *¹ And the fifth angel blew his trumpet, and I saw a star fallen from heaven to earth, and he was given the key to the shaft of the bottomless pit. ² He opened the shaft of the bottomless pit, and from the shaft rose smoke like the smoke of a great furnace, and the sun and the air were darkened with the smoke from the shaft. ³ Then from the smoke came locusts on the earth, and they were given power like the power of scorpions of the earth. ⁴ They were told not to harm the grass of the earth or any green plant or any tree, but only those people who do not have the seal of God on their foreheads. ⁵ They were allowed to torment them for five months, but not to kill them, and their torment was like the torment of a scorpion when it stings someone. ⁶ And in those days people will seek death and will not find it. They will long to die, but death will flee from them.*
>
> *⁷ In appearance the locusts were like horses prepared for battle: on their heads were what looked like crowns of gold; their faces were like human faces, ⁸ their hair like women's hair, and their teeth like lions' teeth; ⁹ they had breastplates like breastplates of iron, and the noise of their*

> *wings was like the noise of many chariots with horses rushing into battle.* ¹⁰ *They have tails and stings like scorpions, and their power to hurt people for five months is in their tails.* ¹¹ *They have as king over them the angel of the bottomless pit. His name in Hebrew is Abaddon, and in Greek he is called Apollyon.*
>
> ¹² *The first woe has passed; behold, two woes are still to come.*

If an insect bigger than a raisin flies around my head, I want to run far away or I want it dead as soon as possible. Or preferably both. So, I really can't imagine being caught in a massive swarm of terrifying locusts. But there is a terrifying spiritual reality that isn't as humorous as my squeamish reaction to bugs—the invisible yet very real swarm of evil forces around us. John wrote of their capabilities and their limits, as well as how followers of Jesus should view them, respond to them, and seek refuge from them.

What Would John's Readers Have Noticed?

Locusts and Passover

There are two connections between the locusts in this passage and the plagues on Egypt: the locusts of the eighth plague and Passover as depicted in the tenth plague. In the Old Testament, locusts represented judgment, due to their agricultural and economic destructiveness. We also see the reference to Passover—when the angel of death killed every firstborn in Egypt but was forbidden to harm any Hebrew house that had the blood of a lamb painted over the door.

This passage also links to language from the prophet Joel, connecting to another historic event every Jew would have known about. Some scholars believe Joel prophesied around 845 BC, ten years after the most devasting locust swarm in Israel's history. In Joel 1:4–6, he recounted four separate disasters, the bugs in each one devouring what the previous swarm had left behind:

> *What the cutting locust left, the swarming locust has eaten. What the swarming locust left, the hopping locust has eaten, and what the hopping locust left, the destroying locust has eaten. . . . ⁶ For a nation has come up against my land, powerful and beyond number; its teeth are lions' teeth, and it has the fangs of a lioness.*

Later, in Joel 2:4–9, he used metaphorical language to prophesy about an earthly invasion, a consequence Israel would suffer if it didn't repent:

> *Their appearance is like the appearance of horses, and like war horses they run. ⁵ As with the rumbling of chariots, they leap on the tops of the mountains. . . . ⁶ Before them peoples are in anguish; all faces grow pale. ⁷ Like warriors they charge; like soldiers they scale the wall. They march each on his way; they do not swerve from their paths. ⁸ They do not jostle one another; each marches in his path. . . . ⁹ They leap upon the city, they run upon the walls, they climb up into the houses, they enter through the windows like a thief.*

The threat of judgment in Joel's prophecy may have been what prompted Jehoshaphat, the king of Judah, to lead Israel into national repentance. God, in turn, held back His judgment. These are positive examples of how prophetic cycles work in the Scriptures. Among God's people, they can lead to repentance. But that doesn't always happen. Later, we see in Revelation that the unredeemed resist and persist in going their own way.

WHAT WAS JESUS TELLING THE CHURCHES?

The first four trumpets exposed the fallacy of the idea that any human attempt can bring peace and redemption to a fallen world. The images in this passage come from symbols and details of first-century warfare. Human wisdom always ends in a spirit of conquest, resulting in suffering, death, and destruction—all part of God's judgment. The fifth and sixth trumpets describe another element of God's judgment: the spiritual forces of evil. These are the very forces Paul described in Ephesians 6:12:

> *For we do not wrestle against flesh and blood, but against the rulers, against the authorities, against the cosmic powers over this present darkness, against the spiritual forces of evil in the heavenly places.*

Revelation also speaks of a fallen star possessing the keys to darkness, a reference we see in other places in Revelation. Think of these multiple references as different camera angles on the same subject. The symbolism of a star falling from heaven links directly to Isaiah 14:12: "How you are fallen from heaven, O Day Star, son of Dawn! How you are cut down to the ground, you who laid the nations low!"

This star carries three symbolic meanings. First, in Isaiah, the star symbolizes a prophecy of the fall of Babylon. Then, in Revelation, it's used as the universal symbol of evil and all its arrogance. Finally, it becomes a metaphor for Satan, the father of lies. This fallen angel—called the fallen morning star (translated "Lucifer" in the King James Version of that verse in Isaiah)—has keys to the abyss, which isn't a physical place but is the spiritual realm of darkness.

When Satan opened the abyss, John saw a massive swarm of locusts emerge. These are much worse than the ones Pharaoh endured, because they're not interested in consuming vegetation. Instead, they want to bring suffering to humanity. But God restricts them, much like He restricted Satan when he tested Job, and much like how He restrains evil now during the church age. The swarms are not allowed to kill humanity, because humanity kills enough of its own.

Let's go through John's imagery, which tells us what this locust army is like. (One can almost see John struggling to describe these uncanny beings. And no, they're not a metaphor for Black Hawk helicopters.) They're *like* horses prepared for battle—fast, mobile, and powerful—bearing what look *like* crowns of gold, which symbolize influence over the rulers of the nations. Their faces are *like* human faces, which represent cleverness and cunning, while hair *like* women's hair shows their beauty, unlike the repulsive image often ascribed to demonic forces. Their teeth *like* the teeth of lions symbolizes their ability to inflict pain and damage.

Humanity can't stop these creatures. Their breastplates of iron show their imperviousness to any earthly weapons. Their wings make a loud, terrifying sound. The scorpion tails symbolize the poison of untruth, deceit, and the associated pain and suffering. But they only have power for five months, which is the lifespan of actual locusts. This does not need to be taken literally, though. Instead, it's meant to be a reminder that, as terrible as they are, their flight of terror is only for a period of time and has a definitive end.

WHAT IS JESUS TELLING US TODAY?

There's overwhelming evidence that darkness and evil exist in this world. It's one the easiest ways to prove the existence of God. Even people who refuse to believe in God find it hard to deny the existence of darkness and evil. World history is full of the carnage evil has caused. The massive demonic horde causing pain and torment is thirsty to bring as many people to eternal judgment as possible through their destruction and spiritual deception. They are so good at it that they can make people wish they were dead. But thankfully, this demonic swarm has three limitations: they have a limited life span, they can't take human life, and they cannot touch, hurt, or deceive God's elect—the ones we learned in a previous chapter are being sealed, then and now, by the Holy Spirit. Through that seal put on us by the blood of the Lamb, we are protected from their power, just as Paul tells us in Romans 8:35–39:

> *Who shall separate us from the love of Christ? Shall tribulation, or distress, or persecution, or famine, or nakedness, or danger, or sword?... ³⁷ No, in all these things we are more than conquerors through him who loved us. ³⁸ For I am sure that neither death nor life, nor angels nor rulers, nor things present nor things to come, nor powers, ³⁹ nor height nor depth, nor anything else in all creation, will be able to separate us from the love of God in Christ Jesus our Lord.*

Yes, as followers of Jesus, we still endure this tribulation, suffering the consequences of the first four seals and trumpets. We may even be led astray at times by bad theology or temptation. These are the temporary consequences of universal human depravity and our own flaws, sinfulness, and bad choices. But the demon horde can harm only those without ears to hear, those without faith in the gospel of our Jesus—they can destroy only the weeds, not the wheat.

Just because we are protected doesn't mean we should be reckless; instead, we should be filled with humility and gratitude. While this swarm cannot touch us, it would certainly devour us if it could, and we should remember that. Why would any follower of Jesus consider flirting with the world when this army of darkness lurks nearby? As we're reminded in 1 Peter 5:8,

> *Be sober-minded; be watchful. Your adversary the devil prowls around like a roaring lion, seeking someone to devour.*

John instructs us in his three epistles how critical it is to love one another and to stay away from evil. At the first Passover, Jews were protected from death by the blood on their doorposts, and now we're sealed by the blood of the Lamb, who has authority to open the seals of that redemption scroll. We must not let the busyness of life or the temptations of this world distract us from this promise to the sealed!

CHAPTER TWENTY-THREE

Trumpets of Judgment (Part Three): A World Controlled by Evil

Revelation 9:13–21:

> *13 Then the sixth angel blew his trumpet, and I heard a voice from the four horns of the golden altar before God, 14 saying to the sixth angel who had the trumpet, "Release the four angels who are bound at the great river Euphrates." 15 So the four angels, who had been prepared for the hour, the day, the month, and the year, were released to kill a third of mankind. 16 The number of mounted troops was twice ten thousand times ten thousand; I heard their number. 17 And this is how I saw the horses in my vision and those who rode them: they wore breastplates the color of fire and of sapphire and of sulfur, and the heads of the horses were like lions' heads, and fire and smoke and sulfur came out of their mouths. 18 By these three plagues a third of mankind was killed, by the fire and smoke and sulfur coming out of their mouths. 19 For the power of the horses is in their mouths and in their tails, for their tails are like serpents with heads, and by means of them they wound.*

> [20] *The rest of mankind, who were not killed by these plagues, did not repent of the works of their hands nor give up worshiping demons and idols of gold and silver and bronze and stone and wood, which cannot see or hear or walk,* [21] *nor did they repent of their murders or their sorceries or their sexual immorality or their thefts.*

Do you remember the first time you saw photographs of the concentration camps at Auschwitz, or the first time you read of Stalin's bloody purges and starvation tactics? Millions upon millions died across Europe and the Soviet Union, without even counting the staggering slaughter of combat deaths in the Second World War. Over the past century, we've seen an exponential rise in humanity's ability to kill each other unlike any other period in history. This passage in Revelation brings us the sixth trumpet and how it reveals evil's growing bloody impact in these last days since the resurrection of Jesus.

What Would John's Readers Have Noticed?

The Euphrates

In Genesis, four great rivers marked the boundary of the garden of Eden, the fourth of which was the Euphrates. The Euphrates River was also the border of the promised land God gave Israel after they endured forty years in the wilderness, as detailed in Joshua 1:4:

> *From the wilderness and this Lebanon as far as the great river, the river Euphrates, all the land of the Hittites to the Great Sea toward the going down of the sun shall be your territory.*

Beyond the Euphrates

For Jews of the Old Testament, the land beyond the Euphrates would have been a great dark mystery, a sentiment that continued through the time of the Roman Empire. Anything from that region was seen by Israel as a threat. For example, invaders from Babylon and Assyria originated there. In Rome's time, the formidable Parthians claimed the land from east of the Euphrates all the way to modern-day India as their empire. Readers of Revelation would have clearly seen the reference to horses with stingers on their tails as a reference to Parthian's famed archers, who could shoot on horseback as lethally backward as forward. That was the notorious "Parthian shot," to which modern English alludes when we refer to a "parting shot." Both Jews and gentiles living in the Roman Empire during the first century would have seen the Euphrates as the staging area for any existential threat, much like the West in the twentieth century viewed the Iron Curtain during the height of the Cold War. John employs the Euphrates symbol to describe the coming scope and influence of evil on the world.

WHAT WAS JESUS TELLING THE CHURCHES?

A voice from the four horns on the golden altar orders the release of four angels "bound" beyond the Euphrates River. This is the same incense altar from the sixth seal. It represented the prayers of the saints who are crying out for the judgment of evil, with the altar acting as a portal from heaven into the physical world. John's intention is to remind us of those prayers and to hint that the sixth trumpet is part of God's answer to those prayers. Angels previously bound are released, indicating they're among the forces of evil controlled by Satan, as the fifth trumpet shows. The power in their mouths and serpent-headed tails symbolizes their ability to deceive and manipulate humanity, evocative of the serpent in the garden of Eden. Even today, we call deceptive people *snakes*. The fire, smoke, and sulfur the serpents are expelling represents destruction caused by the wars that the serpents lure the nations into fighting.

God is using imagery to show how horrific evil really is. In evil's final throes, Satan attempts to derail the plan written inside the scroll of redemption, by unleashing his hordes. At several points in the Old Testament, God used nations for either the judgment or the liberation of His people. This was God preparing Israel for its role in the redemption of His church. Revelation teaches that after the resurrection of Jesus, God partially fulfilled His judgment by turning the power of nations and governments over to the forces of evil. The sixth trumpet signals how, after the cross, evil is given temporary power to influence those nations and armies for its purposes. This is how we are to view the present kingdom of God, as having already obtained many aspects of victory but not yet attaining its fullness. In other words, the kingdom has victory *already* but *not yet*.

Jesus told His disciples in Matthew 24:6–14 that this would be a sign we are in the end of times (emphasis mine):

> *And you will hear of wars and rumors of wars. See that you are not alarmed, for this must take place, but the end is not yet. ⁷ For nation will rise against nation, and kingdom against kingdom, and there will be famines and earthquakes in various places. ⁸ All these are but the beginning of the birth pains.... ¹⁰ And then many will fall away and betray one another and hate one another. ¹¹ And many false prophets will arise and lead many astray. ¹² And because lawlessness will be increased, the love of many will grow cold. ¹³ But the one who endures to the end will be saved. ¹⁴* **And this gospel of the kingdom will be proclaimed throughout the whole world as a testimony to all nations, and then the end will come.**

I believe the time period of the sixth trumpet began at Christ's ascension and will continue until His return. Matthew 28:18–20 tells us this is the age when we fulfill the Great Commission by proclaiming the gospel to all the nations. Simultaneously, the desperate forces of evil are opposing humanity with everything they have, as far as God will permit them to go.

John describes this army's size as ten thousand times ten thousand times two—or 200 million. This would have been a staggering number for first-century readers. The largest number the Greeks had a word for was *myriad*, which indicated anything beyond ten thousand. John's estimate is ten thousand times itself, then doubled—a figure that symbolized to first-century readers a force so great that it couldn't be counted.

WHAT IS JESUS TELLING US TODAY?

Make no mistake: the sixth trumpet is a horrifying revelation of how totally broken, hopeless, and corrupt the current world system is. We saw in the previous chapter that the demon hordes of the fifth trumpet were not given permission to kill. Instead, they were allowed to trick the nations into doing the killing, co-opting the spirit of human conquest that's always been active, referenced by the first four seals and trumpets. The sixth trumpet ties the spirit of human conquest together with the forces of evil into a terrifying tool of God's judgment. Evil's impact on the world is deeper than we know. It will never be voted out, legislated away, or eradicated by revolution or war. It doesn't matter which politician, political party, or economic system you believe in; none of them provide the peace and safety the world promises. History clearly shows us humanity is incapable of it. David laments this tendency in Psalm 2:1–2:

> *Why do the nations rage and the peoples plot in vain?* ² *The kings of the earth set themselves, and the rulers take counsel together, against the* Lord *and against his Anointed.*

The deceptive power in the mouths and tails of the evil forces is revealed in their ability to "lead astray, if possible, even the elect" (Matthew 24:24). Even more stunning is how this deception has normalized wrongdoing in society. It's a horrifying revelation of how pervasive evil is in these last days and how frightening life is without faith in Jesus. Psalm 146:3–4 warns against misplacing our faith:

> *Put not your trust in princes, in a son of man, in whom there is no salvation. ⁴ When his breath departs, he returns to the earth; on that very day his plans perish.*

This may sound odd, but this reality isn't depressing for children of God. In fact, if you stop to think about it, it's comforting. This is how we know we're in what Jesus called the "last days" and what John describes in this passage. In Matthew 24, Jesus said we shouldn't be surprised or troubled by this reality because it must take place before the end comes, and it will get worse, as lawlessness, bloodshed, and immorality increase during the spread of evil's influence and deception.

At the same time, God uses these events to call His chosen. Our eyes discern evil. We have ears to hear the gospel. God's message to believers is this: Don't hope in earthly powers. Don't be deceived by nations, kings, or human wisdom. Preach the gospel, as we learn in 1 Peter 2:9–10:

> *You are a chosen race, a royal priesthood, a holy nation, a people for his own possession, that you may proclaim the excellencies of him who called you out of darkness into his marvelous light. ¹⁰ Once you were not a people, but now*

you are God's people; once you had not received mercy, but now you have received mercy.

God doesn't have a most favored earthly nation anymore; instead, He favors His own nation of royal priests! We must let go of our worthless earthly hopes for peace and the burden of trying to defeat evil through politics, economics, and war. Jesus will do that when He returns. In these last days, we are called to a greater hope. Our job as the redeemed throughout the world isn't to fight for our countries to be righteous Christian nations, but to live in step with the values of the kingdom of God. Meanwhile, the unredeemed world will continue, under evil's deception, to toil, rebel, and spin toward its ultimate destruction.

CHAPTER TWENTY-FOUR

Trumpets of Judgment (Part Four): The Bittersweet Gospel

Revelation 10:

1 Then I saw another mighty angel coming down from heaven, wrapped in a cloud, with a rainbow over his head, and his face was like the sun, and his legs like pillars of fire. 2 He had a little scroll open in his hand. And he set his right foot on the sea, and his left foot on the land, 3 and called out with a loud voice, like a lion roaring. When he called out, the seven thunders sounded. 4 And when the seven thunders had sounded, I was about to write, but I heard a voice from heaven saying, "Seal up what the seven thunders have said, and do not write it down." 5 And the angel whom I saw standing on the sea and on the land raised his right hand to heaven 6 and swore by him who lives forever and ever, who created heaven and what is in it, the earth and what is in it, and the sea and what is in it, that there would be no more delay, 7 but that in the days of the trumpet call to be sounded by the seventh angel, the mystery of God would be fulfilled, just as he announced to his servants the prophets.

8 Then the voice that I had heard from heaven spoke to me again, saying, "Go, take the scroll that is open in the hand of the angel who is standing on the sea and on the land." *⁹ So I went to the angel and told him to give me the little scroll. And he said to me, "Take and eat it; it will make your stomach bitter, but in your mouth it will be sweet as honey." ¹⁰ And I took the little scroll from the hand of the angel and ate it. It was sweet as honey in my mouth, but when I had eaten it my stomach was made bitter. ¹¹ And I was told, "You must again prophesy about many peoples and nations and languages and kings."*

Like most pastors, I'm sure I've said things that have made my congregation cringe. I'm not talking about my jokes. I'm referring to harsh realities or bitter-tasting proclamations from God's Word. You know, the ones that leave no wiggle room in our conscience. We'd much rather hear the sweet, promising, and encouraging statements God's Word has for us. But we need to hear everything God tells us in Scripture.

Knowing when, how, and to whom to speak bitter truth is a difficult job, one for which we need heavenly guidance, especially in a world hostile to God's Word. This may be especially true when it comes to what Scripture says concerning sin. Revelation 10 shows us how the church has everything it needs to proclaim successfully and faithfully both the bitter and the sweet words of the gospel, no matter what happens in the world around us.

Trumpets of Judgment (Part Four)

What Would John's Readers Have Noticed?

A Comforting Interlude

Recall the interlude between the sixth and seventh seals, in which John described the 144,000—a representation of all the people in the entire church on earth at any given moment during the church age—and the multitude in heaven as being sealed. John uses the same literary tool here between the sixth and seventh trumpets of judgment. These interludes are like a cutaway from a main plot in a movie, and they are intended to be read as loving, encouraging reminders from Jesus to His chosen, the sealed redeemed.

Thunder and Honey

For John's readers, the phrase "seven thunders" would have triggered a musical connection to a famous song about God's voice in Psalm 29:3–9 (emphasis mine):

> The voice of the Lord is over the waters; the God of glory **thunders**, the Lord, over many waters. ⁴ The voice of the Lord **is powerful**; the voice of the Lord **is full of majesty**. ⁵ The voice of the Lord **breaks the cedars**; the Lord breaks the cedars of Lebanon. ⁶ He makes Lebanon to skip like a calf, and Sirion like a young wild ox. ⁷ The voice of the Lord **flashes forth flames of fire**. ⁸ The voice of the Lord **shakes the wilderness**; the Lord shakes the wilderness of Kadesh. ⁹ The voice of the Lord **makes the deer give birth and strips the forests bare**, and in his temple all cry, "Glory!"

Notice the bolded phrases throughout the verses. This song has *seven* descriptions of the thunderous, commanding voice of God. The readers of Revelation would have known John was saying that he heard the voice of God, and that's who is speaking in this passage.

The image of John eating the scroll also triggers a well-known image found throughout the Hebrew Bible. John's readers knew this meant studying, memorizing, and meditating on God's Word in order to proclaim it, just as we can see in Ezekiel 3:1–3:

> *And [God] said to me, "Son of man... eat this scroll, and go, speak to the house of Israel." ² So I opened my mouth, and he gave me this scroll to eat. ³ ... Then I ate it, and it was in my mouth as sweet as honey.*

WHAT WAS JESUS TELLING THE CHURCHES?

When describing the authoritative angel, John uses many of the same symbols attributed to Jesus on the throne in heaven in Revelation 4. So, is Jesus the angel? After all, His voice is the seven thunders—the voice of God—and He's wrapped in clouds, which has always symbolized God's presence. There's a rainbow aura around His head, which we also saw around the throne, serving as a symbol of God's covenant with His people. He has one foot on the sea and one on the earth and a hand raised to heaven, symbolizing dominion over creation. His face is like the sun, and His legs are like pillars of fire (understood as the light of truth and the authority to judge, a symbol we also saw in Revelation 1:14–15). He also has this little scroll in His hand containing vital information. Doesn't He sound like Jesus? But he can't be, because Jesus doesn't return to earth until the seventh trumpet for final judgment. So, who else would heaven send? I believe this angel is the Holy Spirit, the Helper whom Jesus promised in John 16:7–11 (which the King James Bible translates as *Comforter*):

> *I tell you the truth: it is to your advantage that I go away, for if I do not go away, the **[Comforter]** will not come to you. But if I go, I will send him to you. ⁸ And when he comes, he will convict the world concerning sin and righteousness and judgment: ⁹ concerning sin, because they do not believe in me; ¹⁰ concerning righteousness, because I go to the Father, and you will see me no longer; ¹¹ concerning judgment, because the ruler of this world is judged.*

Verses 8 and 9 are the bitter words contained in the little scroll—judgment and conviction of sin for those who refuse to believe. How is this to play out? That won't be revealed until the seventh trumpet. When John started to write what the seven thunders said, another voice from heaven said, "Don't write it, seal it up!" Compare this to what Jesus said in the next few verses (John 16:12–15, emphasis added):

> ***I still have many things to say to you, but you cannot bear them now.*** *¹³ When the Spirit of truth comes, he will guide you into all the truth, for he will not speak on his own authority, but whatever he hears he will speak, and he will declare to you the things that are to come. ¹⁴ He will glorify me, for he will take what is mine and declare it to you. ¹⁵ All*

that the Father has is mine; therefore I said that he will take what is mine and declare it to you.

What are the "sweet as honey" words in the little book John eats in Revelation 10? I believe they are Jesus' words in John 16:13–15, which tell us the kingdom of God is now! The Comforter, who was sent by Jesus, carried the scroll of redemption that Jesus unsealed, and He gave it to John. Its message? "Despite judgment and horrific evil in this world, be comforted—the Word is getting out!"

In Matthew 24:12, Jesus told us, "Because lawlessness will be increased, the love of many will grow cold." We see it everywhere in our world, even among some in churches. People are angry and divided. We are polarized and easily triggered over just about everything. Jesus assured us, though, in Matthew 24:14, "This gospel of the kingdom will be proclaimed throughout the whole world as a testimony to all nations, and then the end will come."

John read words both sweet and bitter from the scroll. Jesus' letters to most of the churches earlier in Revelation (2:7, 2:17, 2:29, 3:13, and 3:22) also brought both bitter and sweet truths to God's people. They held promises but also correction and judgment. He who has an ear, let him hear what *the Spirit* says to the churches! This interlude reminds us that, as evil and darkness grow, Jesus' plan, contained in the little scroll, will not be hindered nor derailed.

Trumpets of Judgment (Part Four)

What Is Jesus Telling Us Today?

The gospel is sweet, but it is also bitter. We want to know all its mysteries, yet some of them will be concealed until the day of the Lord. It has warnings and judgment. When confronted with our sin, isn't that bitter? But the gospel is also sweet as honey, because we know it ends with the defeat of evil. We are redeemed and will overcome. However, even with the honey, it's hard to live in this bitter world. We need Jesus constantly! The question "How is He with us?" is answered by Jesus Himself in Matthew 28:18–20:

> "All authority in heaven and earth has been given to me. [19] Go therefore and make disciples of all nations, baptizing them in the name of the Father and of the Son and of the Holy Spirit, [20] teaching them to observe all that I have commanded you. And behold, I am with you always, to the end of the age."

This interlude in Revelation 10 is tightly connected to Matthew 24 and 28, in which Jesus tasked us with making disciples of all nations. The Holy Spirit, sent from heaven with the authority of Jesus, brings us God's Word, and we're to eat it, meditate on it, and proclaim it. The bittersweet plan of redemption isn't easy to proclaim. It sets us at odds with the world. Warning a world with no desire to repent provokes backlash: "Who do you think you are? God is going to judge me? I thought God is love!" There is a reason some churches ignore the bitter and focus only on the sweet. Sharing the bitter is not a very marketable message.

But there are also churches who resent those who reject the gospel (or who hate us for proclaiming all of it). As followers of Jesus, we might be tempted to vilify nonbelievers, but they're the ones to whom the Comforter from heaven is prompting us to proclaim this bittersweet plan of redemption. The church must not get sucked into being angry at or obsessed with fixing this world. Our job is to proclaim the gospel, with both its condemnation and its redemption.

When I was a high school basketball coach and my team faced adversity, I had to keep them focused. I would call a time-out to calm them and say with a smile, "Don't you love this? These tense moments are why we practice. Don't worry about the score. Just do what we've learned together to the best of your ability. No matter what, I am so proud of you." That's the Comforter's role—to provide the Word, which convicts and corrects the heart of sin and leads us to repentance, with the command to believe in the gospel of grace.

CHAPTER TWENTY-FIVE

Trumpets of Judgment (Part Five): The Story of Two Witnesses

Revelation 11:1–14:

> *[1] Then I was given a measuring rod like a staff, and I was told, "Rise and measure the temple of God and the altar and those who worship there, [2] but do not measure the court outside the temple; leave that out, for it is given over to the nations, and they will trample the holy city for forty-two months.[3] And I will grant authority to my two witnesses, and they will prophesy for 1,260 days, clothed in sackcloth."*
>
> *[4] These are the two olive trees and the two lampstands that stand before the Lord of the earth. [5] And if anyone would harm them, fire pours from their mouth and consumes their foes. If anyone would harm them, this is how he is doomed to be killed. [6] They have the power to shut the sky, that no rain may fall during the days of their prophesying, and they have power over the waters to turn them into blood and to strike the earth with every kind of plague, as often as they desire. [7] And when they have finished their testimony, the beast that rises from the bottomless pit will make war on them and conquer them and kill them, [8] and their dead bodies will lie in the street of the great city that*

> *symbolically is called Sodom and Egypt, where their Lord was crucified. ⁹ For three and a half days some from the peoples and tribes and languages and nations will gaze at their dead bodies and refuse to let them be placed in a tomb, ¹⁰ and those who dwell on the earth will rejoice over them and make merry and exchange presents, because these two prophets had been a torment to those who dwell on the earth. ¹¹ But after the three and a half days a breath of life from God entered them, and they stood up on their feet, and great fear fell on those who saw them. ¹² Then they heard a loud voice from heaven saying to them, "Come up here!" And they went up to heaven in a cloud, and their enemies watched them. ¹³ And at that hour there was a great earthquake, and a tenth of the city fell. Seven thousand people were killed in the earthquake, and the rest were terrified and gave glory to the God of heaven.*
>
> *¹⁴ The second woe has passed; behold, the third woe is soon to come.*

If you've ever seen a big painting or mural telling a complicated story, you know it's critical to interpret each image in the order it appears. Think of this passage as a verbal mural of the church's story as it proclaims the gospel throughout the age. Revelation 11 describes that entire age of the gospel and the church—the past, the present, and the not yet. It's a sort of halftime pep talk, preparing us for what is to come, sketching out our story as God's witnesses throughout the age.

WHAT WOULD JOHN'S READERS HAVE NOTICED?

More than a Building

Revelation 11:1–2 declares the subject of this mysterious mural: the temple of God.

> Then I was given a measuring rod like a staff, and I was told, "Rise and measure the temple of God and the altar and those who worship there, ² but do not measure the court outside the temple; leave that out, for it is given over to the nations, and they will trample the holy city for forty-two months.

In the Bible, the temple was never about a mere building. It was an overlap of heaven and earth, where God could dwell with His people. Throughout the Old Testament, Scripture describes the garden of Eden, where Adam walked with God, in similar temple-like terms. Likewise, before the temple was built, God's presence was in the tabernacle, a mobile tent. A brick-and-mortar building can be used as a temple, but Scripture tells us God's temple was about *much* more.

Jesus Is the Temple

Jesus clearly taught in John 2:19 and 21 that He is the temple:

> *Jesus answered them, "Destroy this temple, and in three days I will raise it up." . . . ²¹ But he was speaking about the temple of his body.*

In Revelation 21:22, we'll see John declare that he "saw no temple in the city, for its temple is the Lord God the Almighty and the Lamb." So, we are meant to recognize Jesus as the true temple.

The apostles later expanded this temple to include those who are in Christ. In 1 Peter 2:5, the apostle tells believers, "You yourselves like living stones are being built up as a spiritual house, to be a holy priesthood." This is the correct way to interpret temple references throughout Revelation, as the presence of God among His people. Likewise, measuring the temple was about discovering how many of God's people would fill this space.

In the Old Testament, measuring and counting were used as an expression of God's complete knowledge and His detailed, loving care for His people. Noah's ark, another salvation temple, was perfectly measured and built for that purpose. The command given to John to measure the temple is taken directly from Zechariah 2:1–2, in which the prophet saw a man with a measuring line setting out "to measure Jerusalem, to see what is its width and what is its length." It's a beautiful symbol of God's intimate knowledge of His church. In Luke 12:7, Jesus assured us that "even the hairs of your head are all numbered. Fear not." When it comes to His temple, our God cares about every detail!

John was told to ignore the outer court because it wasn't part of the temple. It would be trampled by gentiles (unbelievers). There was no love or protection for those who were not part of the temple, so it didn't need to be measured. This trampling is a symbol of the ongoing tribulation of the first four seals and trumpets. We learned in Revelation 1:9 that we are partners in tribulation, because John identified himself as "your brother and partner in the tribulation and the kingdom and the patient endurance that are in Jesus." And the message John received in his tribulation? "Fear not! God has taken full measure of His temple, setting us apart for redemption."

What Was Jesus Telling the Churches?

Why does this passage describe two witnesses? In Old Testament law, the proof of a true historical event required the testimony of two witnesses before a charge could be validated and put to a judge to determine guilt, as Numbers 35:30 shows:

> *If anyone kills a person, the murderer shall be put to death on the evidence of [two or more] witnesses. But no person shall be put to death on the testimony of one witness.*

Jesus followed this two-witness method when He sent out His disciples. We're told in Luke 10:1 that He "appointed seventy-two others and sent them on ahead of him, two by two, into every town and place where he himself was about to go." In verses 10 to 12, He instructed them:

> *"Whenever you enter a town and they do not receive you, go into its streets and say, ¹¹ 'Even the dust of your town that clings to our feet we wipe off against you. Nevertheless know this, the kingdom of God has come near.' ¹² I tell you, it will be more bearable on that day for Sodom than for that town."*

Jesus also gave us insight into this heavenly authority of the witnesses in Matthew 18:18–20:

> *"Whatever you bind on earth shall be bound in heaven, and whatever you loose on earth shall be loosed in heaven. ¹⁹ Again I say to you, if two of you agree on earth about anything they ask, it will be done for them by my Father in heaven. ²⁰ For where two or three are gathered in my name, there am I among them."*

The testimony of the two witnesses condemns those who refuse to believe. They have spiritual authority to declare the unrepentant guilty, without excuse. This is the nature of their witness: "Repent, for the kingdom of God is now! Repent or be judged with eternal death." This is the bitterness of the gospel.

John says the witnesses are the two olive trees and the two lampstands. It's a clear fulfillment of a prophecy in Zechariah 4:3–6. When the angel asked Zechariah what he saw, he responded,

> *"There are two olive trees by it [a golden lampstand bearing a bowl and seven lamps], one on the right of the bowl and the other on its left." ⁴ And I said to the angel who talked with me, "What are these, my lord?" ⁵ Then the angel who talked with me answered and said to me, "Do you not know what these are?" I said, "No, my lord." ⁶ Then he*

> said to me, "This is the word of the LORD to Zerubbabel: Not by might, nor by power, but by my Spirit, says the LORD of hosts."

It's important to note that Zerubbabel, king of Judea, was a direct ancestor of Jesus. He built the Second Temple in Jerusalem. A few verses later (4:12–14), Zechariah asked the angel,

> "What are these two branches of the olive trees, which are beside the two golden pipes from which the golden oil is poured out?" [13] He said to me, "Do you not know what these are?" I said, "No, my lord." [14] Then he said, "These are the two anointed ones who stand by the Lord of the whole earth."

So, whom do the lampstands in Revelation represent? John described witnesses as possessing the power of a kingdom and the spiritual authority of priests. Similarly, Paul said in 1 Corinthians 6:2–3, "Do you not know that the saints will judge the world? . . . Do you not know that we are to judge angels?" John was making a clear connection to Zechariah's passage, which his readers would have recognized. It's not during their testimony when the witnesses wield supernatural power but afterward, on the day of the Lord and as part of God's army.

Later in the passage, we read about the beast making war against the witnesses, because he and the nations under his control hate their testimony. This part of the story is dark. The church doesn't get through this tribulation unscathed. But we read in Daniel 7:21–22, "As I looked, this horn made war with the saints and prevailed over them, until the Ancient of Days came, and judgment was given for the saints of the Most High, and the time came when the saints possessed the kingdom." This is that glorious day we're awaiting, when Jesus will return and we'll meet Him in the clouds in our resurrected states.

The whole mural of images in this passage of Revelation describes the fulfillment of the seventieth week in the timeline of Messiah and us, His new temple, as depicted in Daniel 9:27 (emphasis mine):

> *He shall make a strong covenant with many for one week,* ***and for half of the week he shall put an end to sacrifice and offering.*** *And on the wing of abominations shall come one who makes desolate, until the decreed end is poured out on the desolator.*

There is a poetic rhythm to interpreting Revelation, especially when it comes to specific numbers. We already broke down the symbolism of the 200-million-man army, the 144,000, and a few others. Daniel's week isn't seven literal days—it's a metaphor, just like the seven years in Revelation 11:2–3 (42 months plus 1,260 days). Both symbolize the era of Jesus.

The first half of the week referenced in Daniel 9 represents the life of Jesus,[19] including His earthly ministry and leading up to His death on the cross, His resurrection, and His ascension. He destroyed the old temple, ending blood sacrifices, and after His resurrection began building His new temple, which is us—the two witnesses. In fact, He continues to build His Temple throughout the church age, even today. This is another beautiful example of the *already*, *right now*, and *not yet* nature of Revelation. His new temple has been prophesying, is prophesying, and will continue to prophesy through the entire age, and many have and will believe and repent. The gospel is honey to them and to us (Psalm 119:103). But to many others, it is a bitter prophesy of condemnation and future judgment, not just for those who refuse to repent but also for Egypt (slavery and oppression) and Sodom (immorality and sin).

WHAT IS JESUS TELLING US TODAY?

This is a beautiful mural of the story of God's new temple, the church, a nation of royal priests throughout the age, with spiritual power and authority over the nations meant to inspire our faithfulness as witnesses. But it is also sobering to think God would entrust us with His spiritual authority of both grace and judgment. Paul explained in Ephesians 3:10, "Through the church the manifold wisdom of God might now be made known to the rulers and authorities in the heavenly places."

Do you see what a high, glorious view Revelation gives to the church of Jesus? That is us, His holy, measured temple! It's why Jesus said the world would hate us: our testimony is condemnation to all the unrepentant. The world will witness the moment when Jesus calls us to meet Him in the clouds, and reality will hit them hard. What a beautiful mural of the plan of redemption to explain the *already*, the *right now*, and the *not yet*. No matter how difficult our role of proclamation becomes, we know how it ends. As Jesus says in Matthew 28:20, He is with His witnesses until the end of the age.

CHAPTER TWENTY-SIX

Trumpets of Judgment (Part Six): A New Kind of Government

Revelation 11:15–19:

> *15 Then the seventh angel blew his trumpet, and there were loud voices in heaven, saying, "The kingdom of the world has become the kingdom of our Lord and of his Christ, and he shall reign forever and ever." 16 And the twenty-four elders who sit on their thrones before God fell on their faces and worshiped God, 17 saying, "We give thanks to you, Lord God Almighty, who is and who was, for you have taken your great power and begun to reign. 18 The nations raged, but your wrath came, and the time for the dead to be judged, and for rewarding your servants, the prophets and saints, and those who fear your name, both small and great, and for destroying the destroyers of the earth."*
>
> *19 Then God's temple in heaven was opened, and the ark of his covenant was seen within his temple. There were flashes of lightning, rumblings, peals of thunder, an earthquake, and heavy hail.*

I make many references to earthly governments in this book because, if there is one thing Revelation makes clear, it's that earthly politics, regardless of party or platform, are never something followers of Jesus should put their hope in. People tend to be attracted to earthly saviors, which explains how dictators like Hitler and Lenin could come to power. American Christians are often tempted to place hope in a political ideology, like Liberal Progressivism or Christian nationalism, to make our nation righteous and to gain God's blessing. But can a nation ever be truly righteous? Should churches make "transforming government" part of their mission? Israel had a direct, tangible relationship with God manifested in so many ways, and even they couldn't do it right! It's fine to be patriotic citizens of our earthly home, but the kingdom of our God is our only true hope, and it transcends the boundaries of every nation.

What Would John's Readers Have Noticed?

The Sounding of Trumpets

Can you think of places in the Old Testament where trumpets were used in conjunction with the fall of earthly kings? One prime example is found in Joshua 6:20, which details the toppling of Jericho:

> *The people shouted, and the trumpets were blown. As soon as the people heard the sound of the trumpet, the people shouted a great shout, and the wall fell down flat, so that*

the people went up into the city, every man straight before him, and they captured the city.

The Jericho story features the number 7 prominently, with its seven trips around the wall. The trumpets sounding at each pass are direct links to the seven trumpets of judgment in Revelation. After the seventh trip, following the seventh sounding of trumpets, Jericho's walls collapsed, as did its government. God's people went in and took control of an impenetrable city without firing a single arrow. Trumpets are associated with God and His people rising up against evil throughout the prophetic books, too. Isaiah 27:13 tells us, "And in that day a great trumpet will be blown, and those who were lost . . . will come and worship the LORD on the holy mountain at Jerusalem."

The Fate of Earthly Governments

Psalm 2:1–2 asks, "Why do the nations rage and the peoples plot in vain? The kings of the earth set themselves, and the rulers take counsel together, against the LORD and against his Anointed." This is the instinctive response of every political entity throughout human history. Nations don't rage out of anger but out of their insatiable drive for power and control. Who is sovereign over the affairs of mankind: God or government? Government will often ally itself with religion to preserve its secular and spiritual power. But one thing God's people have always hoped for is the day God brings earthly government to an end, as Psalm 110:5 reminds us:

"The Lord is at your right hand; he will shatter kings on the day of his wrath."

This is the most quoted Old Testament passage in the New Testament. The frustration of enduring the authority of kings and kingdoms of this world is something John's readers would have understood well. Israel had suffered under hostile powers like Babylon, Persia, and Greece. Then, Rome's domination carried over into the Christian era. First-century believers would have connected the seventh trumpet to Jericho, seeing it as a reminder of future fulfillment of the day Jesus will return and put an end to earthly human governments.

WHAT WAS JESUS TELLING THE CHURCHES?

The seventh trumpet is another camera angle on the return of Jesus, specifically its ramifications for all governments. Scripture has much to say about the fate of earthly rulers and administrations, as foretold in Daniel 2:44:

> *In the days of those kings the God of heaven will set up a kingdom that shall never be destroyed, nor shall the kingdom be left to another people. It shall break in pieces all these kingdoms and bring them to an end, and it shall stand forever.*

Daniel taught that this ominous fate of earthly governments is the culmination of redemption. He also revealed in Daniel 7:13–14 that all nations exist at God's decree:

> "I saw in the night visions, and behold, with the clouds of heaven there came one like a son of man, and he came to the Ancient of Days and was presented before him. ¹⁴ And to him was given dominion and glory and a kingdom, that all peoples, nations, and languages should serve him; his dominion is an everlasting dominion, which shall not pass away, and his kingdom one that shall not be destroyed."

We long for the day when the kingdoms of this world become the kingdom of our God and of His Son Jesus. Until then, God grants earthly kingdoms authority for a time, for His sovereign purpose. After they have served God's purpose in the plan of redemption, they lose influence or even disappear. Paul said in 1 Corinthians 15:24, "Then comes the end, when [Jesus] delivers the kingdom to God the Father after destroying every rule and every authority and power." And in verse 26, Paul declared that "the last enemy to be destroyed is death."

Throughout history, all nations, no matter how powerful, fall from glory and power at God's decree. But on the day of His return, Jesus will scoop up the kingdoms of this world as a single entity and reclaim them under His authority. In the end, every earthly government will pass away. None of them will last forever, including our own. And that's a good thing, isn't it?

Once the fate of earthly governments has been sealed, the kingdom of God will have an attribute no other government has ever had. Since the beginning of nations, leaders have kept themselves separate from the people, granting them merely the mirage of access. All rulers—from emperors to high-ranking elected officials—want to act like they are of the people, but they aren't really. The people they lead do not have free access. It's too risky for the rulers. But the temple in Revelation represents the place where God dwells among His people. Here, the temple in heaven is opened, so everyone can see the ark of the covenant, a symbol of God's full presence. In other words, when Jesus returns to fully establish *His* government, we will have complete, unfettered access to our King!

WHAT IS JESUS TELLING US TODAY?

Today, as God's people, we certainly experience the benefits of spiritual access to God's kingdom, don't we? It began in Matthew 27:51, when "the curtain of the temple was torn in two, from top to bottom. And the earth shook, and the rocks were split." In Revelation, we see this access being exercised as the aroma of our prayers and worship fill the heavenly temple like incense (8:3–4). That's our direct access to the King of kings during the tribulation period we now live in, which started with Jesus' resurrection and will continue until His return. We experience that access to the King in our prayers, our worship, our study of the Word, and our fellowship together. It's present when we serve each other and our neighbors. We see its impact as the kingdom of God expands to every tribe and nation, even as the governments of those nations rage against it!

But let's be real here: we know there's still something missing. Even though we have access to the King, we can't see or touch Him. But on the day Jesus brings the nations under His authority, access will no longer be just spiritual. The day of the seventh trumpet will bust the barrier between this dimension and the heavenly one, just like the seventh trumpet blast brought down the walls of Jericho!

No earthly form of government is worthy of our hope; only the kingdom of God is worthy of that, as Psalm 146:3–7 reminds us:

> *Put not your trust in princes, in a son of man, in whom there is no salvation. ⁴ When his breath departs, he returns to the earth; on that very day his plans perish. ⁵ Blessed is he whose help is the God of Jacob, whose hope is in the Lord his God, ⁶ who made heaven and earth, the sea, and all that is in them, who keeps faith forever; ⁷ who executes justice for the oppressed, who gives food to the hungry. The Lord sets the prisoners free.*

As followers of Jesus, we instinctively long for a world governed with integrity, justice, and equality, which is what every earthly government claims it can provide. But none have ever, or will ever, meet this standard. Every nation rages against the King of kings. Even America does so, no matter which party or politician is in power (yes, including the one you might vote for). However, on the day of the seventh trumpet, when the King of kings takes over, all of that will change! But who will be in charge then? In 1 Peter 2:9, Peter described a holy nation that will rule with Jesus when He comes at the sound of that seventh trumpet.

> *But you are a chosen race, a royal priesthood, a holy nation, a people for his own possession, that you may proclaim the excellencies of him who called you out of darkness into his marvelous light.*

As Christians, we should abandon our obsession with striving to seize power, to fix an earthly government that can never fulfill its promises and will one day be acquired by the King of kings when He returns anyway. The seventh trumpet teaches followers of Jesus that no earthly nation, no matter how great, can be God's chosen nation. Only the church has been given this role. Our loyalty and passion should always be for the King of kings and His holy nation—His people, His church, His mission—before any pitiful earthly government or ruler.

CHAPTER TWENTY-SEVEN

The Woman vs. the Dragon

Revelation 12:1–6:

> *¹ And a great sign appeared in heaven: a woman clothed with the sun, with the moon under her feet, and on her head a crown of twelve stars. ² She was pregnant and was crying out in birth pains and the agony of giving birth. ³ And another sign appeared in heaven: behold, a great red dragon, with seven heads and ten horns, and on his heads seven diadems. ⁴ His tail swept down a third of the stars of heaven and cast them to the earth. And the dragon stood before the woman who was about to give birth, so that when she bore her child he might devour it. ⁵ She gave birth to a male child, one who is to rule all the nations with a rod of iron, but her child was caught up to God and to his throne, ⁶ and the woman fled into the wilderness, where she has a place prepared by God, in which she is to be nourished for 1,260 days.*

Are you ever troubled by all the wickedness throughout human history? Do you get weary of the seemingly relentless struggle against evil or trying to understand why Christians are often the target of evildoers? That's tribulation! These trials are especially difficult if we don't understand why evil and the suffering it causes seem so ubiquitous. As followers of Jesus, it's important to zoom out of the day-to-day so we can wrap our heads around the bigger picture. God knows it's necessary to gain perspective on the iniquity we see all around us, so He gives us "aha!" passages like this one, which kicks off a powerful three-chapter section to introduce what's coming next.

WHAT WOULD JOHN'S READERS HAVE NOTICED?

The Story of Redemption

Revelation isn't a linear timeline, narrative, or prophecy, as many have explained it. It's a series of wide-angle descriptions of the major influences shaping the *already*, the *right now*, and the *not yet*. Revelation summarizes the four main movements of redemption's story in broad strokes from the beginning of the Bible to the end.

First, we learn of *creation* in Genesis 1 and 2, when God made the world without sin to be a place where He could dwell with mankind. Genesis 3 records the *fall* of humanity, when Satan successfully tempted Adam and Eve and set God's entire creation at odds with its Creator.

Then Genesis 4 through Revelation 20 tells the story of *redemption*. The Old Testament's history of Israel demonstrates God's preservation of His chosen and the line of Jesus. The New Testament starts with the four Gospels, revealing

Jesus and His words and actions. Then the book of Acts chronicles God's transformation of His scared disciples into an international movement. The Epistles address issues of Kingdom living in a fallen world as we wait for Jesus to return. Throughout, we see how God guides, protects, and redeems His people.

The *completion* comes in Revelation 21 and 22, when Jesus returns for the final judgment of evil and restores earth as the place where He can be with His people. These four major movements throughout Scripture were the framework God's people used when reading the Old Testament and processing world events around them.

WHAT WAS JESUS TELLING THE CHURCHES?

This passage reveals the heart of the battle—why evil and the nations rage and why God's people suffer as a result. It contains five symbols: the woman, the dragon, birth pains, the child, and the wilderness. These symbols would have been familiar to John's readers, as they're all pulled directly from the Old Testament.

The first thing John's readers would have recognized is a reference to when God cursed the serpent for tempting Eve in Genesis 3:14–15, saying "I will put enmity between you and the woman, and between your offspring and her offspring; he shall bruise your head, and you shall bruise his heel."

Second, they would have connected the woman described in Revelation 12:1, who was "clothed with the sun, with the moon under her feet, and on her head a crown of twelve stars" with Joseph's vision in Genesis 37:9, which is an unmistakable metaphor for the faithful in Israel:

> *Then he dreamed another dream and told it to his brothers and said, "Behold, I have dreamed another dream. Behold, the sun, the moon, and eleven stars were bowing down to me."*

God used Joseph's visions in Genesis 37 and his interpretation of Pharaoh's dreams in Genesis 41:25–36 to preserve Israel, along with the lineage of Jesus, through the famine in Egypt. But that isn't the only place in Scripture where Israel is described as a woman rejected by the world but chosen by God. We see in Isaiah 54:6, "The Lord has called you like a wife deserted and grieved in spirit, like a wife of youth when she is cast off . . ." John's readers would also have made the obvious connection to Mary, the mother of Jesus, the woman who bore the offspring whose heel bruised the serpent.

The descriptions used for the faithful in Israel were also used for the church: in Ephesians 5:25, Paul described the church as the bride of Christ, saying, "Husbands, love your wives, as Christ loved the church and gave himself up for her." Later, John also described the church as a bride who has adorned herself in pure fine linen for her wedding to the Lamb in Revelation 19:6–8.

The dragon appears in Revelation 12:9:

> *And the great dragon was thrown down, that ancient serpent, who is called the devil and Satan, the deceiver of the*

whole world—he was thrown down to the earth, and his angels were thrown down with him.

Again, John's readers would have recognized "that ancient serpent" from God's curse of the serpent in Genesis 3:14.

The seven heads represent the dragon's cunning, the seven horns represent his earthly power, and the seven crowns represent his authority over the world's kingdoms. The dragon is the mastermind behind the entire world system and its governments, influencing every goal and action. The third of the stars pulled down represent the dragon's power over fallen angels—the same demon locust horde we studied earlier. God's curse in Genesis 3:15–16 made the dragon's opposition clear:

> *"I will put enmity between you and the woman, and between your offspring and her offspring; he shall bruise your head, and you shall bruise his heel."* [16] *To the woman he said, "I will surely multiply your pain in childbearing; in pain you shall bring forth children."*

Birth pains are a metaphor for the suffering God's faithful remnant endured because of the dragon. Ever since Cain killed Abel, the dragon's primary obsession has been his war on Jesus' lineage. Those brothers' enmity (Genesis 4), Pharaoh's attempted genocide (Exodus 1:15–22), and King Saul's bloodlust toward David (1 Samuel 18–24) are just a few examples of his work.

God's faithful were caught in this frontline battle from the fall of Adam and Eve until Jesus was born. But God protected the woman, her offspring, and Jesus' line. Do you see how the Old Testament is a beautifully woven epic narrative of the battle between the dragon and the bloodline of Jesus? It's a major part of the even bigger story of redemption.

Finally, the child was born in Bethlehem. Galatians 4:4 recounts, "When the fullness of time had come, God sent forth his Son, born of woman, born under the law." God became man, went to the cross, and defeated sin and death. Every day Jesus walked this earth, the enemy wanted to destroy Him. We saw it when Herod tried to kill all the Jewish male children when Jesus was born (Matthew 2:16–18), and again when the Pharisees wanted to arrest and kill Jesus but couldn't touch him because the hour had not yet come (John 7:31–53). But after the cross, Jesus ascended to heaven until the day He will return to rule the world's kingdoms at the sounding of the seventh trumpet we learned about in Revelation 11.

In Revelation 12, we see that after Jesus was born, the woman was whisked into the wilderness, where God is protecting her until the end of the tribulation. The wilderness is harsh and desolate, a test of human endurance. But it was where God's faithful people would flee in order to escape their enemies. David, who featured prominently in Jesus' lineage, fled there when Saul and, later, Absalom wanted to kill him (1 Samuel 23, 2 Samuel 15). Moses (Exodus 2), Elijah (1 Kings 19), Hagar (Genesis 21), and countless others—including Jesus—sought the same refuge. In fact, forty years before Rome invaded Jerusalem, Jesus warned the first-century church to flee to the wilderness when it happened.

For us, we are in a type of wilderness today, and it's not easy. But we, too, are protected from the dragon who wants to devour us.

WHAT IS JESUS TELLING US TODAY?

The five symbols of the woman, the dragon, birth pains, the child, and the wilderness illustrate the catalyst behind every major event in human history, the present age, and in the future. They provide a 30,000-foot view of the battle, depicting the constant struggle between evil and God's faithful that will rage until Jesus returns. In this battle, the woman represents the prize. She is the object of the dragon's wrath but also the recipient of the Father's love, grace, mercy, and protection. She symbolizes every human recipient of every redemptive act of God throughout history—from Eve, to Mary, and now the church.

But the greatest miracle of God's grace is that not only does the woman represent the church, but so does the child. As Paul reminded us in Romans 16:20, "The God of peace will soon crush Satan under your feet." The church is our mother. We, along with Jesus, are her offspring, and we, along with Jesus, will crush the dragon's head.

No wonder the dragon hates us so much! No wonder he rages against the woman and her offspring with all his power. In 1 Peter 4:12–13, the apostle said:

> *Beloved, do not be surprised at the fiery trial when it comes upon you to test you, as though something strange were happening to you. ⁱ³ But rejoice insofar as you share Christ's sufferings, that you may also rejoice and be glad when his glory is revealed.*

Redemption and the role God has allowed us to play in it are insulting slaps to the devil's face. Paul went on to say in 2 Corinthians 4:8–9 that "we are afflicted in every way, but not crushed; perplexed, but not driven to despair; persecuted, but not forsaken; struck down, but not destroyed." Living through the tribulation in the wilderness means suffering, but the good news is that we the faithful are marked and protected by the Spirit of God. Just as God preserved the line of Jesus, so He will preserve us. The dragon has been, is, and will be thwarted at every turn, even though he is constantly probing, looking for a way in, and nipping at our heels!

And so we pray God will continue to thwart the dragon's schemes and grant perseverance to us as we live through this tribulation in the wilderness until Jesus returns. As the dragon walks around seeking offspring to devour, we have each other's backs, encouraging one another with the story of redemption! With those same beautiful feet that God will use to crush the dragon's head, we will boldly proclaim the gospel and call others with ears to hear what the spirit says to the churches.

CHAPTER TWENTY-EIGHT

The Accuser Evicted and Bound

Revelation 12:7–12:

> [7] Now war arose in heaven, Michael and his angels fighting against the dragon. And the dragon and his angels fought back, [8] but he was defeated, and there was no longer any place for them in heaven. [9] And the great dragon was thrown down, that ancient serpent, who is called the devil and Satan, the deceiver of the whole world—he was thrown down to the earth, and his angels were thrown down with him. [10] And I heard a loud voice in heaven, saying, "Now the salvation and the power and the kingdom of our God and the authority of his Christ have come, for the accuser of our brothers has been thrown down, who accuses them day and night before our God. [11] And they have conquered him by the blood of the Lamb and by the word of their testimony, for they loved not their lives even unto death. [12] Therefore, rejoice, O heavens and you who dwell in them! But woe to you, O earth and sea, for the devil has come down to you in great wrath, because he knows that his time is short!"

Have you ever been embarrassed by someone who made a loud public accusation against you? Or have you known someone who seemed to enjoy telling everyone about your missteps?

At my first full-time ministry job, I had a coworker who came after me at a public meeting for an error I'd made. When my accuser began airing my blunder, what could I say? This coworker's self-righteousness didn't make the accusations false. I'd made a mistake. By human standards, I had no defense.

But my mentor defended me, anyway: "Joe came to me a week ago when he realized his mistake, then asked for forgiveness and my help in resolving it. He has done everything asked of him. The matter has been fully resolved. Is there anything else?"

I felt humbled and loved by his defense, and his advocacy for me completely disarmed the ammunition my coworker was trying to use against me. Likewise, this passage of Revelation pulls back the cosmic veil to reveal the utter failure of our greatest accuser when our advocate, Jesus, stands up for us.

WHAT WOULD JOHN'S READERS HAVE NOTICED?

The Ancient Accuser

There are two names given to the dragon in verse 9: *devil*, which means *slanderer*,[20] and *Satan*, which means *adversary* or *accuser*.[21] The latter was the name given to him in the story found in the book of Job. Before Jesus came to earth, Satan's favorite pastime was accusing the chosen, whom God loves. He knows if he can destroy the redemption of just one of God's chosen, the whole plan of redemption is called into question and will fail.

If you are a follower of Jesus, Satan resents you because God chose you, loves you, and has redeemed you. It's the core motivation behind why Satan scours the earth, looking for God's redeemed to accuse. John's readers would have associated this accuser with several Old Testament stories of Satan accusing one of God's redeemed. The most memorable occurrence was recorded in Job 1:6–11:

> *Now there was a day when the sons of God came to present themselves before the* LORD, *and Satan also came among them. ⁷ The* LORD *said to Satan, "From where have you come?" Satan answered the* LORD *and said, "From going to and fro on the earth, and from walking up and down on it." ⁸ And the* LORD *said to Satan, "Have you considered my servant Job, that there is none like him on the earth, a blameless and upright man, who fears God and turns away from evil?" ⁹ Then Satan answered the* LORD *and said, "Does Job fear God for no reason? ¹⁰ Have you not put a hedge around him and his house and all that he has, on every side? You have blessed the work of his hands, and his possessions have increased in the land. ¹¹ But stretch out your hand and touch all that he has, and he will curse you to your face."*

Satan knew Job before God pointed him out. Satan was always hunting down people who had received God's undeserved favor. Job was a righteous man not because of his own character but because God had chosen and redeemed him.

Satan came before God in heaven and claimed Job was righteous only because of all God had given him. Satan then happily brought great suffering (or tribulation) to Job's life. But God kept Job's soul safe! The story of Job isn't a celebration of his patience but of how the accuser's attempts to discredit God's chosen have, do, and always will fail.

Another example is the story of Satan accusing a high priest of failing to follow Levitical clothing laws for the temple in Zechariah 3:1:

> *Then he showed me Joshua the high priest standing before the angel of the* LORD, *and Satan standing at his right hand to accuse him.*

Satan accused Joshua of wearing ritually soiled garments in the temple and wanted God to kill Joshua for it! His goal was and is to turn God against those He has chosen for redemption, to set us at odds with the Father.

WHAT WAS JESUS TELLING THE CHURCHES?

Revelation provides critical insights into when and how Satan was expelled from heaven and bound to earth. The archangel Michael is described throughout Scripture as a key player in heavenly warfare and the story of redemption. He is one of the strongest of angels, and he appears in Daniel 10:13, battling with the forces of Satan:

> *The prince of the kingdom of Persia withstood me twenty-one days, but Michael, one of the chief princes, came to help me, for I was left there with the kings of Persia.*

And again, in Jude 9a:

> *But when the archangel Michael, contending with the devil...*

Many believe Satan and his demons were cast out of heaven before creation. I used to believe this, too. From the book of Job, however, we know the Accuser regularly went before the throne of heaven prior to Christ's birth. Revelation 12 also indicates the war in heaven stretched from Adam and Eve's fall until just before Jesus was born. When Satan's war failed to destroy the line of Jesus, Michael and his angels evicted Satan and his demons from heaven, binding them to earth by God's authority.

Recall when Jesus sent out the seventy-two disciples by pairs in Luke 10:17–18 and they "returned with joy, saying, 'Lord, even the demons are subject to us in your name!' And he said to them, 'I saw Satan fall like lightning from heaven.'" This seems to indicate He was aware of what had happened in heaven after His conception.

The dragon also failed to "devour" Christ during His earthly ministry. When Jesus was crucified and resurrected, after which He ascended to heaven, He defeated sin and death and was no longer within reach of the Accuser. The arrival of Messiah had far-reaching impacts across the entire realm of creation. Satan could no longer go before God to accuse His redeemed.

With Satan's eviction, the heavenly host celebrates! The accuser of our brethren has been cast down (Revelation 12:10)! The multitude in Christ who have passed from this earthly realm also celebrate Satan's inevitable demise, as hinted in Deuteronomy 19:18–19: "...and if the witness is a false witness and has accused his brother falsely, then you shall do to him as he had meant to do to his brother. So you shall purge the evil from your midst."

The passage ends with a dire warning to earth's inhabitants. This binding of Satan to earth limits what the Accuser can do—and when and where he can go—until the end of the age. As a result, Satan is livid. He knows he's bound to our dimension. But he can still cause havoc and destruction. That's why John says, "But woe to the inhabitants of the earth" (Revelation 12:12).

Satan can no longer accuse us or do anything to stop our redemption. However, he can still do to us what he did to Job. That's the only power he has left. It marks the beginning of the tribulation age we're currently experiencing. He can't war against heaven anymore, so he turns against the woman—Christ's church.

WHAT IS JESUS TELLING US TODAY?

The victory won by Jesus at the cross was so complete that Satan isn't even allowed to accuse us of being sinners anymore! Perhaps you remember what happened in John 8:9–

11, when Jesus defended a woman accused of adultery, whom a hypocritical group of men wanted to stone:

> But when they heard it, they went away one by one, beginning with the older ones, and Jesus was left alone with the woman standing before him. ¹⁰ Jesus stood up and said to her, "Woman, where are they? Has no one condemned you?" ¹¹ She said, "No one, Lord." And Jesus said, "Neither do I condemn you; go, and from now on sin no more."

Jesus seemed unimpressed by their accusations, even though she was totally guilty! He was writing something on the ground—probably the law in Deuteronomy regarding the fate of hypocritical false witnesses. He said the one without sin should cast the first stone, and then they all began to leave, until Jesus was there with her alone. Imagine how precious that moment must have been for the accused! What did Jesus mean when he told her to go and sin no more?

Remember when the Accuser attributed Job's righteousness to God's benevolence (Job 1:9–11)? Well, he was right! In 2 Peter 1:3 we read, "His divine power has granted to us all things that pertain to life and godliness, through the knowledge of him who called us to his own glory and excellence." That day, Jesus sent the accused woman out with power for everything she would need for life and godliness, just as He did the seventy-two disciples!

Colossians 2:14–15 explains that He cancelled "the record of debt that stood against us. . . . This he set aside, nailing it to the cross. He disarmed the rulers and authorities and put them to open shame, by triumphing over them in him." Before the cross, Satan was able to go to and fro on the earth, compiling a long list of dirt on the redeemed that he could take before God and accuse us of. After the cross, our dirty garments were replaced with white robes of righteousness. No matter how much Satan hates you and wants you to be judged, he can't even talk about you to God anymore!

Remember the story I told you about the time I was accused? We read in 1 John 2:1, "My little children, I am writing these things to you so that you may not sin. But if anyone does sin, we have an advocate with the Father, Jesus Christ the righteous."

A relentless advocate has replaced our accuser before the throne of God—our Jesus, who took our sins to the cross. So, when you hear the enemy whispering accusations in your ear, it's a weak, pitiful attack. Your Jesus has shut the Accuser's obnoxious mouth, evicted him from the heavenly realm for all eternity, and Jesus himself has become your eternal advocate. It's good to have a friend in high places, isn't it?

CHAPTER TWENTY-NINE

Waiting in the Wilderness

Revelation 12:13–17:

> [13] And when the dragon saw that he had been thrown down to the earth, he pursued the woman who had given birth to the male child. [14] But the woman was given the two wings of the great eagle so that she might fly from the serpent into the wilderness, to the place where she is to be nourished for a time, and times, and half a time. [15] The serpent poured water like a river out of his mouth after the woman, to sweep her away with a flood. [16] But the earth came to the help of the woman, and the earth opened its mouth and swallowed the river that the dragon had poured from his mouth. [17] Then the dragon became furious with the woman and went off to make war on the rest of her offspring, on those who keep the commandments of God and hold to the testimony of Jesus. And he stood on the sand of the sea.

Over two decades ago, my wife, Laura, and I were given a trip to Israel. One night, our guide arranged a wilderness camping experience in Bedouin tents. They were huge, luxurious tents—probably more than 800 square feet. Our

Bedouin hosts provided everything we needed—food, beverages, electricity—but they warned our group, "Don't wander off into the wilderness alone. There are dangerous animals that come out at night. Stay with the camp and remain in your tents. You have everything you need until the morning when we come to get you."

In the middle of the night, we heard a shriek right outside from an eighteen-year-old girl who hadn't heeded their warnings. Our Bedouin hosts rushed to her aide and slayed a huge scorpion, which we later learned was the deadliest species in Israel. When we heard the news, all twenty-five of us moved our cots into a four-foot-square area in the center of our tent to wait for sunup.

WHAT WOULD JOHN'S READERS HAVE NOTICED?

The Gospel of Exodus

As we've seen, the seven trumpets were linked to the ten plagues that Egypt suffered when Pharaoh refused to set Israel free (Exodus 7–12). This passage in Revelation links to the second part of that story, after Israel finally left Egypt. Their campfires were barely cold when Pharaoh scrambled to bring his military might to bear to retrieve them, pursuing them to the shores of the Red Sea (Exodus 14). After Israel escaped Pharaoh's army by crossing the parted Red Sea, God led them safely into the wilderness. There, He protected them, allowing them to grow as a nation while He prepared them to take possession of the land He'd promised to Abraham.

In Exodus 19:4, right after God rescued Israel and destroyed Pharaoh's army, He told them, "You yourselves have seen what I did to the Egyptians, and how I bore you on eagles' wings and brought you to myself." When John's readers saw that "the woman was given the two wings of the great eagle so that she might fly from the serpent into the wilderness" (Revelation 12:14), they would have immediately made the connection to the Exodus story. In fact, every Old Testament reference to eagles' wings is used as a metaphor for God rescuing the faithful from their enemies.

John had already established that the woman represented all God's chosen throughout history. Here, I believe the woman pursued by the dragon represents the early church under intense persecution. The next few chapters of Revelation use Israel's exodus story to foreshadow the next great exodus—ours, from this evil world—when Jesus returns to set things right.

Sustained in the Wilderness

Israel's life in the wilderness wasn't easy. They had no food or water. They suffered harsh weather conditions. At one point, the people began to complain constantly to Moses, "Life is terrible here. We want to go back to Egypt!"

Just like us in our own time in the wilderness of this world, Israel's daily survival depended on God patiently sustaining them for forty years as they waited for the promised land. Every day, He displayed miracles such as feeding them with manna from heaven (Exodus 16) and providing water from rocks (Exodus 17:1-7 and Numbers 20:1-13). He provided clouds for shade during the day and a pillar of fire at night (Exodus 13:17-22). They also needed correction and guidance, so He gave them the Ten Commandments (Exodus 20:1-17).

In verse 6, we saw that the woman's time in the wilderness would be 1,260 days. John's readers would have seen this number, which is three and a half years, as a reference to the "time, times, and half a time" of Daniel 7:25 and Daniel 12:7, where the prophet describes the "wear[ing] out [of] the saints of the Most High" and the "shattering of the power of the holy people." Israel had been repeatedly attacked by foreign invaders, and during these persecutions, God's people often fled to the wilderness for protection. John called back to the symbolism of "time, times, and half a time" to paint the era which we are still in, where the dragon and his demon horde of invaders constantly seek to persecute God's people.

WHAT WAS JESUS TELLING THE CHURCHES?

When Satan lost the war in heaven, he became filled with rage and panic. After failing to destroy the line of Jesus and Jesus Himself, he had only one target left: the woman, whom we've seen is the church. Just as Pharaoh gathered his army to pursue Israel, the dragon gathered his demon horde and went after the early church, but God rescued her on the great eagle's wings. Think of those wings as the Holy Spirit, who calls God's chosen out of darkness into light (1 Peter 2:9).

The dragon failed again to kill the woman, so he tried to use a flood from his mouth to carry her away. We have seen several times in Revelation what flows from the mouth of the devil: deception. The waters flowing from the dragon's mouth represent the devil's relentless attempt to flood the church with untruths.

In Matthew 24:24, Jesus warned the church that once the tribulation started, the enemy would come after her with powerful deceptions:

> *For false christs and false prophets will arise and perform great signs and wonders, so as to lead astray, if possible, even the elect.*

With Satan's raging river of lies, he has repeatedly attempted to destroy the church from within through false teaching.

But the earth swallows up his flood of falsehoods. The earth becomes personified in this war—as it does many times in the story of redemption—as an ally to the woman. We see it in Romans 8:22–23, when Paul said, "the whole creation has been groaning [for] . . . redemption," and in Luke 19:40, when Jesus said, "the very stones would cry out." The symbolism of being swallowed by the earth is an undeniable link to Exodus 15, verses 9 and 12:

> *"The enemy said, 'I will pursue, I will overtake, I will divide the spoil, my desire shall have its fill of them. I will draw my sword; my hand shall destroy them.'... ¹² You stretched out your right hand; the earth swallowed them."*

Remember how God destroyed Pharaoh's army in the Exodus story? He swallowed them up in the Red Sea. Throughout the Old Testament, being swallowed by the earth is a metaphor for a shocking, catastrophic defeat. It's a symbol of all the times in Israel's history when God preserved His people from evil, even when all seemed lost.

John was describing the catastrophic defeat of the dragon and his flood of lies. The dragon, even more desperate and running out of time, turns his rage toward the woman's offspring, who keep God's commandments and remain faithful. The offspring is us—the church through this current age of tribulation, from the second century to today.

WHAT IS JESUS TELLING US TODAY?

All these symbols paint a picture of a story that teaches us how to see our life in the wilderness of this earth, right now, today. In Ezekiel 34:25, the Lord ensured the protection of His chosen, saying, "I will make with them a covenant of peace and banish wild beasts from the land, so that they may dwell securely in the wilderness and sleep in the woods."

Ezekiel's prophecy, this "covenant of peace with people sleeping in the woods," is about us—you and me. Spiritually, we are camping in the wilderness. It's not a permanent home. God sustains us daily while we wait. He has banished the beasts who desire to destroy us. Before we became followers of Jesus, the dragon chased us, trying to destroy our souls before the Spirit of God could carry us into the wilderness with the rest of His people. For those of us who have been led there and given the gift of faith, we remain safe in the wilderness until the morning, when Jesus will come to get us!

Like Israel from Egypt and the woman from the dragon, God's spirit carried us on eagles' wings to safety in the wilderness. Yes, we are surrounded by a flood of lies, but the dragon's lies don't work against God's people. Jesus promised He would be with us throughout this tribulation until the day He returns and evicts the evil invaders. Hebrews 13:14 reminds us, "For here we have no lasting city, but we seek the city that is to come."

This wilderness we are camping and waiting in is temporary. Jesus will make a new heaven and earth, free of the dragon. *That* will be our permanent home. When He returns, He will swallow the evil invaders up and restore the earth. On that day, we will return to *our* promised land—a world that has been rid of all evil.

Sadly, I think too many Christians get distracted. We fall in love with camping in the wilderness. We become obsessed with trying to make this world our promised land, thinking we can turn it into heaven on earth. I'm not saying we can't try to make life in the wilderness better, but it will always be wilderness until Jesus returns. That's why Jesus reminded us in John 16:33, "I have said these things to you, that in me you may have peace. In the world you will have tribulation. But take heart; I have overcome the world."

As we wait, God nourishes us through this tribulation. We know that no weapons of the dragon will prosper. No matter how powerful his schemes may be, the earth will swallow them up in total defeat. Until then, we carry the gospel, warning others about the dragon and this war between good and evil.

CHAPTER THIRTY

The Beast from the Sea

Revelation 13:1–10:

> *1 And I saw a beast rising out of the sea, with ten horns and seven heads, with ten diadems on its horns and blasphemous names on its heads. 2 And the beast that I saw was like a leopard; its feet were like a bear's, and its mouth was like a lion's mouth. And to it the dragon gave his power and his throne and great authority. 3 One of its heads seemed to have a mortal wound, but its mortal wound was healed, and the whole earth marveled as they followed the beast. 4 And they worshiped the dragon, for he had given his authority to the beast, and they worshiped the beast, saying, "Who is like the beast, and who can fight against it?"*
>
> *5 And the beast was given a mouth uttering haughty and blasphemous words, and it was allowed to exercise authority for forty-two months. 6 It opened its mouth to utter blasphemies against God, blaspheming his name and his dwelling, that is, those who dwell in heaven. 7 Also it was allowed to make war on the saints and to conquer them. And authority was given it over every tribe and people and language and nation, 8 and all who dwell on earth will worship it, everyone whose name has not been written before the foundation of the world in the book of life of the Lamb who was slain. 9 If anyone has an ear, let him hear:*

> **10** *If anyone is to be taken captive, to captivity he goes; if anyone is to be slain with the sword, with the sword must he be slain.*
>
> *Here is a call for the endurance and faith of the saints.*

I don't like talking about politics during sermons or when I'm writing a book, but Revelation demands it. The book is full of encouragements, but also warnings about the folly of being too invested in this world. There was a time in my life that I was overly obsessed with American politics. But, thankfully, God has been teaching me how political obsession was compromising my kingdom loyalty. My passion and energy for the Great Commission was being sucked away by passion and energy for political drama, election results, and the latest headlines. I confused patriotism with godliness.

There's nothing wrong with loving America or even working in government, but we must keep those aspects in their places. While government is subject to God's sovereign plan, *no* earthly government will ever make the gospel its priority. This passage reveals a sober truth: every government since the fall of Adam and Eve—even the ones we like—is influenced by evil.

What Would John's Readers Have Noticed?

Daniel's Beasts

When the dragon couldn't kill Jesus or the woman, he turned his anger toward her offspring, the church. John's

THE BEAST FROM THE SEA

Jewish-Christian audience, who were living in a brutal time of persecution in Rome under Domitian, would have linked his vision to the one in Daniel 7:2–6:

> Daniel declared, "I saw in my vision by night, and behold, the four winds of heaven were stirring up the great sea. ³ And four great beasts came up out of the sea, different from one another. ⁴ The first was like a lion . . . ⁵ [and] a second one, like a bear. . . . ⁶ After this I looked, and behold, another, like a leopard . . ."

The sea, the three creatures, horns, and deception—they all share the same symbolism. Anyone trying to interpret this passage from Revelation without having Daniel 7 open right next to it has no chance of getting it right. In Jewish culture, the sea symbolized the place where destruction and danger resided—powerful storms, mysterious creatures, and invading navies. The image of the dragon on the shore, summoning this beast from the depths, would invoke fear and awe.

The early church would easily identify the lion with Babylon, the bear with Persia, and the leopard with Greece—three empires that had successfully conquered Israel. Daniel's vision listed them in order from first to last, but John reverses the order, listing them from last to first. Daniel's vision was looking forward into the future, while John's vision was looking back into history. Because of this clear link to Daniel, John's readers knew these beasts weren't representative of a person or an "antichrist" but were metaphors for those three historic invading empires.

A Terrifying New Empire

We also see a fourth, more powerful beast in Daniel 7:7–8 (emphasis mine):

> *After this I saw in the night visions, and behold, a fourth beast, terrifying and dreadful and exceedingly strong.* **It** *had great iron teeth;* **it** *devoured and broke in pieces and stamped what was left with its feet.* **It** *was different from all the beasts before* **it***, and* **it** *had ten horns.* *⁸ ... behold, there came up among them another horn, a little one, before which three of the first horns were plucked up by the roots. And behold, in this horn were eyes like the eyes of a man, and a mouth speaking great things.*

The fourth beast was clearly meant to portend a new empire, greater than the other three, greater than any empire that has ever existed.

WHAT WAS JESUS TELLING THE CHURCHES?

Fortunately, Daniel provided an interpretation for his confusing visions in Daniel 7:16–25:

> *"I [Daniel] approached one of those who stood there and asked him the truth concerning all this. So he told me, ... ¹⁷'These four great beasts are four kings who shall arise out of the earth.'... ¹⁹ Then I desired to know the truth about the fourth beast, which was different from all the rest, exceedingly terrifying, ... ²⁰ and about the ten horns that were on its head, and the other horn that came up....* *²¹ As I looked, this horn made war with the saints and prevailed over them, ²² until the Ancient of Days came.... ²³ Thus he said: 'As for the fourth beast, there shall be a fourth kingdom on earth, which shall be different from all*

The Beast from the Sea

the kingdoms, and it shall devour the whole earth, and trample it down, and break it to pieces. ^{24} As for the ten horns, out of this kingdom ten kings shall arise, and another shall arise after them; he shall be different from the former ones, and shall put down three kings. ^{25} He shall speak words against the Most High, and shall wear out the saints of the Most High, and shall think to change the times and the law; and [the saints] shall be given into his hand for a time, times, and half a time.'"

Once John's readers understood what the three beasts represented, they would have quickly determined that Daniel's fourth beast was Rome. They lived with that fourth beast in the very tribulation Daniel had described. But then John rolls all four of Daniel's beasts into one, revealing how, although they look different, they are really the same. No matter what form a government takes, the dragon has and always will control the worldly systems within which it operates.

Notice that the word *it* occurs fourteen times in this passage in Revelation and several times in Daniel's vision as well. The dragon is a *who*, and the beast is an *it*. Interpreting the beast as a *who* would require you to ignore the text. The beast is the dragon's most effective weapon against the woman's offspring. From its mouth come lies, deceptions, and blasphemies. Everything this beast says and does is so influential, the inhabitants of the world worship the beast and see *it* as their hope.

One head of the beast suffers a mortal wound, dies, and returns to life. Since we know the beast can't be an individual, it's clear this wasn't a reference to an "antichrist" mimicking the cross. Instead, John was using an urban legend from the time as a metaphor for how the beast will always be in the world.

When Nero committed suicide in AD 68, many believed he would come back to life and lead Rome once again. Nero's death left Rome in crisis. Would the empire collapse? Each time an emperor died, the church was hopeful the tribulation would end, but it seemed Rome would never end. When one emperor died, another would rise to take his place. Later in Revelation 13, Nero will be identified with the number 666, the numerical value of the Hebrew letters in his name. John teaches that the beast remains until Jesus returns, no matter what man or empire rules. The beast's resilience is so influential, unbelievers worship it. As John writes in Revelation 13:4, "Who can fight it?"

WHAT IS JESUS TELLING US TODAY?

Revelation 13 reveals what all earthly governments are and how Christians should interact with them. This beast is every government system under the dragon's control throughout history. The end of one ruler's reign doesn't stop the beast or change its goals. Another always rises. Can you see how even our hope in and desire for the American dream can make us vulnerable to the beast's lies? The illusion and promise of peace and prosperity can be a powerful weapon of distraction against the church. The beast seeks our allegiance through making threats or great promises, as we see in Revelation 13:8–10 (emphasis mine):

> *And all who dwell on earth will worship **it**, everyone whose name has not been written before the foundation of the world in the book of life of the Lamb who was slain.* ⁹ *If anyone has an ear, let him hear:* ¹⁰ *If anyone is to be taken captive, to captivity he goes; if anyone is to be slain with the sword, with the sword must he be slain. Here is a call for the endurance and faith of the saints.*

"All who dwell on earth" are those not written in the Book of Life: they live as either captives or slain victims. The beast has them under complete control. But those with "ears to hear"—those who are written in the Book of Life—are encouraged to stay faithful. Paul reminded us in Romans 13:1, "Let every person be subject to the governing authorities. For there is no authority except from God, and those that exist have been instituted by God."

This is the difficult mystery: how to live with the beast that's controlled by the dragon yet still under God's sovereign authority. Jesus said to render to Caesar what belongs to Caesar. He meant taxes, true, but also submission to authority, which He referenced obliquely in Matthew 10:16 when He said, "I'm sending you out as sheep in the midst of wolves, so be wise as serpents and innocent as doves."

Living faithfully in this wilderness alongside this beast isn't easy. The dragon's beast is always actively trying to deceive, distract, or destroy the woman's offspring—the church. To be faithful, we must be as shrewd and wise as serpents, not foolish, obnoxious, arrogant, judgmental, or rebellious. We also cannot be mindless lemmings, going along with whatever the beast says is good. Peter instructed us in 1 Peter 2:16–17 to "live as people who are free, not using your freedom as a cover-up for evil, but living as servants of God. Honor everyone. Love the brotherhood. Fear God. Honor the emperor." Remember, he was writing to Christians who lived under a corrupt, brutal regime that hated them. He encouraged them to be free from the useless burden of beast worship.

Today, perhaps many of us in the church, on either side of the aisle, are too focused on the beast. Maybe we are too invested in fighting the beast, buying into it, or trying to change it into something we think it should be. As Christians, we can love our country, vote, pray for our leaders, obey laws, and work in the government—provided we are shrewd and discerning. But we should never put hope in any earthly government; that's the devil's bait. Keep your hope in the kingdom of heaven.

CHAPTER THIRTY-ONE

The Number of the Beast

Revelation 13:11–18:

11 Then I saw another beast rising out of the earth. It had two horns like a lamb and it spoke like a dragon. 12 It exercises all the authority of the first beast in its presence, and makes the earth and its inhabitants worship the first beast, whose mortal wound was healed. 13 It performs great signs, even making fire come down from heaven to earth in front of people, 14 and by the signs that it is allowed to work in the presence of the beast it deceives those who dwell on earth, telling them to make an image for the beast that was wounded by the sword and yet lived. 15 And it was allowed to give breath to the image of the beast, so that the image of the beast might even speak and might cause those who would not worship the image of the beast to be slain. 16 Also it causes all, both small and great, both rich and poor, both free and slave, to be marked on the right hand or the forehead, 17 so that no one can buy or sell unless he has the mark, that is, the name of the beast or the number of its name. 18 This calls for wisdom: let the one who has understanding calculate the number of the beast, for it is the number of a man, and his number is 666.

Reading Revelation incorrectly can make it seem like a horror movie. Reading it correctly reveals its true purpose, to be a blessing to those who follow Jesus. Flawed interpretations of this passage are a big reason people see Revelation as frightening, because it contains two of the most talked-about symbols in Revelation: the mark of the beast and the number of the beast. The number 666 has been equated to everything from vaccines to Social Security numbers to computer chips.

Both the mark and the number are misinterpreted so often by so many that it would be comical if it weren't so dangerously misleading.

So, why did John put these images in Revelation?

John knew that believers would be blessed by reading his letter (Revelation 1:3). He wanted us to reflect on the mark and number of the beast so that whenever we as believers see the number 666 pop up, it blesses us, not frighten us!

What Would John's Readers Have Noticed?

The Imperial Cult

The real-time relevance of this passage for John's audience is directly connected to life under Roman rule. We already know that John's readers saw the first beast as the visible, tangible power the Roman emperor had over everyday life. The first beast symbolizes the dragon's control over earthly government and its capacity to control or oppress humanity.

Imagine living under constant oppression as a Christian in modern-day China, North Korea, the Middle East, or the old Soviet Union. That's how John's original readers lived. Likewise, they would have known the second beast symbolized the influence Rome's imperial priesthood had over society. Using propaganda and fraudulent miraculous claims, the imperial cult-imposed emperor worship combined with immense social and economic pressure to create what we might refer to today as "cancel culture."

The Emperor's Mark

Nero was known for his construction projects. He not only rebuilt Rome after the Great Fire of AD 64 but ordered the construction of buildings—including temples—all over the empire.[22] His most impressive project was the massive "Golden House" palace complex he began constructing for himself, which occupied one-third of the city![23] The Colossus Neronis—the one-hundred-foot-tall statue of himself for which the Colosseum is named—depicts him as the sun god.[24] The early Christian writer Tertullian called Nero "the first persecutor of the Christians."[25] The roots of his persecutions were the Christians' refusal to participate in the imperial cult.

Remember how, in Jesus' letter to Pergamum (the regional capital of the cult),[26] He spoke of the place "where Satan's throne is" (Revelation 2:13)? You could practice any religion you wanted, but only after pledging your primary worship to the emperor. And, since worship was a public act, your very act of worship "marked" you. People noticed if you did (or did not) go to the temple or perform sacrifices, and they also noticed which temple (or synagogue) you performed them at. Since Christians abstained from the imperial cult, they were regarded with suspicion. Their refusal to accept the emperor's "mark" was a very real mark against them in the eyes of Roman society. Under Nero (and several emperors after him, including Domitian, who was in power when John wrote Revelation), noncompliance, or refusal to receive your mark, often resulted in persecution of Christians across the empire: being barred from essential economic activities, imprisoned, or otherwise punished—even killed.

666

Ancient languages like Hebrew, Greek, and Latin didn't use numeric symbols. Instead, they assigned numeric value to letters of the alphabet. A modern-day example would be the Roman numerals (Latin letters) used to number the Super Bowl. Most literate people knew how to calculate a corresponding number to their names alphabetically. Remember, John wrote Revelation around AD 90, about twenty-two years after Nero committed suicide. After his suicide, many Romans believed, or even hoped, he would soon be resurrected to lead the empire again.[27] (Spoiler: didn't happen!) The Greek letters John wrote may be translated as "six hundred and sixty-six." And when the name of Nero Caesar is written in Aramaic, this happens to equal the same number. Therefore, John's readers would have associated 666 with

Nero's name and his failure to conquer death, which foreshadowed the fatal weakness of the first beast. What is that fatal weakness? Just like Nero, every earthly empire, no matter how fierce or powerful, will someday come to an end, but not the kingdom of heaven. That will endure forever!

WHAT WAS JESUS TELLING THE CHURCHES?

John was using the life experience of first-century Christians in Rome to provide a 30,000-foot view of how the dragon would wage war on the church throughout the rest of the church age until Jesus returns. John described how the dragon and his two beasts work together in this tribulation as an unholy trinity. They're a counterfeit of the Holy Trinity, who works in the hearts of God's chosen to mark them for salvation: the Father on the throne, the Lamb who conquers the world by His death, and the Comforter with the little scroll. Throughout the tribulation, the unholy trinity has worked together to tighten its grip over the world. John used these two symbols—the mark and the number of the beast—to explain the reason for the suffering they were enduring, and also to prepare his readers for more tough times ahead.

Both the first beast's dominance and destruction and the second beast's deception come from the dragon, who is the father of lies. This is foreshadowed by Jesus' warning in Matthew 7:15: "Beware of false prophets, who come to you in sheep's clothing but inwardly are ravenous wolves." The second beast is the power behind every manner of deception swirling around the church from the first century through today. It is the dragon's control over unredeemed hearts and minds, binding them to the invisible, abstract philosophies of the day. The second beast is masterful at convincing the unredeemed to trust the first beast for hope, wisdom, prosperity, and peace.

The second beast appeared as a peaceful lamb compared to the first beast, who assumed the form of predators—the lion, bear, and leopard. Presenting itself as a lover of peace, the second beast pointed people to the first as the conduit to bring about that peace. The second beast was, and is, the spirit behind any thought or philosophy used by the dragon to draw the church away from Jesus.

Remember, people in Rome took note of those who participated in emperor worship. Participation gave people the privilege of participating in Roman society culturally, socially, and economically. John used that participation in the imperial cult to reveal how the second beast marks those he has in bondage. This mark transcends any manifestation of modern technology or government control. It's not a physical earthly mark, but an invisible spiritual one, with eternal consequences. It symbolizes spiritual bondage to the second beast's deception: a mark on the forehead, to symbolize its influence over the thoughts and beliefs of the unredeemed, and on the hand, to symbolize its influence over their actions. This is another example of how evil tries to counterfeit what God does with His chosen, the church.

Compare these counterfeit marks with the mark of God, as described in Revelation 7:3:

> *"Do not harm the earth or the sea or the trees, until we have sealed [marked] the servants of our God on their foreheads."*

Paul also mentioned this mark in 2 Corinthians 1:21–22:

> *And it is God who establishes us with you in Christ, and has anointed us, ²² and who has also put his seal on us and given us his Spirit in our hearts as a guarantee.*

The power of the dragon and the two beasts will ultimately fail. Just as Nero couldn't come back from the dead, 666 symbolizes the truth that the first beast cannot conquer death either. The beast empowered by the dragon and the spirit of antichrist has no control over anything or anyone eternal. Anything it exercises authority over will one day perish and face judgment. It cannot endure, so its power to carry out its plans on earth relies on its ability to control unredeemed humanity's thoughts and actions. John was conveying to his readers this truth: No matter how powerful the first beast gets, it will one day fall to the King of kings. Therefore, 666 is not a number to fear, but a mockery—a constant reminder of how frail the unholy trinity actually is!

What Is Jesus Telling Us Today?

Let's be honest: we need constant reminders that nothing humanity can build, accomplish, or promise is worthy of our hope or allegiance.

You might be familiar with the popular interpretation of the second beast as some future evil charismatic leader of a world government. This Antichrist has been depicted as a brilliant silver-tongued deceiver with the power to do miracles and entice the world into global Satan worship. That interpretation is wrong and falls into the trap of what I like to call "prophetic narcissism": the assumption that the prophecies in Revelation are all about us, in our time, and were irrelevant to John's original readers. Any interpretation that ignores the historical context makes this passage completely irrelevant to John's first-century audience. It makes more sense to interpret these Scriptures as a reminder of how we can tell the difference between real hope and the dragon's lies.

The second beast is any religious, philosophical, or political message that directs our hope and worship away from Jesus and toward the earthly wisdom, power, and glory of the first beast, which is represented by 666. It is any system or ideology that is a human-made, human-controlled alternative to the promises of what the kingdom of heaven will be. The second beast convinces the unredeemed to place their hope in these alternatives and then marks those people as its own. Without realizing it, their daily obsession is on the first beast; it consumes their thoughts, actions, hopes, and passions.

In Colossians 2:8, Paul wrote that we are to "see to it that no one takes you captive by philosophy and empty deceit," because "he disarmed the rulers and authorities and put them to open shame, by triumphing over them" (verse 15). In other words, we are to fight a daily battle against the second beast, because hopes placed in the first beast are doomed to eternal disappointment. In Matthew 16:24, we are called to take up our cross and follow Jesus, because, as 1 John 2:17 says, "The world is passing away along with its desires."

Don't get me wrong—the second beast is a powerful distraction! Sometimes it succeeds in siphoning our passions, time, talents, and treasure. But, as followers of Jesus, we must remember that none of these systems will ever bring hope and redemption to this world. As the unholy spirit of Antichrist beckons the world into darkness, God's Holy Spirit calls us out of darkness into light. As the unholy spirit marks the deceived for death and judgment, the Holy Spirit revives our hearts with truth and the gospel and marks the faithful for redemption.

Instead of running from the number 666, take it as a precious daily reminder to pick up our cross and follow our Jesus. That number reminds us how the dragon's earthly human kingdom is just a temporary evil imitation of the eternal kingdom of heaven. Its unholy trinity is a pathetic, false impersonation of the Holy Trinity who has given us salvation! That means 666 serves as a blessing, helping us decipher and diagnose any potential fixation we may develop with the things of this world. We need that daily check on our hopes and passions to ensure they are placed in Christ and not in empty promises.

One day, when Jesus returns and all is revealed, I believe we will be stunned at how complex and brilliant the lies of the unholy trinity were. We'll understand and say, "Wow, if the Holy Spirit had not put His mark on me first, the second beast surely would have!" Until then, we are called to live in peace and wisdom, and in gratitude for God's mark on us that protects us from the lies of the beast. Thank You, Jesus, for sealing us with Your mark!

CHAPTER THIRTY-TWO

The Lamb's Faithful Followers

Revelation 14:1–5:

> Then I looked, and behold, on Mount Zion stood the Lamb, and with him 144,000 who had his name and his Father's name written on their foreheads. ² And I heard a voice from heaven like the roar of many waters and like the sound of loud thunder. The voice I heard was like the sound of harpists playing on their harps, ³ and they were singing a new song before the throne and before the four living creatures and before the elders. No one could learn that song except the 144,000 who had been redeemed from the earth. ⁴ It is these who have not defiled themselves with women, for they are virgins. It is these who follow the Lamb wherever he goes. These have been redeemed from mankind as firstfruits for God and the Lamb, ⁵ and in their mouth no lie was found, for they are blameless.

Have you ever heard this phrase? "I have good news and bad news. Which do you want first?" I always reply, "The bad news," because I want to process it emotionally, physically, and spiritually, and then hear something hopeful.

That's how Revelation 13 and 14 is laid out. John presents the bad news first. Chapter 13 revealed how Satan wages war against the woman's offspring—God's people, the church. He weaponizes every government, religion, philosophy, and economic system against us. This is why it is foolish to put our hope or allegiance in any of these things.

But chapter 14 declares the good news! It reveals what Jesus is doing at the same time the dragon is trying to weaponize this world against God's chosen people. It also reveals how we will survive this tribulation—how we will ultimately overcome this corrupt world system.

What Would John's Readers Have Noticed?

Symbols of Redemption

John's readers, like most of the church in the world today, faced a daily barrage from the dragon. That's bad news. You can see how John's readers would need the "here's the good news" side of this battle. At the very end of Revelation 13, John sets up the good news with the number 666, as a visual reminder that the Dragon's power is mortal. Revelation 14 starts off a beautiful revelation of the good news. It's full of symbols and metaphors that describe the history of God's plan of redemption for His chosen throughout the tribulation, including us.

Look at Psalm 14:7: "Oh, that salvation for Israel would come out of Zion! When the LORD restores the fortunes of his people, let Jacob rejoice, let Israel be glad." Throughout the Old Testament, Mount Zion is a theological metaphor for a restored Jerusalem where the enemy is vanquished. During John's time, Romans occupied Jerusalem, so for John's readers, Zion became symbolic of a future victory.

The metaphor is similar to how we use *heaven* today—a place to long for. The moment in time when all God's chosen are united together in the presence of the Lord in His holy temple with His people. It's the day our Jesus returns in power and glory, retrieves His church, and completes our victory over evil in the final battle.

The Church in Battle

Back in Revelation 7, we learned about another powerful symbol—the number 144,000—which represents "the church in battle"—every follower of God since the beginning of time who is alive on the earth at any given point in history. Recall that the number is calculated as 12 x 12 x 1,000, which comes from the twelve gates (the sealed Old Testament faithful), the twelve foundations (the sealed New Testament faithful), and 1,000 (for a multitude). This calculated number in Revelation 7:5–8 provides an undeniable reference to the book of Numbers. In that book, the fighting forces of Israel are calculated by tribal name and then by the number of fighting men in each tribe.

When fighting men prepared for a military expedition, abstinence was part of their preparation. We see this in 1 Samuel 21:5:

> David answered the priest, "Truly women have been kept from us as always when I go on an expedition. The vessels of the young men are holy even when it is an ordinary journey. How much more today will their vessels be holy?"

John's readers would have understood the description of the 144,000 as virgins as a clear symbol of a faithful, spiritual army of God. In Hebrew literature, the concept of virginity is about more than just sexual purity. It's a symbol of the dedicated strength, focus, and devotion of a fighting force.

WHAT WAS JESUS TELLING THE CHURCHES?

Mount Zion symbolizes our future hope for a community of God's people who are dwelling with God Himself. Hebrews 12:22 explains, "But you have come to Mount Zion and to the city of the living God, the heavenly Jerusalem, and to innumerable angels in festal gathering." It's a theological expression of the day God vanquishes all evil from earth and establishes His kingdom with us.

In Revelation 13, those with the beast's mark on their forehead and hands are seen as slaves to this world. In Revelation 14, God marks the foreheads of His people with the name of Jesus. They are liberated from slavery to this world—sealed, redeemed, and transformed. Note that Ephesians 6:12 says, "For we do not wrestle against flesh and blood, but against the rulers, against the authorities, against the cosmic powers over this present darkness, against the spiritual forces of evil in the spiritual places."

These marks aren't physical, but they carry eternal consequences, visible only in the transcendent spiritual realm. They are like military markings of a sort, drawing battle lines between spiritual forces of good and evil in this world. The dragon is powerless to save those he has marked with 666 from the coming judgment, but our Jesus saves everyone He marks. Not one soldier among the symbolic 144,000 will be lost to the dragon and his forces of evil.

Ancient armies would sing before a battle and after a victory. The songs helped to build camaraderie, but the singing armies also intimidated the enemy with their thunderous sounds. The army of 144,000 sings about our future victory over the dragon. This is what we do when we worship! The unredeemed don't know the words to our song, their meaning, or the reason we sing it. Nobody can learn it from a distance. Only those marked, sealed, and drawn into the ranks of the 144,000 by the Spirit of God know the words. Our song is the unifying worship of the church in battle and can only be sung by those who follow the Lamb.

Our virginity is a spiritual metaphor for our Holy Spirit–inspired, unwavering courage and faithfulness as we refuse the beast's mark, no matter what he might offer us. It represents our continued faithfulness, strength, and devotion, and the integrity of the gospel we preach. Paul used this symbolism in 2 Corinthians 11:2–3:

> *For I feel a divine jealousy for you, since I betrothed you to one husband, to present you as a pure virgin to Christ. ³ But I am afraid that as the serpent deceived Eve by his cunning,*

> *your thoughts will be led astray from a sincere and pure devotion to Christ.*

In the Old Testament, the first harvest was consecrated to God and dedicated to the priesthood. The second harvest was then designated for everyone and everything else. John declares that the "firstfruits for God and the Lamb" (Revelation 14:4)—those God has marked for redemption—symbolize His spiritual harvest of those He is calling out from all the nations of this world. This means there is also a second harvest yet to come out of the nations. We will learn later that this "second harvest" belongs to the dragon—but, for now, take my word for it, you won't want to be in it!

What Is Jesus Telling Us Today?

Jesus best described these 144,000 on Mount Zion, these unblemished faithful followers, in John 10:27–28 (emphasis mine): "My sheep hear my voice, and I know them, *and they follow me.* I give them eternal life, and they will never perish, and no one will snatch them out of my hand."

We the church are the redeemed 144,000 without blemish, who follow the Lamb wherever He goes. As the dragon marks the unredeemed, the Lamb is marking us, carrying out His plan of redemption and salvation for us. Paul confirmed this plan in Romans 8:35–39:

> *Who shall separate us from the love of Christ? Shall tribulation, or distress, or persecution, or famine, or nakedness, or danger, or sword? . . . [37] No, in all these things we are*

> *more than conquerors through him who loved us. ³⁸ For I am sure that neither death nor life, nor angels nor rulers, nor things present nor things to come, nor powers, ³⁹ nor height nor depth, nor anything else in all creation, will be able to separate us from the love of God in Christ Jesus our Lord.*

Nobody, not even the most powerful of those marked and controlled by the dragon and his beasts, can separate us from the love of Jesus! The faithful 144,000 are all those who have followed, are following, and will follow Jesus for as long as we are alive on this earth. When we depart this earth, we leave the "Church in Battle" and become part of the "Church in Victory," all those who have died and are now in the presence of God. With voices like thunder, the 144,000 sing about how Jesus laid down his life for us, defeated death, and sent the Comforter to mark us, transform us, and lead us in battle.

While we're here, fighting this battle, it might lead to poverty, nakedness, persecution, danger, and even death. But no matter what weapons or evil alliances the dragon forms against us, *he will fail*. We may not think we have it in us to follow the Lamb wherever He goes, but we do, because our song is not about us—it's about the work of the Lamb, as Psalm 23:4–5 reminds us:

> *Even though I walk through the valley of the shadow of death, I will fear no evil, for you are with me; your rod and your staff, they comfort me. ⁵ You prepare a table before me in the presence of my enemies; you anoint my head with oil; my cup overflows.*

The "shadow of death" is always symbolic of tribulation. Yet, even in this valley of darkness, our Great Shepherd is with us. And as we fight, we sing our battle song woven with themes of redemption from both the Old and New Testaments. Even while evil and darkness rage in this world, God is calling, transforming, and preserving His people.

CHAPTER THIRTY-THREE

Faithful Proclamation

Revelation 14:6–13:

6 Then I saw another angel flying directly overhead, with an eternal gospel to proclaim to those who dwell on earth, to every nation and tribe and language and people. 7 And he said with a loud voice, "Fear God and give him glory, because the hour of his judgment has come, and worship him who made heaven and earth, the sea and the springs of water."

8 Another angel, a second, followed, saying, "Fallen, fallen is Babylon the great, she who made all nations drink the wine of the passion of her sexual immorality."

9 And another angel, a third, followed them, saying with a loud voice, "If anyone worships the beast and its image and receives a mark on his forehead or on his hand, 10 he also will drink the wine of God's wrath, poured full strength into the cup of his anger, and he will be tormented with fire and sulfur in the presence of the holy angels and in the presence of the Lamb.11 And the smoke of their torment goes up forever and ever, and they have no rest, day or night, these worshipers of the beast and its image, and whoever receives the mark of its name."

> ¹² *Here is a call for the endurance of the saints, those who keep the commandments of God and their faith in Jesus.*
>
> ¹³ *And I heard a voice from heaven saying, "Write this: Blessed are the dead who die in the Lord from now on." "Blessed indeed," says the Spirit, "that they may rest from their labors, for their deeds follow them!"*

In the Great Commission, Jesus directed His church to go into all the world, preaching the gospel just as He taught us (Matthew 28:18–20). That gospel is God's precious message of grace and mercy, but it's also a warning of judgment for those who reject it.

God's people have always battled the temptation to soften the gospel's warnings of judgment, focusing primarily on its promises of mercy. The church is under constant pressure to truncate the gospel, to make it only about grace and mercy, because the world doesn't want to hear the gospel's warning of judgment for those who reject it. But we can't be silent about judgment. It's what convinces us we need the grace and mercy we love so much!

What Would John's Readers Have Noticed?

"Babylon the Great"

A proper understanding of this passage requires knowing how John's readers would interpret the symbolism of Babylon. The Babylonian captivity was the darkest era in Jewish Old Testament history. It left traumatic cultural scars. In

Jewish culture, Babylon was an iconic symbol of an ancient enemy who were constantly at war with the people of God.

John's readers understood that Babylon was the first of four world empires, represented by the first of Daniel's beasts in Daniel 7, the lion with eagle's wings. That wasn't Babylon's first appearance in a vision, though. In Daniel 2, the empire was depicted as the head of gold in an enormous statue made up of Babylon and all the kingdoms that would follow. Because it was first in both of these visions, Babylon came to be used as a metaphor for the entire history of earthly kingdoms controlled by the first beast, a world full of nations intoxicated with power, cruelty, and immorality.

Jews in the first century also used Babylon as a theological code word for Rome, indicating that they recognized Rome as part of Daniel's beast vision as well. In fact, the apostle Peter used this idiom in his closing in 1 Peter 5:13 when he said, "She who is at Babylon, who is likewise chosen, sends you greetings," referencing a treasured saint who lived in Rome.

John's readers also used Babylon as a metaphor for any attempt by Satan to create his own evil counterfeit of Mount Zion, the kingdom of God. The first such example was the Tower of Babel in Genesis 11, when every human spoke one language, and the spirit of evil gathered them all together to build a tower as a monument to their greatness.

Mount Zion and Angels

We've already learned how Jews used Mount Zion the same way we use the word *heaven*. It was a reference to a future age when God's people are brought together as one tribe under the reign of Messiah. But the three angels in this passage are more than literal; they're also symbolic. In Jewish literature, angels weren't only seen as heavenly beings, but also momentous or important proclamations sent from God. John's readers would have interpreted those three angels as three distinct, important messages sent from heaven. These were three different proclamations given to the people by God to proclaim to all the earth at three different moments in redemptive history.

WHAT WAS JESUS TELLING THE CHURCHES?

The first proclamation "directly overhead" is a proclamation declared to every tribe and nation on earth. The phrase *directly overhead* means this message is visible and audible to everyone. No one could miss it. Paul explained in Romans 1, verses 18 and 20, "For the wrath of God is revealed from heaven against all ungodliness and unrighteousness of men . . . So they are without excuse."

In the past, God's proclamations had always been to one nation or another—Israel, or an enemy of Israel. This one was different. It was the widest proclamation from God since the creation in Genesis. It's a call to heed the gospel, telling us that each person will be on one side or the other. Acts 17:30–31 explains that there is no middle ground:

> *The times of ignorance God overlooked, but now he commands all people everywhere to repent, ³¹ because he has fixed a day on which he will judge the world in righteousness by a man whom he has appointed.*

This passage is an ominous call for all humanity to repent, fear God, and worship Him, because judgment is coming soon. Jesus gave us this exact proclamation before He ascended, and it's a proclamation the dragon hates. He wants to silence it, downplay it, or corrupt it, just like he did in Genesis when he tempted Eve. This proclamation is the gospel, which faithful churches should constantly preach.

The second proclamation about the fall of Babylon will be our celebration on the day Jesus returns and destroys the beast, a fulfillment of Daniel 2:34–35:

> *A stone cut out by no human hand . . . struck the image on its feet of iron and clay and broke them in pieces. ³⁵ Then the iron, the clay, the bronze, the silver, and the gold, all together were broken in pieces, and became like the chaff of the summer threshing floors; and the wind carried them away, so that not a trace of them could be found. But the stone that struck the image became a great mountain and filled the whole earth.*

The second proclamation is the same as the loud singing John heard from the 144,000 in the previous passage—a declaration of our victory. This will be our proclamation on the day Jesus vindicates His redeemed and smashes everything the dragon ever built at its foundation.

Throughout Scripture, sexual sin is used as a metaphor for spiritual unfaithfulness. Since it's often the primary symptom, this isn't surprising. The most heartbreaking, shameful failures of spiritual leaders often stems from sexual immorality. Notice the powerful contrast between the sexual sin of Babylon described in Revelation 14:8 and the purity of the 144,000 in the previous passage. Later, in Revelation 17:5, we read that "on her forehead was written a name of mystery: 'Babylon the great, mother of prostitutes and of earth's abominations.'"

Remember, Hebrew literature often used the concept of virginity as a metaphor for faithfulness, strength, focus, and devotion. Likewise, the sexual sin of Babylon is a graphic metaphor of how God sees those who choose their love of this world over the gospel.

The third angel's proclamation will be our declaration of the final sentence on Babylon and all who received her mark. It's the fulfillment of the judgment part of the gospel we proclaim to all nations, a warning which the world, sadly, ignores. Psalm 75:8 puts it this way:

> *For in the hand of the* Lord *there is a cup with foaming wine, well mixed, and he pours out from it, and all the wicked of the earth shall drain it down to the dregs.*

God's cup of foaming wine symbolizes the pouring out of His wrath. We'll learn more about this when we get to the seven bowls of judgments later.

John then provided another contrast between the "earth dwellers" from verse 6 who worship Babylon and the people of God: as we experience the joy of eternal worship with Jesus in verse 13, those who worshiped Babylon will experience eternal judgment described as "torment forever and ever, day and night." This is the fate of the unredeemed. The doctrine of eternal judgment of the unredeemed being declared here is undeniable!

WHAT IS JESUS TELLING US TODAY?

Any proclamation of the gospel that ignores, omits, or denies its warnings of eternal judgment is a false gospel. When we consider these three proclamations of the church, it's no wonder Jesus said the world will hate us (John 15:18). These ominous warnings about God's wrath and the command to repent are crucial to the gospel we preach. It's tempting to soften our proclamation—to skip over the warnings of eternal judgment and jump right to grace and mercy.

Considering how the world resents this side of the gospel, you can certainly understand why that would be appealing to the church. In fact, many churches throughout church history have given in to that temptation and still do today. Here's the problem: if the gospel has no judgment, then grace and mercy are pointless. It's the danger of judgment that makes the promise of grace, mercy, and forgiveness from our Jesus so precious!

John is reminding the church it must remain faithful to the first proclamation—the Great Commission (Matthew 28:18–20)—throughout the church age and this age of tribulation we are still living in today. Don't cheat on Jesus by proclaiming a Babylonian gospel! Resist temptation and you will be blessed. In Matthew 26:39, Christ said, "My Father, if it be possible, let this cup pass from me; nevertheless, not as I will, but as you will." These words from our Jesus are the inspiration and the motivation for our faithful proclamation of the full gospel. The wine of wrath poured out on Babylon is the same cup Jesus drank for us.

For all who have ears to hear this proclamation, we know Jesus has provided for His redeemed a way of escape from the judgment we deserve. That's how this bold proclamation becomes our passionate, earnest, loving plea to the unredeemed. This is why we proclaim to all nations, "Please, while there's still time, abandon your foolish hope in Babylon and follow Jesus!"

CHAPTER THIRTY-FOUR

Waiting on the Harvest

Revelation 14:14–20:

> [14] Then I looked, and behold, a white cloud, and seated on the cloud one like a son of man, with a golden crown on his head, and a sharp sickle in his hand. [15] And another angel came out of the temple, calling with a loud voice to him who sat on the cloud. "Put in your sickle, and reap, for the hour to reap has come, for the harvest of the earth is fully ripe." [16] So he who sat on the cloud swung his sickle across the earth, and the earth was reaped.
>
> [17] Then another angel came out of the temple in heaven, and he too had a sharp sickle. [18] And another angel came out from the altar, the angel who has authority over the fire, and he called with a loud voice to the one who had the sharp sickle, "Put in your sickle and gather the clusters from the vine of the earth, for its grapes are ripe." [19] So the angel swung his sickle across the earth and gathered the grape harvest of the earth and threw it into the great winepress of the wrath of God. [20] And the winepress was trodden outside the city, and blood flowed from the winepress, as high as a horse's bridle, for 1,600 stadia.

The toughest parts of Revelation are yet to come. They are filled with ominous, graphic, and violent symbolism describing the wrath of God against evil. I believe the purpose of these descriptions is not to scare unbelievers, but to encourage followers of Jesus. John is telling us, "Hang in there. Our Jesus is coming!" He isn't trying to scare you. He's trying to comfort you.

What Would John's Readers Have Noticed?

The Harvest

I have no idea when tomato season is anymore. I eat tomatoes year-round. The same goes for watermelon and grapes. I can go to the store any time of year and get just about any kind of produce I want, in season or out of season.

Life wasn't like that in the Old Testament. The ancient world had no choice but to live in rhythm with the seasons. Everyone from farmers to shepherds to fishermen knew every harvest season for just about every crop. This made harvesting a powerful symbol throughout both the Old and New Testaments. In the Old Testament, *harvest* is often used as a metaphor for waiting on salvation and judgment. Jesus used the same image at least ten times.

The Wine

Similar to the harvest, the winemaking process was as essential to the ancient world as the internet is for us. There was no refrigeration to preserve anything that wasn't water, so wine was the second-most-consumed beverage. Fermentation was the only way to preserve grape juice and other beverages over an extended period. This is why we see wine and winemaking as another common metaphor for God's judgment throughout the Old Testament.

The Unclean

And then there's the powerful image of the uncleanness outside the city walls. That's where anything unsanitary, from human waste to spoiled food, was taken to be burned or disposed of. This was done to protect the city from the spread of sickness and disease. People with contagious illnesses like leprosy were banished there as well. Mountains of burning refuse and carcasses, both human and animal, smoldered outside the city walls day in and day out. When the wind blew the wrong direction, the stench in some parts of the city was overwhelming.

WHAT WAS JESUS TELLING THE CHURCHES?

The description of the first harvest seems to be a grain harvest, linked to the firstfruits we saw in the description of the 144,000 in Revelation 14:4: "These have been redeemed from mankind as firstfruits for God and the Lamb." Remember, the 144,000 is a symbolic number representing the faithful throughout history who follow the Lamb wherever He goes. If you are a follower of Jesus, you are part of the 144,000. The firstfruits were a grain offering—at the Feast of Firstfruits, Jews would bring their first sheaf of wheat or barley to be waved before the Lord by a priest (Leviticus 23:9-14).

In verse 14, John described someone "like a son of man" coming on a cloud with a crown. This is clearly Jesus on the day of His return. An angel emerges from the heavenly temple and calls out a proclamation from God the Father to Jesus, declaring the harvest "ripe," which means dry. Grain crops are ready for harvest when the stalk at the top withers, because the dry stalk is easy for the reaper to cut. Harvesting too soon would mean the grain isn't fully developed yet, and since the green stalk is difficult to cut, cutting would damage the fruit. That's why Jesus needed to wait until the firstfruits were ripe before harvesting—so He wouldn't gather immature or damaged fruit.

The second harvest, symbolized by the process of harvesting grapes and crushing them into wine, is a judgment harvest. This connects directly to the theme of the wine of God's wrath John used earlier in Revelation 14:10: "He also will drink the wine of God's wrath, poured full strength into the cup of his anger." This imagery of winemaking as a metaphor for God's wrath is borrowed directly from Joel 3:13, when the prophet wrote, "Put in the sickle, for the harvest is ripe. Go in, tread, for the winepress is full. The vats overflow, for their evil is great."

After Jesus gathers the firstfruits, two more angels are dispatched for the wine harvest. The first one has a sickle and the second comes from the altar with authority over "the fire." Who was this second angel? What fire was he in charge of? Let's take a closer look at Revelation 8:3–5:

> *And another angel came and stood at the altar with a golden censer, and he was given much incense to offer with the prayers of all the saints on the golden altar before the throne, ⁴ and the smoke of the incense, with the prayers of the saints, rose before God from the hand of the angel. ⁵ Then the angel took the censer and filled it with fire from the altar and threw it on the earth, and there were peals of thunder, rumblings, flashes of lightning, and an earthquake.*

The prayers asking Jesus to return and judge the wicked are finally answered! The slain saints cried, "How long, oh Lord?" This second angel took the censer full of their prayers, filled it with hot coals from the altar he oversees, and hurled it to earth on the wicked, where the grapes of wrath will be harvested at last! This graphic symbolism comparing God's wrath to a winepress is taken directly from His words in Isaiah 63:1–6:

> *"It is I, speaking in righteousness, mighty to save.... ³ I have trodden the winepress alone, and from the peoples no one was with me; I trod them in my anger and trampled them in my wrath; their lifeblood spattered on my garments and stained all my apparel. ⁴ For the day of vengeance was in my heart, and my year of redemption*

> had come. . . . ⁶ I trampled down the peoples in my anger; I made them drunk in my wrath, and I poured out their lifeblood on the earth."

The harvested grapes were poured into the top of the winepress and crushed underfoot. The juice, called the "lifeblood" of the wicked in Isaiah, completely filled the bottom vat. The vat was as high as a horse's bridle (or about six feet tall) and 1,600 stadia wide (or about 184 miles). That's a lot of blood.

This gruesome depth and width is symbolic of how no wickedness or evil escapes the wrath of God's winepress. This winepress was outside the city, indicating the wine was unclean, contaminated with disease and poisons that would kill anyone who drank it. Notice who will do the crushing in Revelation 19:15—Jesus Himself: "He will tread the winepress of the fury of the wrath of God the Almighty."

WHAT IS JESUS TELLING US TODAY?

Jesus doesn't need our help judging the wicked. When that day comes, He'll do just fine by Himself. We all regularly get frustrated, discouraged, and even angry about the things the wicked do in this world. With all the inequity, injustice, and unfairness, our anger and frustration seem like reasonable responses to this world, right? So, we turn to political battles, culture wars, or posts on social media. We even obsess over doling out our own personal justice on individuals who have wronged us, such as those "depraved" drivers on the highway who dare to cut us off! All of these become our own personal winepress as we take on the job of crushing the grapes of wrath in this world.

Why are we obsessed with taking on the role of grape smasher, picking one grape at a time and smashing it ourselves? That isn't a job we're qualified to do, for many reasons. What about the times *we* are the depraved driver on the highway? Not only that, do you really think your own personal winepress of wrath is going to make one bit of difference in this world?

As followers of Jesus, we're better off waiting for the day John describes in this passage. The day of the Lord, the day of judgment—the day the angel from the altar takes our prayers, combines them with fiery coals, and flings them to earth. Revelation 6:10 reminds us what those prayers are: "O Sovereign Lord, holy and true, how long before you will judge and avenge our blood on those who dwell on the earth?" John is teaching us that the answer to our prayers for justice is, "Wait and be patient, because it's coming."

With that promise in mind, this graphic description of the day of judgment becomes a blessing, a comfort, and a reminder to us, the redeemed, to be patient. This promise provides the freedom to wait on Jesus, leaving judgment to Him, while we focus on the first and most important proclamation, as written in Revelation 14:7:

> "Fear God and give him glory, because the hour of his judgment has come, and worship him who made heaven and earth, the sea and the springs of water."

The world has no reason to fear your little winepress, nor does it need our individual brand of wrath and judgment. There is plenty of real wrath and judgment to come later. But until that day, what the world does desperately need is our proclamation of the Good News. When people are given ears to hear the gospel we preach, they will receive mercy and forgiveness, become a part of our church family, and, most importantly, escape the great winepress of His wrath. Instead of one day facing Him as judge, they will learn the joy of worshiping God and of following Jesus wherever He goes.

CHAPTER THIRTY-FIVE

A Song of Anticipation

Revelation 15:

¹ Then I saw another sign in heaven, great and amazing, seven angels with seven plagues, which are the last, for with them the wrath of God is finished.

² And I saw what appeared to be a sea of glass mingled with fire—and also those who had conquered the beast and its image and the number of its name, standing beside the sea of glass with harps of God in their hands. ³ And they sing the song of Moses, the servant of God, and the song of the Lamb, saying, "Great and amazing are your deeds, O Lord God the Almighty! Just and true are your ways, O King of the nations! ⁴ Who will not fear, O Lord, and glorify your name? For you alone are holy. All nations will come and worship you, for your righteous acts have been revealed."

⁵ After this I looked, and the sanctuary of the tent of witness in heaven was opened, ⁶ and out of the sanctuary came the seven angels with the seven plagues, clothed in pure, bright linen, with golden sashes around their chests. ⁷ And one of the four living creatures gave to the seven angels seven golden bowls full of the wrath of God who lives forever and ever, ⁸ and the sanctuary was filled with smoke from the glory of God and from his power, and no one could

> *enter the sanctuary until the seven plagues of the seven angels were finished.*

Why do we read the book of Revelation? What are we hoping to learn when we take the time to study it carefully? Are we supposed to treat it like a manual for predicting the end times? How many predictions from well-meaning people about the return of Jesus based on Revelation have been right?

Revelation reveals beautiful, inspiring truth about the return of Jesus, but its purpose isn't to help us predict it. Jesus warned about that foolishness when he said no one except the Father knows the day and hour (Matthew 24:36). Instead, in the book's first chapter, the Spirit revealed that those who read it will be "blessed." The word means encouraged, inspired to endure, and press on. The true purpose of Revelation is to teach us how to live with the joy of anticipation so we can follow and worship Jesus with confidence, no matter what the world might bring against us.

What Would John's Readers Have Noticed?

The Exodus Story

John's readers would have connected Revelation 15 with the Exodus—just as they would have with the seven trumpets of Revelation 8—by linking the chapter with an ancient story of redemption. After Israel endured four hundred years of slavery in Egypt, as God told Abraham in Genesis 15:13, He sent Moses to command Pharaoh to let Israel go. God sent ten separate plagues to force Pharaoh's obedience (Exodus 7–12). Finally, under immense pressure, Pharaoh relented—but he didn't really repent. Incredibly, he changed his mind and attempted to chase Israel with the most lethal army in history. God then saved Israel by drowning that powerful army in the Red Sea (Exodus 14).

You can imagine the flood of awe and gratitude Israel had for God on that day. Scripture tells us how Moses led the entire nation in a massive celebration of this redemptive act in Exodus 15, culminating in a song about what God had done that was bookended by the jubilant declaration, "sing to the LORD, for he has triumphed gloriously; the horse and his rider he has thrown into the sea" (verses 1 and 21). This song came to be known in Jewish culture as the "Song of Moses." I believe it's the epitome of human expression of praise for the redemptive power of God. Jews still sing it in community to this day. In many ways, so do we.

The Tabernacle

But leading Israel out of Egypt wasn't the end of the miracle. In Exodus 40, God gives detailed instructions on how to build a structure He would fill with His presence in verses 34 and 35:

> *Then the cloud covered the tent of meeting, and the glory of the LORD filled the tabernacle. ³⁵ And Moses was not able to enter the tent of meeting because the cloud settled on it.*

The tabernacle became a place where a righteous and holy God could reside among His people. It and the other temples built later were earthly prototypes of the heavenly temple, which God's glory filled with thick smoke in Revelation 15:8.

WHAT WAS JESUS TELLING THE CHURCHES?

We can't understand the purpose of this passage from an American Christian perspective using today's headlines. Interpreting its symbolism requires reading it through the lens of first-century Jewish Christians. And those first-century believers would have seen direct links back to that story in Exodus.

The seven angels from heaven with seven bowls of judgment ready to pour out seven plagues point to God's use of plagues to rescue the Israelites from Pharaoh and carry them to safety in the wilderness. Those plagues didn't impact Israel. In the same way, these bowls of judgment won't touch the redeemed—those who have been marked by the Holy Spirit and given to Jesus. To make it clear, that's us, the church. This beautifully ties back to Revelation 12, where the woman (the church) is rescued from the dragon and taken into the wilderness.

The Exodus had two stages: from Egypt into the wilderness, and, forty years later, from the wilderness into the promised land. Just as God used the plagues in Exodus to lead His people out of Egypt into the wilderness for safekeeping, God will use these plagues John describes to lead us out of the

A Song of Anticipation

wilderness of tribulation where we have been living since the resurrection of Jesus.

As I mentioned in chapter 29, being "swallowed up by the earth" was used throughout the Old Testament as a metaphor for a shocking, catastrophic defeat. Similarly, in Jewish culture, and particularly throughout Hebrew literature, the sea is used as a metaphor for mysterious danger. It's a place of unknown horror and judgment. Recall how God destroyed Pharaoh's army in the Exodus story by swallowing it up in the Red Sea!

John describes the first beast as coming out of the sea. But here, the sea is described as glass, symbolizing peace and safety. This is the second time we see this sea of glass in Revelation; the first time was with the redeemed around the throne singing songs of redemption in chapter 4. Just like He did from the boat during the storm on the Sea of Galilee (Mark 4), Jesus calms the sea, transforming it from a place of judgment to a place of peace. Once evil is purged from all of creation, the sea becomes a beautiful location where we gather to worship Jesus.

This is a future scene of the complete church, including every person God has saved throughout the history of redemption—those who have faithfully resisted the lies of the second beast as well as all who refused to worship the first beast. The entire congregation of believers will assemble in complete and total victory, and the "Song of Moses" will be their spiritual fight song. It's like the song a college football team might sing before a big game. At that moment, we will know we're soon to exit the wilderness and enter our promised land to rule with Jesus forever, the hints of which we see in John 10:9 when Jesus said, "If anyone enters by me, he will be saved and will go in and out and find pasture."

After the song has been sung, the temple in heaven is opened and seven bowls of God's wrath are made ready. Anticipation builds, because the judgment of evil is at hand. This is what the redeemed have all been waiting for! When the sanctuary opens, it's filled with the smoke of God's presence, smoke so thick no one can enter. We must wait for all seven bowls of judgment to be poured out and for evil to be purged from creation.

Only later, when the new Jerusalem (the bride of the Lamb, the church of all His redeemed) descends in Revelation 21, do we enter the new temple where God lives among His people and fills the whole earth with His glory! The faithful can come and go while finding rest in His presence without fear, burden, or judgment.

What Is Jesus Telling Us Today?

Instead of expecting Revelation to predict the future, we should read it to discover all the reasons we should continue to faithfully worship and follow Jesus as we wait for His return. I don't know about you, but I am full of anticipation for that day. It's become the lens through which I process everything I see in this world.

Jesus' return is the moment we should all be living for—the moment God begins the final act of the story of redemption. It's the day that the heavenly temple will descend, so that God's presence can fill the entire earth and we can be with Him forever. When that day comes, we will sing the "Song of Moses" in full force with all the redeemed from throughout history. That's why, for us, this day of judgment isn't ominous but exhilarating and inspiring. We'll witness the removal of the last barrier between the Father and His people.

The reason Israel sang the "Song of Moses," the reason we can sing it, and the reason the church in heaven will sing it is because of Jesus' amazing redemptive work on the cross and His future day of judgment upon the wicked. Hebrews 13:14 reminds us, "For here we have no lasting city, but we seek the city that is to come." Yes, it's true, we're in the wilderness now, protected from the dragon and his two beasts. But they hate us, and they come after us constantly. That's why life here is hard. The sea is still stormy, and the city we seek still feels very far away.

But we shouldn't be discouraged. The Spirit has given us this Revelation so we know how we should see this world and how we should live in it—with great anticipation for that day! This passage teaches us to live with anticipation of the great and marvelous things He has done, is doing, and will do. We know that once the bowls of judgment purge the earth of evil, we will exit this wilderness—this age of tribulation—and live forever in the tabernacle of the new heaven and new earth side-by-side with our Jesus.

We anticipate the day we will sing our "Song of Moses" with all the redeemed from every nation and tribe. We anticipate our excitement for what we will witness Jesus do on that day. But for now, the closest we can get to that is when we gather together to worship our Jesus as a church family and read His Word in community—to be reminded of His return to establish His forever kingdom.

CHAPTER THIRTY-SIX

Wickedness Is Stubborn

Revelation 16:1–16:

> [1] Then I heard a loud voice from the temple telling the seven angels, "Go and pour out on the earth the seven bowls of the wrath of God."
>
> [2] So the first angel went and poured out his bowl on the earth, and harmful and painful sores came upon the people who bore the mark of the beast and worshiped its image.
>
> [3] The second angel poured out his bowl into the sea, and it became like the blood of a corpse, and every living thing died that was in the sea.
>
> [4] The third angel poured out his bowl into the rivers and the springs of water, and they became blood. [5] And I heard the angel in charge of the waters say, "Just are you, O Holy One, who is and who was, for you brought these judgments. [6] For they have shed the blood of saints and prophets, and you have given them blood to drink. It is what they deserve!"
>
> [7] And I heard the altar saying, "Yes, Lord God the Almighty, true and just are your judgments!"

> *⁸ The fourth angel poured out his bowl on the sun, and it was allowed to scorch people with fire. ⁹ They were scorched by the fierce heat, and they cursed the name of God who had power over these plagues. They did not repent and give him glory.*
>
> *¹⁰ The fifth angel poured out his bowl on the throne of the beast, and its kingdom was plunged into darkness. People gnawed their tongues in anguish ¹¹ and cursed the God of heaven for their pain and sores. They did not repent of their deeds.*
>
> *¹² The sixth angel poured out his bowl on the great river Euphrates, and its water was dried up, to prepare the way for the kings from the east. ¹³ And I saw, coming out of the mouth of the dragon and out of the mouth of the beast and out of the mouth of the false prophet, three unclean spirits like frogs. ¹⁴ For they are demonic spirits, performing signs, who go abroad to the kings of the whole world, to assemble them for battle on the great day of God the Almighty. ¹⁵ ("Behold, I am coming like a thief! Blessed is the one who stays awake, keeping his garments on, that he may not go about naked and be seen exposed!") ¹⁶ And they assembled them at the place that in Hebrew is called Armageddon.*

Do you ever get frustrated with the world's stubborn commitment to wickedness? Does it seem like the world takes pleasure in its relentless rejection of God and the gospel? Even if they don't verbally reject God, they constantly redefine Him in their own terms. Evil seems like an uncontrollable weed popping up everywhere, constantly needing to be rooted out. The difference between the righteous and the wicked isn't sinlessness. It's a question of passionate devotion to either good or evil.

WHAT WOULD JOHN'S READERS HAVE NOTICED?

Belligerent Pharaoh

Because the descriptions of these plagues connect symbolically with the Egyptian plagues, John's readers would have continued to view this passage through the lens of that very familiar story in Exodus, In Exodus 14:5–9, even as the plagues came upon Egypt, Pharaoh's irrational allegiance to wickedness was manifested:

> *The mind of Pharaoh and his servants was changed toward the people, and they said, "What is this we have done, that we have let Israel go from serving us?" ⁶ So he made ready his chariot and took his army with him . . . ⁸ And the* LORD *hardened the heart of Pharaoh king of Egypt, and he pursued the people of Israel . . . ⁹ The Egyptians pursued them, all Pharaoh's horses and chariots and his horsemen and his army, and overtook them encamped at the sea.*

Pharaoh refused to repent and submit to God's authority. He only agreed to let Israel go after the tenth plague, but, even then, he quickly changed his mind. He was so dedicated to evil that he foolishly gathered his army together to pursue Israel.

Mount Megiddo

John also made another Old Testament reference, though it's a bit disguised. The valley of Megiddo near Jerusalem is described in the Old Testament several times as a flat plain (2 Chronicles 35:22, Zechariah 12:11). The cultural history of this valley made it a great symbol of the last battle between good and evil. Many battles were fought there. Sometimes Israel lost; other times, it won. But why is it called Armageddon here?

Armageddon is a Hebrew word meaning "Mount Megiddo," which is a critical clue for readers.[28] There is no such thing as *Mount Megiddo*—it's flat. This isn't John's error but rather a common Hebrew wordplay to symbolize significance. It would be like us calling the battle of Gettysburg "Mount Gettysburg," even though there's no such mountain.

John's readers would have understood this wasn't necessarily about the topography or location of the place, but more about the significance of a future event. They wouldn't have read it as pertaining to a single geographical location but, instead, as a broader representation of the future final battle with evil.

WHAT WAS JESUS TELLING THE CHURCHES?

The first plague brings painful sores, revealing the frailty of humanity and its susceptibility to sickness and disease. The second and third plagues poison the sea, cutting off major food and water sources. These same plagues endangered Egyptians' lives in the Exodus story, and yet the wicked refused to repent. The same will happen here.

Then we see three more plagues. The fourth is a heat wave that scorches people, crops, and livestock—another strike against what humanity needs to survive on earth. The fifth angel darkens the sun. Now the wicked are suffering from their sores from the first plague and the scorching heat of the fourth plague, yet they still won't repent. The sixth angel brings the sixth plague—a drought so bad it dries up the Euphrates, a metaphor for the removal of the only barrier between the world and the power of the beast's great army.

All these bowls transform the earth into a place where provision and security for the unredeemed are gone. The symbolism is intriguing, but the two important things we learn are what evil deserves and how evil responds. Their lack of desire to even hear or understand the gospel and the call to repentance is also part of the judgment, as Romans 1:19–20 reminds us:

> *What can be known about God is plain to them, because God has shown it to them. 20 For his invisible attributes, namely, his eternal power and divine nature, have been clearly perceived, ever since the creation of the world, in the things that have been made. So they are without excuse.*

These stages of judgment are part of the fulfillment of this passage in Romans. They remove any doubt who the wicked are. They have everything they love taken from them except one thing: Babylon (or the seventh bowl). But sadly, as the plagues didn't convince Pharaoh to repent, these six bowls won't convince the wicked to repent. Even if they wanted to, there's no more room for repentance. This is the well-deserved final judgment.

Christians popularly equate Armageddon with "the final battle". But if that were the case, why isn't Armageddon at the end of Revelation? It's because Revelation isn't a book of chronological events, but rather like different movie clips of the last days, which began with the resurrection of Christ. (Acts 2:15–17; Hebrews 1:1–2). As we will learn in the next chapter, Armageddon is another camera angle on that second harvest and the winepress of God's wrath from a couple chapters ago. All the unredeemed still under the spell of the second beast are mustered together for evil's last stand. But anything coming from the mouth of the dragon or the beast is deception. These people and demons aren't just struggling with sin. They're devoted to evil up to the very end.

It's what Jesus was describing at the end of His parable of the wheat and the weeds in Matthew 13:30 when He said, "Gather the weeds first and bind them in bundles to be burned." Like Pharaoh, the wicked refuse to turn to God and, in the process, become even more entrenched with evil. And just like Pharaoh gathered his army to pursue Israel, the dragon and his two beasts gather the wicked for a final suicide mission.

This is what *Armageddon* symbolizes: Satan gathering all of evil's power from every corner of the earth for the seventh bowl—every king, weapon, effort, and bitter resentment gathered in one place for the ultimate showdown against

God. Through their hatred of the gospel and foolish commitment to evil, they have set themselves up as sitting ducks for final judgment.

WHAT IS JESUS TELLING US TODAY?

God's judgment exposes the senseless absurdity of the wicked. It also inspires the joy and gratitude of the redeemed. Keep in mind, these symbolic plagues aren't coded clues revealing secrets about what to look for on that day. The purpose is to connect to the lesson learned with Pharaoh: they expose the obstinate, wicked insanity of the unredeemed.

It's hard for us to fully understand the extent of evil's corruption. It has infiltrated this world at every level. But judgment reveals the difference between sinfulness and wickedness. Every human is sinful, but not all are wicked. In 2 Corinthians 4:4, we read the warning that "in their case the god of this world [the dragon] has blinded the minds of the unbelievers, to keep them from seeing the light of the gospel of the glory of Christ."

Like Pharaoh, the wicked are hopelessly hardened against the gospel, against God, and against us, His redeemed. Does God really need six bowls of judgment? Is He sadistic? God doesn't take joy in destroying the wicked, but their irrational wickedness will never change and must be eradicated. Each bowl further exposes the depth of disdain the wicked have for the gospel and for God. Each bowl and the consequent rejection of the call to repent from the wicked incriminates them even further.

It seems like total insanity to answer God's power and judgment this way. The willful dedication to wickedness of the unredeemed has no place in the presence of God. But we the redeemed have been spared from this insanity. Instead, we're committed to the gospel, to the kingdom values Jesus taught us. As the redeemed, we're dedicated to the qualities of the priesthood—proclamation, integrity, and industry.

But living this way is in direct opposition to the wicked. They don't understand it, so they resent it. And so, until Jesus returns, we will always be swimming upstream. This should encourage us to let go of our deep frustration with the world's stubborn wickedness. So, Christian, please relax.

Despite our sinful acts, God convinces us to abandon wickedness, not to ally with it. We have been made recipients of grace and mercy, which we ourselves would never have wanted to accept. The bowls remind us that, by grace, we've been spared the burden the wicked have embraced. And because we have been set free, we don't deserve any of this judgment!

That's how God's judgment of the wicked should inspire even more worship. We have been given ears to hear the truth! And instead of being frustrated with the world's relentless pursuit of evil, we are filled with gratitude for the miraculous gift of our desire to wholeheartedly follow the Lamb wherever He goes!

CHAPTER THIRTY-SEVEN

Armageddon Celebration

Revelation 16:16–21:

> ^{16} *And they assembled them at the place that in Hebrew is called Armageddon.*
>
> ^{17} *The seventh angel poured out his bowl into the air, and a loud voice came out of the temple, from the throne, saying, "It is done!"* ^{18} *And there were flashes of lightning, rumblings, peals of thunder, and a great earthquake such as there had never been since man was on the earth, so great was that earthquake.* ^{19} *The great city was split into three parts, and the cities of the nations fell, and God remembered Babylon the great, to make her drain the cup of the wine of the fury of his wrath.* ^{20} *And every island fled away, and no mountains were to be found.* ^{21} *And great hailstones, about one hundred pounds each, fell from heaven on people; and they cursed God for the plague of the hail, because the plague was so severe.*

When someone mentions Armageddon, what comes to mind? Many people have assigned an erroneous meaning to *Armageddon*, much like they have with the word *apocalypse*. When we began our journey through Revelation, we learned that *apocalypse* means "revealing" and is not intended to be a metaphor for the horrific events of the end of the world.[29] Similarly, most people use *Armageddon* as a geopolitical metaphor to describe something like a potential nuclear war between powerful nations.

But as we just learned in the previous chapter, *Armageddon* is a symbolic Hebrew word that is original and exclusive to the book of Revelation.[30] It's a reference to the final spiritual battle between good and evil, a metaphor for the theological concept of the day God unleashes His full wrath to flush all the forces of wickedness out of hiding into plain sight. It's something that could happen at any time and that the redeemed should live in hope for.

What Would John's Readers Have Noticed?

This passage has Old Testament words and phrases John's readers would immediately recognize: *hail*, *Babylon*, and *the Great City*.

Hail

As we begin, this seventh bowl of judgment poured out at Armageddon continues to borrow symbolism from the story of Exodus, specifically Exodus 9:23–26:

> The Lord rained hail upon the land of Egypt. *24* There was hail and fire flashing continually in the midst of the hail,

very heavy hail, such as had never been in all the land of Egypt since it became a nation. ²⁵ *The hail struck down everything that was in the field in all the land of Egypt, both man and beast. And the hail struck down every plant of the field and broke every tree of the field.* ²⁶ *Only in the land of Goshen, where the people of Israel were, was there no hail.*

Babylon

When John's readers read "God remembered Babylon," they would have recalled the story of the Tower of Babel (Genesis 11). *Babel* and *Babylon* are derived from the same Hebrew word for "confusion."³¹ The people in Genesis 11:4 said to themselves, "Come, let us build ourselves a city and a tower with its top in the heavens, and let us make a name for ourselves, lest we be dispersed over the face of the whole earth." The purpose of their gathering was to build a tower that would unify all the inhabitants of earth. God saw this plan and put a stop to it by causing them all to speak different languages. The city of Babel would eventually come to be known as Babylon, and the connection between Babylon and the gathering of the wicked in this Revelation passage would have been clear. Like Armageddon, the Tower of Babel was a gathering point for all the rebellious inhabitants of the earth.

The Great City

We see the phrase "great city" several times in the Old Testament, always referring to either a judgment event or a warning to repent and avoid judgment. We see an example of this in the second verse of the book of Jonah, when God says, "Arise, go to Nineveh, that great city, and call out against it, for their evil has come up before me."

John used the term *great* earlier in Revelation 11:8, as a metaphor for the world system of government that opposes God's plan of redemption, when he wrote, "their dead bodies will lie in the street of the great city that *symbolically* is called Sodom and Egypt, where their Lord was crucified" (emphasis mine). The symbolic names of Sodom, Egypt, and Babylon represent a trinity of evil tools the dragon uses to control the world. Sodom stands for moral decay, Egypt represents evil's desire to conquer and enslave the redeemed, and Babylon indicates idolatry and false teaching.

What Was Jesus Telling the Churches?

The first beast, represented by Babylon, is deeply corrupt, and yet it seemed to John's readers like God doesn't do much about it. But John reminds us that God will never forget what the wicked have done. Remember, there is a difference between those struggling with sin and those who are completely committed to wickedness: the latter are persistent in their rebellion. Instead of seeking repentance, they stand in rebellion and rage against God's justice.

There's a reason God waits to judge them: He also remembers His redeemed and patiently waits for all of us to be safely preserved, as we see in Romans 9:22–24:

> *What if God, desiring to show his wrath and to make known his power, has endured with much patience vessels of wrath prepared for destruction, ²³ in order to make known the riches of his glory for vessels of mercy, which he has prepared beforehand for glory— ²⁴ even us whom he has called, not from the Jews only but also from the Gentiles?*

We should remember that the first six bowls were poured out on the earth to flush out those who inhabit it, but the seventh was "poured out into the air" (Revelation 16:17). This bowl targets the realm of wickedness that controls the unredeemed. Ephesians 2:1–2 hints at this when Paul writes,

> *And you were dead in the trespasses and sins ² in which you once walked, following the course of this world, following the prince of the power of the air, the spirit that is now at work in the sons of disobedience.*

This pouring of the seventh bowl is the eradication of the architect of the Great City and all the wickedness in this world. It targets the spiritual forces of deception that have influenced the wicked to gather together against God.

John's descriptions of the impact of this seventh bowl is another great lesson about how we should interpret Revelation. Armageddon should be seen as the same event described three prior times in Revelation, each one from different camera angles, as we see here:

Revelation 4:5 — *From the throne came flashes of lightning, and rumblings and peals of thunder.*

Revelation 8:5 —*There were peals of thunder, rumblings, flashes of lightning, and an earthquake.*

Revelation 11:19 — *Then God's temple in heaven was opened.... There were flashes of lightning, rumblings, peals of thunder, an earthquake, and heavy hail.*

There is no escaping the seventh bowl. The Great City's fate is far worse than that of Babel, Sodom, or any others we see in the Bible. Unlike Nineveh, there's no call to repent. Unlike Sodom, God isn't targeting just wickedness. This is the final judgment. There's no tomorrow and nowhere for evil to run or hide.

What Is Jesus Telling Us Today?

Armageddon shouldn't be feared. Instead, the redeemed should take comfort in knowing it will be a precursor to the greatest worship service in church history. But for the wicked, Armageddon will be a catastrophic, painful end to their world system.

Some who claim to follow Jesus say that God won't remember and judge the world's wickedness, that there's no Armageddon, and that everyone will be redeemed and there will be no final day of judgment. But they are wrong. God will remember. He won't forget. One day evil will pay for what it has done to this world, as we learn in 2 Peter 3:9–10:

> *The Lord is not slow to fulfill his promise as some count slowness, but is patient toward you, not wishing that any should perish, but that all should reach repentance.* [10] *But*

> *the day of the Lord will come like a thief, and then the heavens will pass away with a roar, and the heavenly bodies will be burned up and dissolved, and the earth and the works that are done on it will be exposed.*

God is patiently holding back Armageddon. But it would be a big mistake to interpret His patience as proof that judgment won't be coming. Armageddon is far more than some future earthly geopolitical event. It's the moment of the complete eradication of every earthly and spiritual enemy of righteousness. Think of it as the day our God remembers everything the wicked have ever done, said, and thought. The seventh bowl will leave no stone unturned. It will expose and eradicate every drop of evil.

So, what should our reaction be when we hear the word *Armageddon*? Recall the massive worship celebration in heaven we've read about throughout Revelation? It's especially bold in Revelation 7:9–10:

> *After this I looked, and behold, a great multitude that no one could number, from every nation, from all tribes and peoples and languages, standing before the throne and before the Lamb, clothed in white robes . . . ¹⁰ and crying out with a loud voice, "Salvation belongs to our God who sits on the throne, and to the Lamb!"*

Each time this worship celebration is mentioned in Revelation, it begins just prior to this same judgment event of thunder, lightning, and an earthquake. While the day God remembers Babylon will be evil's worst nightmare, it will be the cause for our greatest celebration. Think of this: if God were to forget or ignore the wickedness of Babylon, would He really be worthy of worship or celebration? If God never exposes all the works of evil—and the one behind them—can Jesus really be celebrated as our eternal king? If God cannot be trusted to bring perfect justice for the wicked, can He be trusted with grace and mercy for the redeemed?

The fact is, God will remember. He will judge evil. It's one of the biggest reasons He is worthy of worship and celebration. Justice at Armageddon will inspire the single greatest expression of worship the redeemed have ever experienced. We'll celebrate God's acts of power, righteousness, and faithfulness to do what He promised.

CHAPTER THIRTY-EIGHT

The Great Prostitute

Revelation 17:1–7:

> ¹ Then one of the seven angels who had the seven bowls came and said to me, "Come, I will show you the judgment of the great prostitute who is seated on many waters, ² with whom the kings of the earth have committed sexual immorality, and with the wine of whose sexual immorality the dwellers on earth have become drunk." ³ And he carried me away in the Spirit into a wilderness, and I saw a woman sitting on a scarlet beast that was full of blasphemous names, and it had seven heads and ten horns. ⁴ The woman was arrayed in purple and scarlet, and adorned with gold and jewels and pearls, holding in her hand a golden cup full of abominations and the impurities of her sexual immorality. ⁵ And on her forehead was written a name of mystery: "Babylon the great, mother of prostitutes and of earth's abominations." ⁶ And I saw the woman, drunk with the blood of the saints, the blood of the martyrs of Jesus.
>
> When I saw her, I marveled greatly. ⁷ But the angel said to me, "Why do you marvel? I will tell you the mystery of the woman, and of the beast with seven heads and ten horns that carries her."

Let me start off with a small disclaimer: this passage contains graphic imagery.

We've learned in the previous two chapters that there's a difference between struggling with sin and being fully committed to wickedness. We live in a fallen world where people suffer the consequences of the choices we make, even choices we have been forced into.

God's purpose for this passage isn't to shame or condemn people who've been sucked into bad situations. The images in this passage are a metaphor for how seductive evil can be, so followers of Jesus can know what's really going on in the world—how the dragon has created a system that's wholly designed to feed human lust and pride. We're all going to need lots of wisdom if we want to resist that powerful seduction.

What Would John's Readers Have Noticed?

Immorality

After the Armageddon vision, an angel pulled back another curtain for John, revealing the seductive power of wickedness. The passage is a graphic description of how the allure of evil dominates the unredeemed world. It starts by introducing a woman the angel calls "the great prostitute," revealing who she is, and explaining how she will be judged when Jesus returns. Remember that throughout the Old Testament, sexual immorality is used as a metaphor for when God's people chose to be unfaithful to God.

John used the Greek word πορνεύω (*porneuo*), which means "to prostitute oneself"—to fulfill the lust of another in order to gain leverage over them. It describes unfaithfulness as a capitulation to evil's seduction to the point of being, in a spiritual sense, completely naked and exposed.[32]

Drunkenness

The Old Testament used *drunkenness* in a similar way as *sexual immorality*, as a metaphor for someone whose wisdom and discernment have been compromised. We see this in Joel 1:5: "Awake, you drunkards, and weep, and wail, all you drinkers of wine, because of the sweet wine, for it is cut off from your mouth." When people are drunk, their thought processes are impaired. They become easily seduced, manipulated, and exploited. They lose the ability to comprehend reality, which means they can't assess deceptions or threats around them or the consequences of succumbing to them.

Taken together, these two visions of a prostitute and drunkenness create a powerful combined metaphor. The woman is an alluring, beautiful prostitute holding a cup full of intoxicating abominations that dull the senses. John's readers would have understood the purely spiritual meaning.

Babylon

But there's one more image to address. Forty years after the exodus to the wilderness, Israel entered the promised land, and they later became a powerful kingdom. For almost a thousand years, the nation withstood countless invaders, until a civil war split Israel in two. Judah, the southern kingdom, represented the throne of David and the line of Christ. It remained autonomous and intact until 600 BC, when it finally fell to invading Babylon—the first of four foreign occupying empires that would rule Jerusalem, just as Daniel prophesied in Daniel 7.

The Babylonian King Nebuchadnezzar desecrated and destroyed the temple and exiled the Jewish people from their land. Since Babylon was the first to conquer Israel, it became a symbol, a euphemism for any future occupying forces or empires. As we have already seen in previous chapters, first-century Jews symbolically referred to both the Roman occupation and Rome itself as Babylon. We see a clear example of this in 1 Peter 5:13, where the apostle wrote, "She who is at Babylon, who is likewise chosen, sends you greetings."

WHAT WAS JESUS TELLING THE CHURCHES?

Again, this passage is not intended to condemn every person who has ever given in to temptation or who has been forced into a life of abuse and exploitation. It serves as a metaphor for spiritual unfaithfulness. It is, however, an appropriate metaphor. The evil of sexual exploitation and

The Great Prostitute

human trafficking has always been rampant in the fallen world.

Just as the wicked will be exposed when they are gathered together in one place at the battle of Armageddon, the angel exposes who this Great Prostitute is—she carries the mark of the second beast! The name of every blasphemy and deception from the mouth of the dragon is written on her forehead. Even though she's outwardly beautiful and holds a golden chalice, that chalice is filled with disgusting, intoxicating abominations. The bitter dregs inside make the nations drunk with passion for evil and every sinful desire the dragon can offer.

Do you remember the other woman we learned about in an earlier chapter, the one in the wilderness? She and her offspring represented the faithful believers—in other words, the church. But this woman, the Great Prostitute, is a metaphor for the rest of the world—those who love this world more than Jesus, who are content to give in to her seduction and have their senses dulled by her wine. And this prostitute herself is drunk. She's drunk with hatred toward God's redeemed and wants nothing more than to deceive them and destroy them. When her deception and seduction don't work, she turns to violence by seducing the nations, making them drunk with that same wine of hatred and resentment.

John describes this Great Prostitute as riding a scarlet beast with seven heads and ten horns! And yes, it's the same beast we saw in Revelation 13, the beast that controls every world government. So, this Great Prostitute is marked by one beast while she rides the other. This reveals the source of her seduction. She represents everything wicked, evil, and opposed to God in one single stunningly beautiful appearance.

Just as Daniel was troubled and in awe of what was revealed to him, John is also stunned and troubled by the sight of this Great Prostitute who is marked by one beast and riding the other. Why wouldn't he be? To the average person, she's incredibly seductive and irresistible. But she is also extremely powerful and deadly. However, as we'll see in the next chapter, the angel said to John, "Why do you marvel at her? Don't worry, I'm about to expose her every secret. Once I do, you'll understand exactly who she is, what she wants, and why you will always be able to withstand her seduction. I'm going to arm you and the rest of my redeemed with wisdom, so they can resist her and faithfully follow the Lamb wherever He goes."

What Is Jesus Telling Us Today?

The unredeemed world is a temptress who uses anything and everything she can to seduce followers of Jesus into unfaithfulness. It's understandable, then, why even we the faithful often struggle with the constant barrage of seduction from the Great Prostitute, isn't it? She uses everything in her arsenal against the redeemed. She doesn't try to seduce us with unappealing things or ideas; instead, she uses religion, politics, or philosophies that seem beautiful—even outwardly moral—but are substitutes for truth.

This is why Paul warned all believers in 1 Corinthians 15:34 to "wake up from your drunken stupor, as is right, and do not go on sinning. For some have no knowledge of God. I say this to your shame." Like John and Daniel, I think many Christians are often caught marveling at the Great Prostitute that is this world system. Paul warned the Christians in Corinth against sipping dregs of the Great Prostitute's golden cup.

As followers of Jesus, we are sometimes seduced. Peter knew this when he admonished many of the same churches John wrote to in 1 Peter 5:8–9: "Be sober-minded; be watchful. Your adversary the devil prowls around like a roaring lion, seeking someone to devour. Resist him, firm in your faith." Sometimes we get a little tipsy, don't we? We become affectionate or even intimate with the intoxicants the Great Prostitute offers to us.

A true follower of Jesus, who has been marked by the Holy Spirit, might occasionally taste her bitter dregs, but instinctively we will soon spit them out. Followers of Jesus know that her bitter-tasting cup, full of every abomination, is specifically intended to cause us to become unfaithful. 1 John 2:16 reminds us, "For all that is in the world—the desires of the flesh and the desires of the eyes and pride of life—is not from the Father but is from the world." If we are to resist the seduction of the Great Prostitute, it starts with understanding who's behind her beauty. We must be armed with all that is revealed in this passage—who she is, what she wants, and the source of her power. This knowledge will keep us from becoming mesmerized by her like the world around us is. Instead, we will be armed with discernment that can spot her cunning and seductive schemes a mile away!

Pulling back the curtain on the prostitute becomes another one of those blessings John promised in Revelation 1 for all those who read this book. God provides similar wisdom in Proverbs 7:24–27:

> *O sons, listen to me, and be attentive to the words of my mouth. 25 Let not your heart turn aside to her ways; do not stray into her paths, 26 for many a victim has she laid low, and all her slain are a mighty throng. 27 Her house is the way to Sheol, going down to the chambers of death.*

CHAPTER THIRTY-NINE

Who Was, Is, and Is Not

Revelation 17:6–18:

> ^{6} And I saw the woman, drunk with the blood of the saints, the blood of the martyrs of Jesus.
>
> When I saw her, I marveled greatly. ^{7} But the angel said to me, "Why do you marvel? I will tell you the mystery of the woman, and of the beast with seven heads and ten horns that carries her. ^{8} The beast that you saw was, and is not, and is about to rise from the bottomless pit and go to destruction. And the dwellers on earth whose names have not been written in the book of life from the foundation of the world will marvel to see the beast, because it was and is not and is to come. ^{9} This calls for a mind with wisdom: the seven heads are seven mountains on which the woman is seated; ^{10} they are also seven kings, five of whom have fallen, one is, the other has not yet come, and when he does come he must remain only a little while. ^{11} As for the beast that was and is not, it is an eighth but it belongs to the seven, and it goes to destruction. ^{12} And the ten horns that you saw are ten kings who have not yet received royal power, but they are to receive authority as kings for one hour, together with the beast. ^{13} These are of one mind, and they hand over their power and authority to the beast.

> *14 They will make war on the Lamb, and the Lamb will conquer them, for he is Lord of lords and King of kings, and those with him are called and chosen and faithful."*
>
> *15 And the angel said to me, "The waters that you saw, where the prostitute is seated, are peoples and multitudes and nations and languages. 16 And the ten horns that you saw, they and the beast will hate the prostitute. They will make her desolate and naked, and devour her flesh and burn her up with fire, 17 for God has put it into their hearts to carry out his purpose by being of one mind and handing over their royal power to the beast, until the words of God are fulfilled. 18 And the woman that you saw is the great city that has dominion over the kings of the earth."*

Once when my wife and I were driving to meet some friends, we encountered the worst traffic jam I can ever remember. The highway was so backed up, it was like a parking lot. I huffed, shook my head, and complained about the other drivers who don't drive as well as I do.

"We're going to miss dinner," I told Laura. "We're never going to get off this road. We'll be stuck here forever."

She gave me one of those looks and said, "Joe, that's a little bit dramatic, don't you think?"

Can you relate to how I was feeling? Have you ever been in a miserable situation that felt like it had no end? For most in the church today, especially in America, our so-called suffering is nothing compared to the tribulation John's readers were living through. There's no doubt the tribulation they bore under Roman rule felt like it had no end in sight. If they were going to endure, they desperately needed to be blessed and encouraged with fresh wisdom from God. They needed to be able to see beyond the living hell of being a Christian under Roman rule.

They needed to be able to see the bigger picture.

WHAT WOULD JOHN'S READERS HAVE NOTICED?

Life Under Roman Rule

Understanding Revelation begins with knowing all its visions and metaphors were one hundred percent relevant to its original readers. John wrote it to *them* during an era when Rome controlled virtually the whole world. Life under Roman rule for a Christian, especially a Jewish Christian, was full of terrible suffering and tribulation.

We've seen how Jews referred to Rome as "Babylon," clear proof they saw Rome as part of the prophecy in Daniel 7. Because Rome was known throughout the ancient world as the city built on seven hills, the seven heads as seven mountains in this passage clearly places first-century Rome, and John's readers, squarely into the timeline of biblical prophecy. Just as Daniel had prophesied, the fourth empire to control Israel would be so great, it would break all others into pieces. Rome had become the pinnacle of human achievement to that point, greater than any other world empire before.

The Mortal Kingdom

As with every other world empire, other nations and kings around Rome resented her power.

For centuries, those outside kingdoms constantly attacked the empire's eastern borders, probing for weaknesses to exploit. This constant nuisance, combined with the seeds of moral and political rot within, eventually toppled the Roman Empire. We saw earlier in Revelation 13:18, "This calls for wisdom: let the one who has understanding calculate the number of the beast, for it is the number of a man, and his number is 666," which we learned was a reminder to John's readers that even the Roman Empire wouldn't last forever.

Repeating this call for wisdom would point first-century believers back to what John taught them about the number of the beast: the number was a reminder that, no matter how permanent Rome seemed, it was a mortal kingdom and, ultimately, would suffer a mortal fate. This prepared John's readers to receive yet another encouragement about the mortality of earthly empires.

WHAT WAS JESUS TELLING THE CHURCHES?

When John first saw the vision of Babylon the Great Prostitute riding the beast, he marveled at her beauty and power. But the angel challenged him, "Why do you marvel? Let me tell you who this is. It was, and is, but it is not!" This is *the* critical clue to an accurate interpretation of this chapter: recognizing that the beast's timeline has a termination point.

Who Was, Who Is, and Is Not

John's Christian readers would have noticed this and picked up on a stark contrast with Jesus—the one "who was and is and is to come" (Revelation 4:8). Jesus has no beginning or end. But this beast Rome (or Babylon the Great Prostitute) rides has a different fate and timeline. He is not! The *was* alludes to the beast's past greatness. The *is* refers to the present greatness (Rome), while *is not* declares that these earthly empires aren't eternal—they have a beginning and an end.

Once again, we see the number 7 when talking about the heads that are mountains who are kings—but not only that number. There are five kings, then a sixth and a seventh, and also an eighth belonging to the seventh. This sounds complex, but actually these heads are an explanation of how "what was, what is, and is not" plays out over the course of human history.

First, the number 7 represents completion. Seven empires symbolize the beginning and end of human history. The seven heads are a metaphor for seven empires who, at different times, ride the beast, meaning they dominate the world at different times in history. These empires each take their turn as the Great Prostitute who rides the beast, seducing the world into unfaithfulness.

The five kings "who have fallen" are a metaphor for any empire before Rome. They are "who was". The sixth is Rome, which was riding the beast when John wrote Revelation. Then we see a seventh, which will be another empire after Rome, and an eighth "who is not yet" but belongs to the other seven. This means that after Rome there will be another, and then another, and another, all riding the beast—and each was, is, and is not, because, eventually, every empire ends.

The symbolism of the number 10 in the Bible often represents the idea of completion—for example, the Ten Commandments. In this particular use in Revelation, it represents the pinnacle of human achievement and accomplishment. Just like 666, the number 10 teaches us that this pinnacle is a façade that feeds a constant and chaotic cycle of earthly governments. The "ten kings" symbolizes that every king throughout history had, has, or will have the same mind and ambition: to ride the beast. They all want to use their fifteen minutes of fame to take down the Great Prostitute of their time so they can take her place. This chaotic cycle of war here and in Revelation 6 are the catalysts for the tribulation that Jesus warned us would begin after His resurrection in Matthew 24:6–7:

> *You will hear of wars and rumors of wars. See that you are not alarmed, for this must take place, but the end is not yet. ⁷ For nation will rise against nation, and kingdom against kingdom, and there will be famines and earthquakes in various places.*

God allows these rulers to pursue this desire so He can expose all the wicked for final judgment. This entire chaotic world system—the empires and the kings who hate them—sits on many roaring waters, a metaphor for the unredeemed throughout history. They all have blind loyalty to the beast's system of chaos, being seduced by one ruler after another into this bloody, hopeless cycle of history.

WHAT IS JESUS TELLING US TODAY?

Throughout church history, many have tried to interpret this passage through the lens of whatever the world order was in their lifetime. In the Middle Ages, many believed the seventh head was the Ottoman Empire, then the Mongol Empire, and then the Spanish Empire. In modern times, people have linked Russia, Germany, China, the United States, or the European Union to the seven heads or the ten kings. Some have even tried to link the United Kingdom, which, at its peak, was the largest empire in human history!

The problem with trying to interpret this passage literally or contemporarily is there are only seven heads and ten kings on the beast to go around. If you insist on trying to match them to specific ones, you are going to leave out some of the most prime candidates! This was not the intended purpose of this vision. Like I've said before, John didn't write Revelation to scare Christians throughout the church age but to bless and encourage them.

This metaphor reveals the nature of how evil dominates the unredeemed in this world, reminding us there will always be another great prostitute who wants to take their turn riding the beast. This includes the age we are currently living in as well. We should always remember Revelation 1:8: "'I am the Alpha and the Omega,' says the Lord God, 'who is and who was and who is to come, the Almighty.'"

In America, I see a miniature version of the "ten kings" cycle in our attitudes every four years during election time. By trusting in and clinging to Revelation's wisdom, we can see the big picture of this constant chaotic cycle and how it will all end. We won't live in fear of every fleeting temporary political or global power shift. Revelation's wisdom reminds us to live above that fickle cycle and to keep our allegiance to, and our hope in, the eternal kingdom of God over any earthly one.

Jesus encouraged us to pray in Matthew 6:9–10 by saying, "Our Father in heaven, hallowed be your name. Your kingdom come, your will be done, on earth as it is in heaven." I hope studying Revelation is helping you better understand why Jesus taught us to pray like this.

Followers of Jesus don't need to be part of the loud waters of the unredeemed the beast sits on. We drink the living water and, therefore, don't thirst for this world anymore. We the redeemed are inspired to live differently, free from the prison of feckless worldly hope ruled by evil and darkness. People with wisdom don't hope in what was, is, and is not. People with wisdom will hope in the One who was, who is, and who is to come.

CHAPTER FORTY

Come Out of Babylon

Revelation 18:1–8:

> *After this I saw another angel coming down from heaven, having great authority, and the earth was made bright with his glory. ² And he called out with a mighty voice, "Fallen, fallen is Babylon the great! She has become a dwelling place for demons, a haunt for every unclean spirit, a haunt for every unclean bird, a haunt for every unclean and detestable beast. ³ For all nations have drunk the wine of the passion of her sexual immorality, and the kings of the earth have committed immorality with her, and the merchants of the earth have grown rich from the power of her luxurious living."*
>
> *⁴ Then I heard another voice from heaven saying, "Come out of her, my people, lest you take part in her sins, lest you share in her plagues; ⁵ for her sins are heaped high as heaven, and God has remembered her iniquities. ⁶ Pay her back as she herself has paid back others, and repay her double for her deeds; mix a double portion for her in the cup she mixed. ⁷ As she glorified herself and lived in luxury, so give her a like measure of torment and mourning, since in her heart she says, 'I sit as a queen, I am no widow, and mourning I shall never see.' ⁸ For this reason her plagues will come in a single day, death and mourning and famine,*

and she will be burned up with fire; for mighty is the Lord God who has judged her."

As a follower of Jesus, do you ever hear conflicting voices in this world, calling you in two different directions? One voice invites you to come out of the world, while the other urges you to stay comfortably within the world's system. This struggle between two conflicting voices is more subtle than our obvious struggle between righteousness and wickedness.

Would you rather live in this world without any of that tension, or grapple every day with the tug-of-war between Jesus and the world? The thing is, true followers of Jesus will always be caught in this tension. The constant struggle can be exhausting, but it can also be a comfort. It's a struggle we are called to embrace and be prepared to face and fight every day. In fact, if this struggle exists in your life, it's one of the best pieces of evidence that you are a follower of Jesus. It's a sign of spiritual life!

What Would John's Readers Have Noticed?

John's first-century Jewish Christian readers would have recognized language in this passage from two well-known Old Testament themes. Understanding these themes is critical in understanding this passage's beautiful complexity. In fact, you cannot accurately interpret this passage without them.

The Promised Fall of Babylon

The first theme is the many prophecies of Babylon's future fall, given to Israel during their captivity under Babylonian rule. Other than the promise of a Messiah, this was the most precious prophetic promise Jews hoped for. Babylon was the first world empire of its kind, and it seemed it would last forever—but God had other plans, as relayed through Jeremiah 51:55–56:

> For the LORD is laying Babylon waste and stilling her mighty voice. Their waves roar like many waters; the noise of their voice is raised, ⁵⁶ for a destroyer has come upon her, upon Babylon; her warriors are taken; their bows are broken in pieces, for the LORD is a God of recompense; he will surely repay.

And similarly, in Isaiah 13:21:

> But wild animals will lie down there, and their houses will be full of howling creatures; there ostriches will dwell, and there wild goats will dance.

John's readers would pick up on the language about unclean beasts and "howling creatures" taking over the fallen city, a metaphor for how catastrophic the fall would be. Babylon's final defeat was, in fact, surprising and rapid, leaving all who had built a life of comfort in Babylon devastated and destitute.

Judgment for Sodom

The second theme is the warning of Sodom's judgment by fire, including God's warning to Lot and his family in Genesis 19:15 to escape: "As morning dawned, the angels urged Lot, saying, 'Up! Take your wife and your two daughters who are here, lest you be swept away in the punishment of the city.'" This came to pass within a matter of hours. Lot's family was called out of Sodom and thus saved from judgment, but there's a tragic element in verses 24 and 26: "Then the LORD rained on Sodom and Gomorrah sulfur and fire from the LORD out of heaven. . . . But Lot's wife, behind him, looked back, and she became a pillar of salt."

Despite the suffering she and her family had endured and the warning from the angels, she couldn't resist looking back. The lifestyle she had built in Sodom had a powerful grip on her heart, and she was unwilling to let go. But she paid for her affection for that wicked city with her life, because she loved what she was leaving behind more than she loved God.

WHAT WAS JESUS TELLING THE CHURCHES?

Remember Jesus' warning to the churches of Thyatira and Laodicea in Revelation 2 and 3? These two cities were known for their profitable trade guilds, but membership required pagan worship in temples. Refusal meant being locked out of commerce. These churches were struggling with loving the luxuries of Roman life. It competed with their allegiance to and love for Jesus.

Jesus gave the same warning to everyone else that he'd given to them: if you don't reject the world's ways, you'll face the same judgment the world will face. This command to "come out of Babylon" in Revelation 18:4 would take Jewish Christians of that day right back to the same familiar order in Isaiah 48:20: "Go out from Babylon, ... declare this with a shout of joy, proclaim it, send it out to the end of the earth."

Remember, first-century Jews used Babylon as a metaphor for Rome, their oppressor. Earlier references to 666 and the seven hills would have grabbed the attention of John's readers, who likely would have exclaimed, "This is about Rome!" By using language from these Old Testament themes, Revelation teaches them and us how God is actively calling His people to come out of the world and into His kingdom, saving them from judgment throughout history!

But beyond the warning of judgment, this passage includes a beautiful, merciful calling to the redeemed. See if you can connect the dots to what Jesus told His disciples before He left earth after the resurrection in Mark 16:15–16: "He said to them, 'Go into all the world and proclaim the gospel to the whole creation. Whoever believes and is baptized will be saved, but whoever does not believe will be condemned.'"

We can see that both imperatives—to come out of Babylon, and to make disciples—are to be proclaimed throughout the earth! They share the same scope: call out people from every nation and tribe so they won't face judgment. But that's not the only connection between these two proclamations, because in Matthew 28:20, Jesus said, "And behold, I am with you always, to the end of the age."

Remember the seven heads and ten kings representing the cycle of empires taking turns riding the beast through history? Each one seduces the unredeemed into giving full allegiance and love to that world system and its promises. At the same time, God tells His church to proclaim the gospel and come out of the very same system that is propped up by the world's empires. As we obey that call, John tells us, no matter how powerful Babylon gets, He will be with us as we obey His command until the end of the age when He returns! All of this helps us to see this call to the redeemed to come out of Babylon as a metaphor for the Great Commission—the harvest of the redeemed before final judgment!

What Is Jesus Telling Us Today?

The gospel of Jesus is both a prophecy of judgment for the wicked and a loving call to mercy for the redeemed. This call to come out of the world's empires is so relevant for all of us, isn't it? Jesus beckons us, "Come out of Babylon! If you have ears to hear what God says to the churches, listen, and follow *Me*!"

For those who are wholly content with staying in Babylon, this call serves as a declaration of judgment. In 1 John 2:15, we're told, "Do not love the world or the things in the world. If anyone loves the world, the love of the Father is not in him." For followers of Jesus, this call becomes our precious daily struggle. But Babylon is very tempting, even for us. While we don't condone its wickedness, all the pleasure, the luxury, and the *stuff* Babylon offers is very seductive!

Sometimes we fail, sometimes we succeed, but for true followers of Jesus, the desire to come out of Babylon is renewed daily by the Holy Spirit. That's how this call to come out of Babylon to avoid her judgment is a blessing and an encouragement. It was a call for the people of God in the Old Testament; it was a call for John's first-century readers; and it remains a call for followers of Jesus today. His words remind us, in John 10:27–30:

> *My sheep hear my voice, and I know them, and they follow me. [28] I give them eternal life, and they will never perish, and no one will snatch them out of my hand. [29] My Father, who has given them to me, is greater than all, and no one is able to snatch them out of the Father's hand. [30] I and the Father are one.*

We see this theme of *calling out* throughout the Old and New Testaments. God, in love and through grace, repeatedly called His people out of the world, as we see in 2 Corinthians 6:17–18: "Therefore go out from their midst, and be separate from them, says the Lord, . . . and I will be a father to you, and you shall be sons and daughters to me, says the Lord Almighty." And consider Paul's exhortation in Romans 12:2: "Do not be conformed to this world, but be transformed by the renewal of your mind."

The call to come out of Babylon is a call to align our identity with the Lamb of God and His kingdom rather than the kingdoms, rulers, or political movements of this world. Are you among those who cannot hear this call, comfortable but hopelessly trapped in Babylon until her judgment? Are you like Lot's wife, who hears the call and takes a few steps out of the city, only to turn around and go back? Or do you have ears to hear the call to come out of Babylon, to pick up your cross daily (Luke 9:23), and to follow the Lamb wherever He goes?

CHAPTER FORTY-ONE

A Day of Mourning

Revelation 18:9–24:

> [9] And the kings of the earth, who committed sexual immorality and lived in luxury with her, will weep and wail over her when they see the smoke of her burning. [10] They will stand far off, in fear of her torment, and say, "Alas! Alas! You great city, you mighty city, Babylon! For in a single hour your judgment has come."
>
> [11] And the merchants of the earth weep and mourn for her, since no one buys their cargo anymore, [12] cargo of gold, silver, jewels, pearls, fine linen, purple cloth, silk, scarlet cloth, all kinds of scented wood, all kinds of articles of ivory, all kinds of articles of costly wood, bronze, iron and marble, [13] cinnamon, spice, incense, myrrh, frankincense, wine, oil, fine flour, wheat, cattle and sheep, horses and chariots, and slaves, that is, human souls.
>
> [14] "The fruit for which your soul longed has gone from you, and all your delicacies and your splendors are lost to you, never to be found again!"
>
> [15] The merchants of these wares, who gained wealth from her, will stand far off, in fear of her torment, weeping and mourning aloud,

> [16] "Alas, alas, for the great city that was clothed in fine linen, in purple and scarlet, adorned with gold, with jewels, and with pearls! [17] For in a single hour all this wealth has been laid waste."
>
> And all shipmasters and seafaring men, sailors and all whose trade is on the sea, stood far off [18] and cried out as they saw the smoke of her burning, "What city was like the great city?"
>
> [19] And they threw dust on their heads as they wept and mourned, crying out, "Alas, alas, for the great city where all who had ships at sea grew rich by her wealth! For in a single hour she has been laid waste. [20] Rejoice over her, O heaven, and you saints and apostles and prophets, for God has given judgment for you against her!"
>
> [21] Then a mighty angel took up a stone like a great millstone and threw it into the sea, saying, "So will Babylon the great city be thrown down with violence, and will be found no more; [22] and the sound of harpists and musicians, of flute players and trumpeters, will be heard in you no more, and a craftsman of any craft will be found in you no more, and the sound of the mill will be heard in you no more, [23] and the light of a lamp will shine in you no more, and the voice of bridegroom and bride will be heard in you no more, for your merchants were the great ones of the earth, and all nations were deceived by your sorcery. [24] And in her was found the blood of prophets and of saints, and of all who have been slain on earth."

Can you think of moments in recent history when it seemed like the world system was on the verge of collapse? Many of us think of 9/11, when the World Trade Center towers fell, or the massive economic collapse of 2008, or the more recent COVID-19 pandemic. Some might even think of the war between Israel and Hamas that began in late 2023. Perhaps you can relate personally to the anxiety, pain, and loss of those events, or at least empathize with those directly impacted.

As devastating as those events were, the world has recovered each time. However, it won't recover after the events described in Revelation 18. This passage is a prophecy about the day the world will mourn the complete catastrophic collapse of every world system that's ever been built by human hands under the control of the father of lies.

WHAT WOULD JOHN'S READERS HAVE NOTICED?

The fall of every empire or major disruption of world order has always resulted in sorrow and chaos for anyone living within that system. The absence of a central authority and shared values disrupts trade and basic services. As anarchy takes hold, the powerful mourn the loss of luxury, but the poor also suffer, as a new wave of tyranny tightens its grip and exploits them for its own gain. This cycle repeats throughout human history—one system falls, another replaces it, and the world moves on. John's readers would have recognized language from two such prophetic iterations of this historic cycle.

Tyre

We see the first failure in the prophesied judgment and economic collapse of Tyre, an ancient port city known for its lucrative trade in luxury items and slaves. This city dominated ancient commerce for generations until its fall to Babylonian conquest in 573 BC.[33] Ezekiel 27:33–34 predicted Tyre's fall twenty years earlier, to encourage God's people that nothing lasts forever: "When your wares came from the seas, you satisfied many peoples; with your abundant wealth and merchandise you enriched the kings of the earth. Now you are wrecked by the seas, in the depths of the waters; your merchandise and all your crew in your midst have sunk with you." Centuries later, John used Ezekiel's language in Revelation to remind his readers that, just like the great city of Tyre, Rome would also one day fall.

Babylon

The second example of an earthly kingdom's failure Revelation borrows from is the prophecy of Babylon's future in Jeremiah 51:63–64:

> "When you finish reading this book, tie a stone to it and cast it into the midst of the Euphrates, and say, 'Thus shall Babylon sink, to rise no more, because of the disaster that I am bringing upon her, and they shall become exhausted.'"

Remember, first-century Jews and Jewish Christians saw Babylon as a metaphor for the Roman Empire of their day, so they would have understood this passage as a prophecy of Rome's fall. But beyond that, they would also have recognized it as a metaphor for all future cycles of judgment and, ultimately, the complete and final judgment of evil.

A Day of Mourning

WHAT WAS JESUS TELLING THE CHURCHES?

This passage is an expanded close-up of the angelic declaration we learned about in Revelation 14:8: "Another angel, a second, followed, saying, 'Fallen, fallen is Babylon the great, she who made all nations drink the wine of the passion of her sexual immorality.'" It reveals the foolishness of people's allegiance to earthly power, even if it benefits them for the time being. It uncovers how the unredeemed will deeply mourn the loss of the luxurious lifestyles they have grown to expect. And in verse 24, we see the horrible cost of this lifestyle in the persecution and murder of the good and the innocent. Even today, we live very luxurious lives at the expense of others. This is the natural goal of every earthly human system: to find the most efficient way to exploit other people and their resources.

Revelation 18 describes how the unredeemed would respond when Rome fell, but also how they will respond to the fall of the entire world system on judgment day. The rich, the powerful, and those fueled by their success will look on in horror as their wealth is obliterated. And as they mourn, they will "stand back," trying to flee from the collateral damage.

Revelation says Babylon will fall "in a single hour," which is a metaphor for how totally unprepared for it the wicked will be. Doomsday prepping isn't new. The wealthy in Rome were notorious for prepping, but none of their efforts mattered. This concept applies to the day of final judgment, but on an even more catastrophic level. Watch how Jesus describes that day in Luke 17:26–30:

> *Just as it was in the days of Noah, so will it be in the days of the Son of Man.* ^{27} *They were eating and drinking and marrying and being given in marriage, until the day when Noah entered the ark, and the flood came and destroyed them all.* ^{28} *Likewise, just as it was in the days of Lot—they were eating and drinking, buying and selling, planting and building,* ^{29} *but on the day when Lot went out from Sodom, fire and sulfur rained from heaven and destroyed them all—* ^{30} *So will it be on the day when the Son of Man is revealed.*

The fallout from the collapses of Tyre, Babylon, and Rome won't compare to the shock and awe of the world's day of final judgment. The wicked will know that everything they lived for, everything they believed in, was meaningless. But sadly, their mourning won't produce repentance. Their sadness and anger at the realization they have lost everything in the blink of an eye will overpower any notion or desire for contrition or repentance.

WHAT IS JESUS TELLING US TODAY?

Unlike previous collapses affecting a city, empire, or financial system, this impending collapse will impact everything. The sad irony is that people try to prepare for that day without really understanding the nature of it. They think they are preparing for an earthly event, but it's not just an earthly catastrophe, it is also a spiritual one. Some stockpile gold, food, and ammunition, but those things will become part of the rubble. Paul's words in 1 Thessalonians 5:3–6 remind us how quickly we will be overwhelmed:

> *While people are saying, "There is peace and security," then sudden destruction will come upon them as labor pains come upon a pregnant woman, and they will not escape. ⁴ But you are not in darkness, brothers, for that day to surprise you like a thief. ⁵ For you are all children of light, children of the day. We are not of the night or of the darkness. ⁶ So then let us not sleep, as others do, but let us keep awake and be sober.*

The warning is clear: those who are caught up in the daily routine of life are completely unaware of the impending judgment. When that day comes, the unredeemed will watch, horrified, as the house of cards Satan has built throughout human history crashes down on top of them. The unredeemed will realize any systems to which they pledged allegiance or hoped in were all deceptions from the dragon.

But as the world they love disintegrates, they will resent that the kingdom of God is the only empire left standing—the one they rejected for the luxuries of this world. Jesus warned His disciples in Matthew 6:19–21 just how dangerous this could be:

> *Do not lay up for yourselves treasures on earth, where moth and rust destroy and where thieves break in and steal, ²⁰ but lay up for yourselves treasures in heaven, where neither moth nor rust destroys and where thieves do not break in and steal. ²¹ **For where your treasure is, there your heart will be also.*** (emphasis mine)

If I visited your home and asked you to show me where you keep your treasure, where would you take me? Would you show me a safe or lead me to your garage or perhaps point out framed pictures? Jesus teaches us that where our treasure is, there our heart will be as well. It's easy to get distracted by treasures in this world that will be among the rubble on the day of the Lord. How often are you seduced to invest in this earthly house of cards at the expense of heavenly treasures?

As those who hear the call and follow the Lamb wherever He goes, we have the advantage of knowing how this will all end. We understand the temporary nature of earthly riches, especially in light of our greater calling—knowing our earthly treasures are not our own but belong to the kingdom of God. Because God has revealed to us the frailty of the world system, we won't be among those who hopelessly mourn its collapse. Instead, we will be among the redeemed in heaven who rejoice in the glory of the kingdom of God.

CHAPTER FORTY-TWO

The Greatest Party Ever

Revelation 19:1–10:

> *[1] After this I heard what seemed to be the loud voice of a great multitude in heaven, crying out, "Hallelujah! Salvation and glory and power belong to our God, [2] for his judgments are true and just; for he has judged the great prostitute who corrupted the earth with her immorality, and has avenged on her the blood of his servants."*
>
> *[3] Once more they cried out, "Hallelujah! The smoke from her goes up forever and ever."*
>
> *[4] And the twenty-four elders and the four living creatures fell down and worshiped God who was seated on the throne, saying, "Amen. Hallelujah!" [5] And from the throne came a voice saying, "Praise our God, all you his servants, you who fear him, small and great."*
>
> *[6] Then I heard what seemed to be the voice of a great multitude, like the roar of many waters and like the sound of mighty peals of thunder, crying out, "Hallelujah! For the Lord our God the Almighty reigns. [7] Let us rejoice and exult and give him the glory, for the marriage of the Lamb has come, and his Bride has made herself ready; [8] it was granted her to clothe herself with fine linen, bright and*

> pure"—for the fine linen is the righteous deeds of the saints.
>
> ⁹ And the angel said to me, "Write this: Blessed are those who are invited to the marriage supper of the Lamb." And he said to me, "These are the true words of God." ¹⁰ Then I fell down at his feet to worship him, but he said to me, "You must not do that! I am a fellow servant with you and your brothers who hold to the testimony of Jesus. Worship God." For the testimony of Jesus is the spirit of prophecy.

Have you ever been invited to a party or event so special to the host that you felt honored just to be included on the guest list? Or maybe you were excited for a wedding celebration of a close friend or family member. You just knew it was going to be such a great day that you started preparing months in advance. And your preparation wasn't just about you. It was also to honor the person who loved you enough to invite you. This is how I felt studying this next passage from Revelation, about a glorious feast promised for the redeemed when Jesus returns—I not only want to be prepared for the honor of being there, but I also want to be prepared to honor the Lord and the occasion.

What Would John's Readers Have Noticed?

The Feast Circuit

In the first century, the "feast circuit" embodied the supreme trifecta of religious, personal, and business social life.

Feasts were held for a variety of reasons, including celebrations of high holy days or personal milestones or successes, but none were as grand as a marriage feast. The hosts of a marriage feast could easily expect hundreds or, in some cases, thousands of people to attend. They weren't just for one evening or even one full day. They could last several days and up to an entire week.

Feast competition was fierce! Each host wanted to ensure their feast was the biggest, longest, and most lavish. The more influential the host, the more prestigious the guests and the grander the feast. It was essential to include prominent, well-known individuals on the guest list, particularly in Jewish society, where political leaders and respected religious figures were highly sought-after.

For a marriage feast, the invitations would have been very formal and expensive, hand-delivered by the household's most trusted servants. Because these events were typically planned more than a year in advance, excuses for not attending were hard to come by. Guests were carefully selected, so the RSVP rate would be virtually one hundred percent! After all, if you invite dignitaries and nobody shows up, it would be extremely embarrassing for the hosts. Because of this, individuals in lower classes would never think of declining an invitation to a higher-class feast. It would be the end of any aspirations of upward mobility in society.

John's readers would have been very familiar with the feast circuit. They would have linked this foundational cultural custom to the metaphor of the marriage supper of the Lamb in this passage.

WHAT WAS JESUS TELLING THE CHURCHES?

We have learned that Revelation gives two descriptions of the church: the church in battle and the church in victory. The church in battle consists of every living believer at any given time on earth fighting against evil and carrying out the Great Commission. At this moment in redemptive history, it's our turn to be the church in battle. The church in victory, on the other hand, includes all the saints who have died in Jesus or who have been martyred. It includes our brothers and sisters who have gone before us and are excitedly waiting in the presence of God for the moment Jesus returns for the rest of us.

In this passage, there is no more church in battle! Babylon has fallen, the wicked have been judged, and the earth has been cleansed and prepared for its King. All saints throughout redemptive history are together in total victory. This great multitude from every tribe and nation erupts with praise and joy! It's the big payoff for all the redeemed who've been waiting for our vindication—and our greatest moment of gratitude and affection for our Jesus.

The reality of the scope of our victory will only be beginning to dawn on us as we gather around Jesus. We will be preparing to enter the King's banquet hall for our combined wedding and victory feast. The beautiful theology of that marriage feast and how the guest list was filled was taught to us by our Jesus himself. Every detail is important, powerful, and beautiful.

Below, I have written a harmony of this parable from Matthew 22:2–10 (underlined) and Luke 14:16–24. Take note of the words I've bolded for emphasis.

<u>"The kingdom of heaven may be compared to **a king** who gave a wedding feast for his son.</u> And at the time for the banquet he sent his servant to say to those who had been invited, 'Come, for everything is now ready.' But they all alike began to make excuses. The first said to him, 'I have bought a field, and I must go out and see it. Please have me excused.' And another said, 'I have bought five yoke of oxen, and I go to examine them. Please have me excused.' And another said, 'I have married a wife, and therefore I cannot come.' So the servant came and reported these things to his master.

<u>"Again he sent other servants, saying, 'Tell those who are invited, "See, I have prepared my dinner, my oxen and my fat calves have been slaughtered, and everything is ready. Come to the wedding feast."' But they paid no attention and went off, one to his farm, another to his business, while the rest seized his servants, **treated them shamefully**, and killed them. The king was angry, and he sent his troops and destroyed those murderers and burned their city.</u>

"Then the master of the house became angry and said to his servant, <u>'The wedding feast is ready, but those invited were not worthy.</u> Go out quickly to the streets and lanes of the city, and **bring in** <u>to the wedding feast as many as you find.' And those servants went out into the roads and gathered all whom they found, both bad and good</u>—the poor and crippled and blind and lame. And the servant said, 'Sir, what you commanded has been done, and still there is room.' And the master said to the servant, 'Go out to the highways and hedges and **compel** people to come in, that my house may be filled. For I tell you, none of those men who were invited shall taste my banquet.' <u>So the wedding hall was filled with guests."</u>

Not only did the invited guests insult the King by refusing His invitation, but they also beat and mocked the King's servants who tried to deliver the invitation. They preferred their own lives and their own plans over accepting the invitation to the greatest wedding celebration ever. When the feast day comes, and smoke is still rising from the rubble that's left of their world, they will realize what a mistake refusing that invitation was. They will mourn and be filled with rage, but not for themselves. They will be angry with the host for holding them accountable for their decision to refuse His invitation.

The second list of guests—the poor, lame, persecuted, and rejected—have no stature to merit such an invitation. Yet even though they know they're unworthy, the King orders His servants to "compel them." The Greek word there is ἀναγκάζω, a verb with the phonetic spelling *an-ang-kad'-zo*. It means "to use forcefulness."[34]

The writer of Revelation records Jesus' words in John 6:37–39, reminding us that this invitation is one in which we should rejoice: "All that the Father gives me will come to me, and whoever comes to me I will never cast out. For I have come down from heaven, not to do my own will but the will of him who sent me. And this is the will of him who sent me, that I should lose nothing of all that he has given me, but raise it up on the last day." The King has invited us, so we shouldn't be afraid to attend!

WHAT IS JESUS TELLING US TODAY?

The unredeemed are too obsessed with this life to imagine the joy we the redeemed will experience on the day of our celebration feast with Jesus. They have no concept of the great and mighty works Jesus has done, so why would they want to celebrate them? This is why the world is unimpressed by an invitation to the Lord's Table.

But, as the church, we don't have to wait until that day to celebrate perfect justice and our marriage to Jesus. We have been invited, even compelled, to attend. Since the day we accepted that invitation, our lives on earth have become all about our preparation for that celebration. By faith, we are called, inspired, and motivated to practice and prepare ahead of time for that great, festive gathering. That's one of the reasons we gather on Sundays. It's why worshipping together as a church should be one of our highest priorities.

From the moment we were compelled to accept the invitation, our lives became a pre-party preparation for the feast to be held on the day Jesus is united with His church forever. Paul offered this encouragement in Philippians 1:6–7:

> "And I am sure of this, that he who began a good work in you will bring it to completion at the day of Jesus Christ. It is right for me to feel this way about you all, because I hold you in my heart, for you are all partakers with me of grace."

But our preparation isn't just for the celebration on that day; it's also a celebration of what Jesus is doing right now!

He is calling, saving, and transforming us, and then sending us out, as His trusted servants, to invite others to join in on our preparation for the feast. His church is not perfect, yet we celebrate as if she is. We trust our Jesus to fulfill His promises and complete His work in us.

Sometimes that transformation is evident, sometimes not so much. But it's happening and will continue to do so until the day of the wedding feast! We get a great illustration of what this celebration will be like in Isaiah 25:6: "On this mountain the LORD of hosts will make for all peoples a feast of rich food, a feast of well-aged wine, of rich food full of marrow."

Trust me, Jesus knows how to throw a party. It will be way better than any party Babylon could ever throw. For one thing, think about how every wedding or fancy party seems to have appetizer trays. They're so much fun! Something about miniature beef sliders and bacon-wrapped shrimp makes jokes funnier and conversations better. If you think about it, when we celebrate the Lord's Table while gathering for worship and feast practice, it's sort of like an appetizer for that great marriage feast we'll celebrate one day with our King. That's why Paul taught us to hold those moments precious in 1 Corinthians 11:23–26:

> *For I received from the Lord what I also delivered to you, that the Lord Jesus on the night when he was betrayed took bread, 24 and when he had given thanks, he broke it, and said, "This is my body, which is for you. Do this in remembrance of me." 25 In the same way also he took the cup, after supper, saying, "This cup is the new covenant in my blood. Do this, as often as you drink it, in remembrance of me."*

²⁶ For as often as you eat this bread and drink the cup, you proclaim the Lord's death until he comes.

CHAPTER FORTY-THREE

The Power of His Word

Revelation 19:11–21:

¹¹ Then I saw heaven opened, and behold, a white horse! The one sitting on it is called Faithful and True, and in righteousness he judges and makes war. ¹² His eyes are like a flame of fire, and on his head are many diadems, and he has a name written that no one knows but himself. ¹³ He is clothed in a robe dipped in blood, and the name by which he is called is The Word of God. ¹⁴ And the armies of heaven, arrayed in fine linen, white and pure, were following him on white horses. ¹⁵ From his mouth comes a sharp sword with which to strike down the nations, and he will rule them with a rod of iron. He will tread the winepress of the fury of the wrath of God the Almighty. ¹⁶ On his robe and on his thigh he has a name written, King of kings and Lord of lords.

¹⁷ Then I saw an angel standing in the sun, and with a loud voice he called to all the birds that fly directly overhead, "Come, gather for the great supper of God, ¹⁸ to eat the flesh of kings, the flesh of captains, the flesh of mighty men, the flesh of horses and their riders, and the flesh of all men, both free and slave, both small and great." ¹⁹ And I saw the beast and the kings of the earth with their armies gathered to make war against him who was sitting on the horse and

> against his army. ²⁰ And the beast was captured, and with it the false prophet who in its presence had done the signs by which he deceived those who had received the mark of the beast and those who worshiped its image. These two were thrown alive into the lake of fire that burns with sulfur. ²¹ And the rest were slain by the sword that came from the mouth of him who was sitting on the horse, and all the birds were gorged with their flesh.

As a follower of Jesus, would you say you believe in the power of God's word? If so, why do you believe in it? You likely have some theoretical knowledge of its power, but maybe you haven't embraced it in practical ways. If our primary desire is to be faithful followers of Jesus, we must understand this power. This next passage in Revelation offers compelling insights and inspiration which will help you visualize the full power of God's word.

WHAT WOULD JOHN'S READERS HAVE NOTICED?

Battlefield Metaphors

Why did Jesus give John this vision? After all, it may seem like unnecessarily gory battlefield imagery, but John's readers would have known right away these weren't random violent images used for dramatic effect. They would have connected this passage with two Old Testament prophecies describing the return of Jesus.

The Blood-Splattered Warrior

The first is a metaphor of a conquering king with clothes stained with blood from his fallen enemies, similar to what we see in Isaiah 63:1–4:

> *Who is this who comes from Edom, in crimsoned garments from Bozrah, he who is splendid in his apparel, marching in the greatness of his strength? "It is I, speaking in righteousness, mighty to save." ² Why is your apparel red, and your garments like his who treads in the winepress? ³ "I have trodden the winepress alone, . . . their lifeblood spattered on my garments and stained all my apparel. ⁴ For the day of vengeance was in my heart, and my year of redemption had come."*

This is an ancient metaphor of a conquering warrior coming off a battlefield immediately after he has decimated his foes. The evidence of the massive victory is all over him—the blood of his enemies is splattered all over his warrior garb. But this is not about the blood; it's about whose blood has been shed and just how one-sided the battle was. It is metaphor for a complete, total rout.

The Scavenger Birds

The second prophetic image is the scavenger birds feasting on the remains of God's enemies. We see a similar graphic depiction in Jeremiah 12:9: "Is my heritage to me like a hyena's lair? Are the birds of prey against her all around? Go, assemble all the wild beasts; bring them to devour."

In the aftermath of an ancient battle, there was always the problem of what to do with the bodies of the conquered. A common practice was to use this opportunity to send a message to other potential enemies by leaving the bodies of the slain on the battlefield to rot. The stench would attract scavengers of all kinds, including hyenas, which would drag carcasses back to their den.

John's readers would have seen the connection to both of these Old Testament prophecies as a future promise of what will happen to the wicked.

What Was Jesus Telling the Churches?

We have previously established that the correct way to read Revelation is as a depiction of various events from multiple viewpoints, sort of like providing us with different camera angles. For example, we saw Armageddon in Revelation 16:12–21 and, before that, in 14:14–20, with the harvesting of the earth and the treading of the winepress. Here, again, we encounter it from a new perspective. Don't be distracted by the gory details. This is a metaphor for the power of our King and how all He needs to destroy His enemies is His word!

Heaven opens and King Jesus appears in all His glory, riding a white horse. We, too, are dressed in white and riding horses of our own. We follow Jesus as He leads us into battle against the ultimate collection of Satan's forces.

But Jesus doesn't even let evil fire a shot! He captures the two beasts, ordering them by His word into the lake of fire.

The Old Testament foreshadows this over-before-it-even-begins type of showdown in the story of David's victory over the Philistine champion Goliath, won with a single slingshot rock to the forehead. John links three passages from the Old and New Testaments to explain what happens here. Revelation 19:13 tells us "the name by which [Jesus] is called is The Word of God," which refers to the more familiar John 1:1–3: "In the beginning was the Word, and the Word was with God, and the Word was God. He was in the beginning with God. All things were made through him, and without him was not any thing made that was made." We can see how both references to Jesus as the Word of God are foreshadowed from the very beginning by Genesis 1:3: "And God said, 'Let there be light,' and there was light." The weapon the wicked will fear the most isn't some tactical nuke or a predator drone. On that day, they'll fear the Word of God!

Once the beasts are banished, Christ rides through what's left of the forces of darkness, slicing through them like a hot knife through butter with the sword of His mouth. By the power of His word, Jesus created the heavens and the earth, and here, He defeats evil with that same power. Then, before the forces of evil can even fathom what has hit them, the battle is done, and we follow Him through the carnage of the wicked, straight to the entrance into His house, through the door of the banquet hall for the victory celebration.

WHAT IS JESUS TELLING US TODAY?

With just His word, Jesus has authority and power over the forces of evil, and in fact, evil fears His word. We have seen Jesus do this kind of thing before. In Luke 8:31–33, we read of a man who was possessed by a legion of demons, and Jesus ordered those demons out of the man with just His word. The demons pleaded with Jesus not to send them to the abyss, declaring that it was not yet the day of their judgment:

> And they begged him not to command them to depart into the abyss. ³² Now a large herd of pigs was feeding there on the hillside, and they begged him to let them enter these. So he gave them permission. ³³ Then the demons came out of the man and entered the pigs, and the herd rushed down the steep bank into the lake and drowned.

But on the last day, there will be no herd of pigs, no negotiation, no begging, and no mercy for the forces of evil. Judgment day for the powers of darkness will arrive, and the battles lines will be drawn between Jesus' troops (including us) and all of Satan's armies. There we will be on our white horses, in our white robes, following Jesus wherever He goes, while opposite us, the beasts will lead their soldiers of darkness, confidently mocking us, much like Goliath mocked David: "Look at you pathetic sheep on your pretty white horses in your clean white robes, following the Lamb of God!"

Isaiah's prophecy in Isaiah 54:17 puts the enemy's claim to shame: "No weapon that is fashioned against you shall succeed, and you shall refute every tongue that rises against you in judgment. This is the heritage of the servants of the LORD and their vindication from me, declares the LORD."

Before evil can launch a missile or fire a bullet, our Jesus says, "Not today, Satan. In fact, never again!" Jesus accomplishes with the power of His word what no human politician, weapon, or world system could ever achieve. He captures and orders Satan's two beasts, his generals, into the lake of fire, leaving the wicked army without leadership. With just the power of His word, He wipes them out, leaving them to rot where they fall.

Then, in the afterglow of that great victory, we will join together in a chorus of our own powerful words, proclaiming the great and marvelous works of our King: "Our victory has come, and it came with just a word! The same Word that saved us from our sins!" Hebrews 11:1 encourages us by saying, "Now faith is the assurance of things hoped for, the conviction of things not seen." Add that comfort to what John affirmed in 1 John 5:4–5: "For everyone who has been born of God overcomes the world. And this is the victory that has overcome the world—our faith. Who is it that overcomes the world except the one who believes that Jesus is the Son of God?"

It's easy to worry about and obsess over earthly power, but we don't need to. The only power that will one day set this world right is the power of God's word. Therefore, as followers of Jesus, our primary focus is on the kingdom of God, not trying to fix or control the kingdoms of men. When Jesus returns, His word will preserve His redeemed and instantly destroy everything evil has built. Until then, that very same Word will be our shield, our confidence, and our inspiration to follow Him wherever He goes.

CHAPTER FORTY-FOUR

Authority in the Millennium

Revelation 20:1–6:

> [1] Then I saw an angel coming down from heaven, holding in his hand the key to the bottomless pit and a great chain. [2] And he seized the dragon, that ancient serpent, who is the devil and Satan, and bound him for a thousand years, [3] and threw him into the pit, and shut it and sealed it over him, so that he might not deceive the nations any longer, until the thousand years were ended. After that he must be released for a little while.
>
> [4] Then I saw thrones, and seated on them were those to whom the authority to judge was committed. Also I saw the souls of those who had been beheaded for the testimony of Jesus and for the word of God, and those who had not worshiped the beast or its image and had not received its mark on their foreheads or their hands. They came to life and reigned with Christ for a thousand years. [5] The rest of the dead did not come to life until the thousand years were ended. This is the first resurrection. [6] Blessed and holy is the one who shares in the first resurrection! Over such the second death has no power, but they will be priests of God and of Christ, and they will reign with him for a thousand years.

Have you ever been in a situation where you felt powerless? You just knew things were going to end badly, but you couldn't do anything about it? Well, Revelation teaches us that's exactly how Satan feels about God's kingdom. Even with all his power and rage, he is watching the kingdom of God advance. He fumes as the church (whom he hates) uses the authority of Jesus to proclaim the gospel to all the nations.

The thousand-year kingdom of God is an idea not found anywhere in Scripture except Revelation. That means we cannot use our established methods of interpreting its meaning by going to the Old Testament or even parallel passages in the New Testament. There are four main interpretations of this kingdom, which have led to significant division and conflict within the church. That's unacceptable. This passage, like the rest of Revelation, is supposed to be a blessing, providing both joy and unity among us.

WHAT WOULD JOHN'S READERS HAVE NOTICED?

A Thousand Years

Revelation's visions are not chronological prophecies outlining the sequence of specific future events. Instead, they repeat the same events again and again from alternative points of view. So far, we have seen six distinct cycles, each offering different perspectives and descriptions of judgment, including the final battle with evil called Armageddon (described in Revelation 6:12–17; 8:5; 9:1–11; 11:19; 16:18; and 19:11–21). Each one of these cycles provides a unique camera angle on everything happening throughout the church age. That means Revelation 20 is not to be interpreted as chronologically following Revelation 19. Instead, Revelation 20 begins the seventh and final cycle of visions. It zooms out to give us a view of the entire age, from Christ on earth, to His second coming, to our eternal state, and everything in between—past, present, and future.

The Millennial Kingdom

Ancient poetic and apocalyptic literature, especially Jewish apocalyptic literature, regularly used measures of time as symbolic metaphors. For instance, "an hour" or "a day" could stand for an individual's lifespan. Old Testament prophets used weeks, months, and years to represent much longer periods of time, like in the case of Daniel's "seventy weeks" (Daniel 9). This literary practice appears throughout Revelation, such as when we read about kings given power "for one hour" (Revelation 17:12)—meaning until they died.

John does the same thing, using months and years to describe the tribulation. Remember how, in the opening chapter, John reminded his readers they were all partners in this tribulation, which they were already experiencing at the time he wrote Revelation. His use of the number 1,000 follows the same poetic rhythm we have seen in other time metaphors found in Revelation. Throughout history, empires—both ancient and modern—have shared a common aspiration: to be a "millennial kingdom." This phrase represents the goal of any earthly empire rather than its literal lifespan—its desire to establish a legacy of authority and rule that can be passed down to future generations.

After the Babylonian captivity, the Jews hoped for an earthly return to the kind of millennial kingdom they'd experienced under David or Solomon. Early Christians reading this passage would have regarded the millennium as a portrayal of the entire church age, or the entire kingdom of God that Jesus clearly taught had started with Him (in Matthew 4:17; 5:3; 10:7; Mark 1:15; and Luke 17:20–21, among other places). They understood the primary purpose of this number to be a description of the endurance of the kingdom of God as prophesied: where Jesus is Lord, ruling along with His redeemed, who are called "more than conquerors" in this sinful world (Romans 8:37).

WHAT WAS JESUS TELLING THE CHURCHES?

John's vision has three crucial theological elements with profound impact on the age we are living in today: (1) Satan bound, (2) the nations allowed to come to Christ, and (3) the saints given new life to reign with Jesus in His kingdom.

As he did with Job, Satan would often accuse the redeemed before God, but now God will no longer tolerate Satan's nonsense. In Revelation 12, heaven rejoices that Satan has been expelled, unable to levy his lies or accusations against followers of Jesus anymore.

Revelation 20 gives us another camera angle on that event—an angel from heaven, bearing a chain and a key, seizes Satan and binds him. John's readers understood from apostolic teaching in several places that this wasn't a future event but one that had already happened, as we read in Jude 1:6: "And the angels who did not stay within their own position of authority, but left their proper dwelling, he has kept in eternal chains under gloomy darkness until the judgment of the great day."

It's a significant spiritual moment that likely happened during, or just prior to, Jesus' earthly life. But why is Satan bound? So he can no longer deceive the redeemed who are still living among the nations, just as Jesus taught in His parable of the wheat growing among the weeds. After John's account of this binding, he described the slain redeemed who have authority as reigning together with Christ. They are given life; the kingdom has come!

John called this the "first resurrection," which Jesus talked about when He said in John 5:25, "Truly, truly, I say to you, an hour is coming, *and is now here*, when the dead will hear the voice of the Son of God, and those who hear will live" (emphasis mine). In verses 28 and 29, Jesus went on to contrast that first resurrection with another one:

> "Do not marvel at this [that the hour is now here when the dead come to life], for an hour is coming when all who are in the tombs will hear his voice [29] and come out, those who

> have done good to the resurrection of life, and those who have done evil to the resurrection of judgment."

These verses refer to the "second resurrection." This two-resurrection theology appears throughout the New Testament, but my favorite occurrence is in Ephesians 2:1–2 and 2:4–5:

> *You were dead in the trespasses and sins* ² *in which you once walked, following the course of this world, following the prince of the power of the air, the spirit that is now at work in the sons of disobedience.... * ⁴ *But God, being rich in mercy, because of the great love with which he loved us,* ⁵ *even when we were dead in our trespasses, made us alive together with Christ—by grace you have been saved.*

The redeemed are given life both in heaven (those who have died) and on earth (those who are given power by the Holy Spirit to resist the beast's deception). The two resurrections encompass both the church in victory in heaven and the church in battle here on earth. Both groups have been made alive to reign with Christ in both places, as Jesus uncoincidentally taught us to pray in Matthew 6:10: "Your kingdom come, your will be done, on earth *as it is* in heaven" (emphasis mine). The Greek καί used here is a primary particle of cumulative force for an action or being—*also, even so, and also,* etc.[35] In English, we might use a forceful cumulative participle like this: "I ran through the house and even into the street." In Matthew, we use it to pray for God's kingdom to come on earth *as well as* in heaven!

We also know Jesus taught that His kingdom had already come, that its power was a reality for His disciples *and* for us today, as He indicated in Luke 17:20–21 when He said, "The kingdom of God is not coming in ways that can be observed, nor will they say, 'Look, here it is!' or 'There!' for behold, the kingdom of God is in the midst of you."

John's readers also understood the apostolic teaching about the spiritual authority given to the church in this world. The first manifestation of this authority was when Jesus sent out His apostles, first by pairs and then as a large group, as recorded in Luke 10:17–20:

> *The seventy-two returned with joy, saying, "Lord, even the demons are subject to us in your name!"* [18] *And he said to them, "**I saw Satan fall like lightning from heaven**.* [19] *Behold, I have given you authority to tread on serpents and scorpions, and over all the power of the enemy, and nothing shall hurt you.* [20] *Nevertheless, do not rejoice in this, that the spirits are subject to you, but rejoice that your names are written in heaven."*

It's true, Satan can still lash out and cause pain and suffering in this life. That's the tribulation John says we are all partners in. Jesus, meanwhile, patiently waits for His wheat to grow among the weeds until all His elect are gathered. And until this age ends, Satan remains bound, powerless to stop the redemption of God's elect and the advancement of His Kingdom! After Jesus has gathered all His redeemed and His church is complete, Satan will be released for "a little while" to gather what's left of the inhabitants of earth—the weeds—

for that final battle. Spoiler alert: we already know how that goes.

WHAT IS JESUS TELLING US TODAY?

John's readers understood that this millennial kingdom authority wasn't something in the distant future. It was reality for them, just as it is for us now! At first glance, the world might see our claim as arrogant—that Christians hold the spiritual authority in this world. But as followers of Jesus, we know we haven't *earned* the right to this authority. We *received* it through an act of God's unstoppable grace. The fact that God delegates the authority of proclaiming the gospel and the kingdom of God to sinners like us is incredibly humbling. But He didn't send us unprotected into the dragon's lair. First, He prepared the way by binding the enemy. Consider Mark 3:27: "But no one can enter a strong man's house and plunder his goods, unless he first binds the strong man. Then indeed he may plunder his house." Jesus' words assure us that God has bound Satan, clearing the way for us to go out into this world and harvest the souls Satan wants for himself. But God, through His Spirit, has already claimed and marked His chosen for salvation!

In John 10:29–30, Jesus reminded us of the church's security: "My Father, who has given them to me, is greater than all, and no one is able to snatch them out of the Father's hand. I and the Father are one." While Satan is bound, leaving the church free to go throughout the world with the spiritual power and authority of the gospel, the kingdom of God expands. Satan is left with one option: to inflict as much earthly suffering and persecution on the redeemed as he can. Again, this is the tribulation John spoke of, in which all of God's redeemed—past, present, and future—are participants.

It's why Jesus said we should not be surprised when we face tribulation in this world. It's why John said in Revelation 1:9 that we are all partners in the kingdom of God, but we're also partners together in the tribulation. Jesus assured us of our security in His presence in Matthew 28:18–20 when He said,

> "All authority in heaven and on earth has been given to me. [19] Go therefore and make disciples of all nations, baptizing them in the name of the Father and of the Son and of the Holy Spirit, [20] teaching them to observe all that I have commanded you. And behold, I am with you always, to the end of the age."

Through the power and authority of the gospel, we get to participate with God's Spirit as He speaks to His chosen people. Through the power and authority of the gospel, we get to proclaim hope and salvation—but also judgment.

For those without ears to hear, the gospel will seem foolish. Sadly, for them, it proclaims judgment. But for those who have been given ears to hear, the gospel we proclaim is the power of God for their salvation, new life, and resurrection! As we take the gospel to every tribe and nation, the forces of darkness are powerless to stop it. God's Word will never return empty (Isaiah 55:11)—it always accomplishes its purpose. That's why we can have the bold confidence to remain faithful and follow the Lamb wherever He goes, even in this life full of tribulation.

CHAPTER FORTY-FIVE

Gathering with Gog and Magog

Revelation 20:5–10:

> [5] The rest of the dead did not come to life until the thousand years were ended. This is the first resurrection. [6] Blessed and holy is the one who shares in the first resurrection! Over such the second death has no power, but they will be priests of God and of Christ, and they will reign with him for a thousand years.
>
> [7] And when the thousand years are ended, Satan will be released from his prison [8] and will come out to deceive the nations that are at the four corners of the earth, Gog and Magog, to gather them for battle; their number is like the sand of the sea. [9] And they marched up over the broad plain of the earth and surrounded the camp of the saints and the beloved city, but fire came down from heaven and consumed them, [10] and the devil who had deceived them was thrown into the lake of fire and sulfur where the beast and the false prophet were, and they will be tormented day and night forever and ever.

As a Christian, are you ever pulled in two directions, drawn to the promises of this world, even though you cherish the precious promises of Jesus? I know I struggle with this.

But the world's promises always come with a caveat. They cause us to stray and separate us from God's people. It seems the world constantly beckons us, just as Satan beckoned our Jesus in the wilderness (Matthew 4).

No wonder believers get scared they might be missing out on the things of this world and are tempted to drift away from the church. Sometimes we even try to split the difference. Can we really have the best of both worlds? Well, personal experience informs me that time-splitting between the promises of this world and the promises of God has never worked, and it won't end well in the future, either.

WHAT WOULD JOHN'S READERS HAVE NOTICED?

Who Are Gog and Magog?

Once again, Revelation's cyclical nature offers another fresh perspective, another camera angle on the battle of Armageddon. John has a vision of Satan gathering nations from the four corners of the earth, referring to them as Gog and Magog. Both names are a contentious topic. Who are they? Perhaps code names for nations on today's map?

As with the rest of the symbolism in Revelation, proper interpretation requires a first-century Jewish Christian point of view. Gog and Magog pointed John's readers back to a fascinating journey through the Old Testament, revealing Gog and Magog to be descendants of Noah and Jacob.

Gog of the Land of Magog

Our first stop is Ezekiel 38:1–4, written four years after Babylon had captured Israel:

> *The word of the LORD came to me: ² "Son of man, set your face toward Gog, of the land of Magog, . . . and prophesy against him ³ and say, Thus says the Lord GOD: Behold, I am against you, O Gog, chief prince of Meshech and Tubal. ⁴ And I will turn you about and put hooks into your jaws."*

In this prophesy, Gog of the land of Magog brings his armies against God's people and is destroyed. There's no historic record of a battle between Israel and Gog, so we know Ezekiel's prophesy is referring to a future battle to come.

Jacob's Descendants

Our next stop is in 1 Chronicles 5:4: "The sons of Joel: Shemaiah his son, Gog his son . . ." Gog was a son of Joel, a descendant of Reuben, who was one of Jacob's twelve sons. When Israel was conquering the promised land of Canaan, the tribe of Reuben settled in the first fertile-looking spot, separating from most of their family and settling east of the Jordan to get rich raising cattle. They became powerful and wealthy as part of the northern kingdom of Israel, but Reuben's descendants drifted from their spiritual heritage, integrating with the world around them. Ezekiel's prophecy is about the destruction of Reuben's descendants when they come against Israel. It's a sad story.

Noah's Descendants

Next, let's look at Genesis 10, known as "the Table of Nations." It's an outline of the origin of all nations of the world as they descend from Noah's sons. Of the three sons—Shem, Ham, and Japheth—Shem was the middle born, but he was chosen by God as the firstborn, marked as the line of Jesus through Jacob (Israel). Ham, who was cursed because of some serious Jerry Springer-level family dysfunction, settled to the south, becoming the father of the people of Egypt and Cush.

Japheth, Noah's firstborn, no doubt felt slighted that his birthright as the firstborn was given to Shem. Why would he want to play second fiddle? So, he took his family and settled to the east of the Jordan River, becoming isolated from Shem's descendants. He left his family to establish his own legacy, his own nation, and his own kingdom on his own terms. In Genesis 10:2, we see that three of his sons were Magog, Meshech, and Tubal—the lands mentioned in connection with Gog in Ezekiel 38. And that's not all: in Ezekiel 38:5–6, we see a horde of other nations gathered with Gog, including Gomer, Cush, and Put—more tribes descended from Japheth and his brother Ham. The full list of nations mentioned in verses 1 through 6 surrounded Israel on every side.

Tucked away in Genesis 10 is a fascinating connection: one of Ham's descendants was a mighty warrior named Nimrod with even mightier ambitions. He wanted to rule the world! Nimrod's legacy became the empires of what we now call Sumeria (referred to as "the land of Shinar" in Genesis 10:10 and 11:2) and Assyria (Genesis 10:11). After Nimrod's descendants became great nations, they gathered together to immortalize their legacy by building the Tower of Babel (which, you'll remember from chapter 37, became Babylon). They didn't know it, but they were doing Satan's bidding, building an evil counterfeit of the kingdom of God. God intervened, confusing their language and dispersing them.

Clearly, the descendants of Japheth and the descendants of Ham had something in common—they eventually became enemies to God's people.

What Was Jesus Telling the Churches?

Do you follow how the names Gog and Magog would have taken John's first-century Jewish Christian readers back to the Old Testament—to their long history of being besieged by the surrounding nations, who had a habit of gathering and plotting together against God and His people? All of human history is the story of this conflict between two competing kingdoms: Gog and Magog versus God. This desire to gather nations against God has been the desire of every empire, as seen in Psalm 2:1–4:

> *Why do the nations rage and the peoples plot in vain?* ² *The kings of the earth set themselves, and the rulers take counsel together, against the* LORD *and against his Anointed, saying,* ³ *"Let us burst their bonds apart and cast away their cords from us."* ⁴ *He who sits in the heavens laughs; the Lord holds them in derision.*

By the time of John, the phrase "Gog, from Magog" in Ezekiel 38 had changed to "Gog and Magog." It became a popular expression referring to the nations of the earth who allied themselves against God's people. These kingdoms had spread throughout the earth, building their legacy. The first to accomplish this goal was the Babylonian Empire, which forced Israel into exile and captivity. It's why Babylon was shorthand for such a traumatic era in Hebrew history and why, in Revelation, it's a metaphor for every earthly empire, including Rome. But note this—the Babylonians, like all the other nations, were descendants of Noah. They should have known of God's saving grace during the flood!

John wrote in verse 8 that "their number is like the sand of the sea." Does this sound familiar? It should. It's a sad prophecy about the many people who will come against God's kingdom and face God's judgment, which we've seen repeated throughout Revelation. These are those of whom the Lord said, in Ezekiel 38:15–16:

> *"You will come, . . . you and many peoples with you, . . . a great host, a mighty army.* ¹⁶ *You will come up against my people Israel, like a cloud covering the land. In the latter days I will bring you against my land, that the nations may know me, when through you, O Gog, I vindicate my holiness before their eyes."*

Sadly, even though these surrounding nations once came from a godly heritage, they became part of the kingdoms controlled by Satan.

Meanwhile, God had his own plan for the legacy of His kingdom. He was protecting and preserving His remnant—especially one family that would become the line of Jesus, our Messiah and deliverer. This is the story of Seth, Shem, Jacob, Joseph, and David—the tribe of Judah, all preserved, while Gog and Magog raged against them.

But when Jesus came, He reversed the power structure! Satan and his kingdoms are now bound, and the kingdom of God has taken over. From that moment, Gog and Magog became part of this pathetic cycle of one nation swapping power and authority with another. Meanwhile, God unleashes the spiritual power and authority of His kingdom, using the gospel to liberate His elect from the clutches and control of Gog and Magog.

After the church age, when God is done building His Kingdom, Satan will be released for a very short time to gather what's left of his, for that final battle called Armageddon. He'll try one last time what he tried with Babylon, Persia, Greece, Rome, and every other gathering of earthly nations in human history—to replace God's Kingdom with his own. But this last and final gathering of the forces of evil will also be Satan's most pathetic failure. It will be over in an instant, gone, poof! The Lamb of God will ride through them, slaying them all with just the sword of His Word!

So, why doesn't God just rescue His people now? Why go through all this trouble? We already have the answer in 2 Peter 3:9: "The Lord is not slow to fulfill his promise . . . but is patient toward you, not wishing that any should perish, but that all should reach repentance." His delay is because of His love for all of us. He displays patience until all His elect hear His call to come out of the nations.

WHAT IS JESUS TELLING US TODAY?

Gog and Magog aren't nations on a map. They represent the spiritual condition of the kingdoms of this world, which the beast controls. They are a symbol for all who love the kingdoms of this world more than the kingdom of God. Although the citizens of God's kingdom might live within the earthly kingdoms of Gog and Magog, we don't seek dual citizenship. Followers of Jesus make the kingdom of God our first love. As Jesus reminds His followers in John 15:19, "you are not of the world, but I chose you out of the world, therefore the world hates you." But recall what He said to the church in Ephesus in Revelation 2:4: "You have abandoned the love you had at first."

If our loyalty to or our hope in any earthly nation is stronger than our loyalty to or our hope in the kingdom of God, we cannot truly claim to follow the Lamb wherever He goes. God has shown loving patience by delivering us from the world. We should remember Jesus' admonition in John 13:34–35:

> *"A new commandment I give to you, that you love one another: just as I have loved you, you also are to love one another. ³⁵ By this all people will know that you are my disciples, if you have love for one another."*

Followers of Jesus can't be deceived by the promises of darkness. We know His promises are far better! This doesn't mean we live as arrogant religious zealots or isolationists, cut off from the nations. After all, the only reason we are among the redeemed is because God patiently waited for us to hear the gospel. Also, Jesus has commanded us, in Matthew 28:19, "Go therefore and make disciples of all nations, baptizing them in the name of the Father and of the Son and of the Holy Spirit."

We the church don't gather for any kingdom of this world. We gather for a far greater legacy, the kingdom of God. This is why followers of Jesus will never feel at home or be satisfied in any political party or earthly kingdom. We know that their promise of prosperity and legacy is empty. Instead, we will always choose to gather with our King and His people.

CHAPTER FORTY-SIX

The Great White Throne

Revelation 20:11–15:

> [11] Then I saw a great white throne and him who was seated on it. From his presence earth and sky fled away, and no place was found for them. [12] And I saw the dead, great and small, standing before the throne, and books were opened. Then another book was opened, which is the book of life. And the dead were judged by what was written in the books, according to what they had done. [13] And the sea gave up the dead who were in it, Death and Hades gave up the dead who were in them, and they were judged, each one of them, according to what they had done. [14] Then Death and Hades were thrown into the lake of fire. This is the second death, the lake of fire. [15] And if anyone's name was not found written in the book of life, he was thrown into the lake of fire.

Clothes are important, aren't they? We desperately need them. The right clothes cover a multitude of our dietary sins! They can also communicate important associations: ethnic groups, nationalities, sports teams, even music genres. And it's important to wear the right clothes for your destination. You don't wear a tuxedo to meet someone at a coffee shop, just like you wouldn't wear beach shorts and flip-flops to a formal wedding. Wearing the right outfit can be vital, especially when it comes to judgment day.

WHAT WOULD JOHN'S READERS HAVE NOTICED?

The Throne of Fire

As we have seen in the other six cycles, this seventh cycle in Revelation 20 is a broad overview of the events covering the first coming of Christ to His return. John's vision of judgment adds yet another profound image, the Great White Throne. This is the last of the revelatory cycles, and it takes place after Armageddon. John's first-century Jewish readers would have recalled this description from Daniel 7:9–10:

> *"As I looked, thrones were placed, and the Ancient of Days took his seat; his clothing was white as snow, and the hair of his head like pure wool; his throne was fiery flames; its wheels were burning fire. [10] A stream of fire issued and came out from before him; a thousand thousands served him, and ten thousand times ten thousand stood before him; the court sat in judgment, and the books were opened."*

The Book of Life

Revelation 20 and Daniel 7 are just two of several places in the Bible that refer to these books containing records of every person's deeds. Psalm 69:27–28 proclaims, "Add to them punishment upon punishment; may they have no acquittal from you. Let them be blotted out of the book of the living; let them not be enrolled among the righteous." These might be literal books recording the whole spectrum of our deeds or just metaphors of God's all-encompassing memory.

Imagine watching a DVD of your life that shows everything you've ever done and said, with subtitles of what you were really thinking. Would you want anybody to ever see that? That's what the first set of books in John's vision represent.

The Purest White

John's vision is dominated with pure white, a powerful metaphor for purity and righteousness throughout the Old Testament. Here, the Greek word for *white* represents much more than just a color. It also describes unfiltered radiant brightness, much like what Moses experienced in Exodus 33:20–23 when God spoke to him:

> *"But," he said, "you cannot see my face, for man shall not see me and live." [21] And the LORD said, "Behold, there is a place by me where you shall stand on the rock, [22] and while my glory passes by I will put you in a cleft of the rock, and I will cover you with my hand until I have passed by. [23] Then I will take away my hand, and you shall see my back, but my face shall not be seen."*

This whiteness is a sight so pure and clean that it radiates or reflects light perfectly. In Revelation, we see it as a white throne that, in the parallel description in Daniel, was described as having fiery flames. This throne is radiating bright light, like the sun. What do you do when the sun is in your eye? You are forced to turn away. Your natural reflex is to cover your eyes or be blinded.

WHAT WAS JESUS TELLING THE CHURCHES?

The Great White Throne is directly connected to the parable of the wheat and the weeds. Here's how Jesus ends that parable in Matthew 13:41–43: "The Son of Man will send his angels, and they will gather out of his kingdom all causes of sin and all law-breakers, and throw them into the fiery furnace. In that place there will be weeping and gnashing of teeth. Then the righteous will shine like the sun in the kingdom of their Father. He who has ears, let him hear."

Everyone who has ever lived, including humans and demons, will stand before this Great White Throne of Judgment in two groups. The first group to appear before the throne consists of Satan, his demons, and those he convinced to worship his beast, or this world. They have all experienced the first death, either during their lifetime or at Armageddon, and will return to life during the second resurrection to face the second death on judgment day.

They are separated on one side of the throne. A library of open books displays their every word, deed, and thought. It's an archive of all the unrighteousness of humankind. Their shameful true nature will be revealed to all. But Jesus tells us what makes it even more tragic is that they will be shocked, even confused, by how they ended up there.

But there is another group gathered at the throne. These people are dressed to match the Judge and His throne, as described in Revelation 3:5: "The one who conquers will be clothed thus in white garments, and I will never blot his name out of the book of life. I will confess his name before my Father and before his angels." John sees them again in Revelation 7:13–14:

> *One of the elders addressed me, saying, "Who are these, clothed in white robes, and from where have they come?"* [14] *I said to him, "Sir, you know." And he said to me, "These are the ones coming out of the great tribulation. They have washed their robes and made them white in the blood of the Lamb."*

So, to repeat the rhetorical question the elder posed to John, who are those clothed in white before the Great White Throne? They're you. They're me. They're every follower of Jesus! We are the ones dressed in white robes, the ones from verses 4 and 5 who followed Jesus on white horses at Armageddon. We're all on the other side of that throne, and there's only one open book containing a list of our names. John's readers would not have been frightened by this passage, but comforted. The Great White Throne of Judgment would be a reminder that being faithful in the face of immense suffering and tribulation is so worth it.

What Is Jesus Telling Us Today?

The prophet Isaiah reminds us in Isaiah 64:6 that "we have all become like one who is unclean, and all our righteous deeds are like a polluted garment." When I preached this sermon to our church, I stopped and asked my congregation, "Tell me—do these filthy rags make my sin look big?" The correct answer, of course, is "No, Joe, your sin makes your sin look big." Or, better yet, "No, Joe, your sin makes God's salvation look overwhelmingly great."

Throughout history, people have created their own standards of righteousness. For some, adherence to one political extreme or another can replace God's standard. Even generosity or religious fervor can seem an acceptable substitute. Some aspects of these things can appear righteous, and it may even be commendable to participate in them. In fact, as followers of Jesus, we are commanded to do some of these things—but they do not make us righteous. They only make us *self*-righteous.

People dress themselves with these ideals, hoping their legacy will be a righteous one now and after they die, but at the Great White Throne of Judgment, they will all be filthy garments in the eyes of God for those who have not believed the gospel. Jesus warns us of this outcome in Matthew 7:22–23:

> "On that day many will say to me, 'Lord, Lord, did we not prophesy in your name, and cast out demons in your name, and do many mighty works in your name?' 23 And then will I declare to them, 'I never knew you; depart from me, you workers of lawlessness.'"

This is a hard truth for those who refuse to admit that they need the cross to become righteous. It's bad news for the philanthropists, the volunteers, the activists, the patriots, and the religious zealots—anyone who thinks they can live a life that is pleasing to God through human efforts and wisdom.

Only Jesus can clothe us in the kind of righteousness we will need to wear at the Great White Throne. Paul brings this to the forefront in Philippians 3:9 when he says, "be found in him, not having a righteousness of my own . . . , but that which comes through faith in Christ, the righteousness from God that depends on faith." Imagine asking on that day, "Do these white robes make me look righteous?" The answer you might hear is, "No, follower of Jesus, they *make* you righteous!" Or, more accurately, they'll mean you've *already been made* righteous.

This is great news for those of us who understand that our own righteousness is no better than polluted, filthy rags. For the redeemed, judgment day isn't about the DVD of our life. It's about our Savior and all He has done for us!

"But wait," you say, "aren't we supposed to do righteous things on earth? Won't we also be judged by our works?"

Yes! But even those good works are gifts God has given to us. Look at what Paul says in Ephesians 2:8–10:

> *For by grace you have been saved through faith. And this is not your own doing; it is the gift of God, ⁹ not a result of works, so that no one may boast. ¹⁰ For we are his workmanship, created in Christ Jesus for good works, which God prepared beforehand, that we should walk in them.*

Christian, we must abandon the foolishness of trying to dress ourselves in filthy rags and, instead, put on the gospel of Jesus. Wouldn't it be better to let Jesus pick out our clothes on judgment day than to try dressing ourselves in our own righteousness? For those who follow the Lamb wherever He goes—those whom He has dressed in white robes of righteousness—the judgment before the Great White Throne will not be a fearful day; it will be a great day!

CHAPTER FORTY-SEVEN

A New Heaven and a New Earth

Read Revelation 21:1–8.

1 Then I saw a new heaven and a new earth, for the first heaven and the first earth had passed away, and the sea was no more. 2 And I saw the holy city, new Jerusalem, coming down out of heaven from God, prepared as a bride adorned for her husband. 3 And I heard a loud voice from the throne saying, "Behold, the dwelling place of God is with man. He will dwell with them, and they will be his people, and God himself will be with them as their God. 4 He will wipe away every tear from their eyes, and death shall be no more, neither shall there be mourning, nor crying, nor pain anymore, for the former things have passed away."

5 And he who was seated on the throne said, "Behold, I am making all things new." Also he said, "Write this down, for these words are trustworthy and true." 6 And he said to me, "It is done! I am the Alpha and the Omega, the beginning and the end. To the thirsty I will give from the spring of the water of life without payment. 7 The one who conquers will have this heritage, and I will be his God and he will be my son. 8 But as for the cowardly, the faithless, the detestable, as for murderers, the sexually immoral, sorcerers,

> *idolaters, and all liars, their portion will be in the lake that burns with fire and sulfur, which is the second death."*

All of us, at one time or another, have been captivated by the beauty of God's creation. Maybe it was a serene mountain vista or a cascading waterfall. Even people who don't believe in God appreciate nature's beauty. However, our world is far from perfect, plagued by natural disasters and extreme weather. And anyone can see how humanity has left permanent scars on the natural beauty of creation over thousands of years.

Likewise, anyone, including the unbelieving, can observe the spiritual impact of human evil on the world. As beautiful as creation can be, it's full of both physical and spiritual chaos. For the unredeemed, this fallen world is sadly all they have and the best they can hope for.

What Would John's Readers Have Noticed?

Ancient Promises

God promised throughout the Old Testament to create a new heaven, a new earth, and a new Jerusalem. This passage in Revelation borrows several specifics from the most well-known of those passages, including Isaiah 65:17–18, 24:

> *"For behold, I create new heavens and a new earth, and the former things shall not be remembered or come into mind.* ¹⁸ *... I create Jerusalem to be a joy, and her people to be a*

gladness. . . . ²⁴ Before they call I will answer; while they are yet speaking I will hear."

John's readers understood that the primary hope of every Jew was for God to one day restore Israel to its former glory and rebuild Jerusalem. Jews often reminisced about Solomon's kingdom—the era of Israel's greatest expansion, wealth, and global spiritual influence. When Jesus came, He taught that longing for a new earthly Israel was futile, and it was actually the wrong hope. Instead, Jesus revealed that the prophecies in Isaiah and other passages were about God's eternal kingdom, a world where He would dwell among all of His people from all nations.

No More Sea

We've already learned that first-century believers saw the sea as a metaphor for danger and viewed it as the place where invasions by distant empires originated. John's vision in Revelation 13:1 describes the dragon's beast (a metaphor for world empires) rising from the sea. So, when his readers saw "no more sea" in this passage, they would have recognized it as a metaphor for God's eradication of the threat of evil from His creation.

No More Tears

The promise of "no more tears" likewise echoes Old Testament prophecies. Perhaps the most familiar is Isaiah 25:8:

"He will swallow up death forever; and the Lord GOD will wipe away tears from all faces." As with the prophecy of a new heaven and earth, Jews assumed this promise was about life in a restored kingdom of Israel and a rebuilt Jerusalem.

But Jesus told His disciples there would always be tears in this life, and that this promise was also about the kingdom of God. Jesus was clear: life would always be hard. Israel, Jerusalem, and the temple itself were part of that difficulty. First-century Christians would have understood that this was a promise about life in the kingdom of God when Jesus returns.

WHAT WAS JESUS TELLING THE CHURCHES?

The theological concepts in this passage trace back to the beginning of Genesis and the first creation. Both Genesis and Revelation 21 contain three elements: creation, sin and death, and the promise of restoration.

In Genesis 1:31, we read, "And God saw everything that he had made, and behold, it was very good." Throughout the creation story, God declares His complete satisfaction with each phase. Everything about creation was perfectly in sync. God appointed Adam and Eve as the king and queen of His creation, which He meant as a gift for them to fill with perfect, sinless kids and families. Humans were to populate, care for, and, foremost, enjoy it.

Fun fact: after the fall of Adam and Eve, the phrases "it was good" and "it was very good" don't appear again in the

Bible until God expresses His complete satisfaction with Jesus at His baptism, an account of which we see in Mark 1:10–11:

> *And when he came up out of the water, immediately he saw the heavens being torn open and the Spirit descending on him like a dove. ¹¹ And a voice came from heaven, "You are my beloved Son; with you I am well pleased."*

From Adam and Eve down to the smallest grain of sand, there was no sin, no sorrow, no pain, and no strife. God walked with them each day in Eden. The world was physically and spiritually perfect, with breathtaking beauty and harmony between creation and its Creator.

But Adam and Eve somehow became discontent with Eden and their perfect relationship with God, and they chose to rebel. They listened to the false promises from the serpent—that God was holding something greater back, and they could have even more. John reminds us in Revelation 12:9 that the enemy is "that ancient serpent, who is called the devil and Satan, the deceiver of the whole world."

The serpent convinced Adam and Eve they didn't have to settle for obedience to the Creator. They could be their own gods. They could be creators instead of just creations—and Adam and Eve believed him. Their rebellion initiated a long, painful history of sin and strife. Humanity spiraled downward into a wicked abyss, a descent vividly depicted throughout the Old Testament and Revelation.

Their rebellion also subjected creation to that same curse. The creation they were told to care for had been marred. Natural disasters persist to this day as creation groans for its redemption. That's the narrative of all Scripture, as both the redeemed and creation eagerly anticipate the day when someone will make it all right again.

Amid this tragic story, in the first moments after the fall, God promised in Genesis 3:15 to redeem both His people and His creation through Jesus: "'I will put enmity between you [the serpent] and the woman, and between your offspring and her offspring; he shall bruise your head, and you shall bruise his heel.'"

The first part of the promise includes the eradication of all the evil Adam and Eve introduced into this world. The second part is the renewal of creation and the restoration of perfect harmony between God and His people, as they were in Eden. Jesus started with the second part first when He conquered the curse of sin and death through the cross and His resurrection.

John's vision looks to the future, when Jesus will fulfill the first part by rendering eternal judgment for every wicked person. This isn't only for those who have committed the sins listed in verse 8, or everyone who has committed a specific sin of any kind. If so, we'd all be in trouble! What we're seeing is the Great White Throne Judgment of Satan and those who hoped in his false promises instead of Jesus. It's after this that Jesus will create a new heaven and earth, better than the original, in fulfillment of His original plan to dwell with His people.

WHAT IS JESUS TELLING US TODAY?

If you think God's creation is breathtaking now, just wait for the new heaven and the new earth! John's vision of the new Jerusalem, which is described in detail in the next passage, is the key to understanding how we apply this one. Old Jerusalem was beloved by God's people because the temple was there, and God dwelt in that temple. In this chapter of Revelation, the new Jerusalem descends from heaven dressed like a bride coming down the aisle for her wedding. That's the same way Jesus, John, and the rest of the apostles described the church upon Jesus' return! In fact, in Revelation 21:9, an angel refers to the new Jerusalem as "the Bride of the Lamb." Do you understand how the new Jerusalem is a metaphor for us—the redeemed, the church of Jesus?

John confirmed to his readers that the prophecies about a new Jerusalem aren't merely about a new physical city but a new civilization, culture, and people. Put that together with what Paul taught us in 1 Corinthians 3:16: "Do you not know that you are God's temple and that God's Spirit dwells in you?" This is another example of the *already*, the *right now*, and the *not yet*. Even though we have not been perfected yet, the church already functions as the temple of God. Through His Word and through His Spirit, He dwells among His people today!

Just as the first creation was a gift to Adam and Eve, this new creation will be a gift to us—a wedding gift! The universe God created was breathtaking. It can still be breathtaking today, but it's been damaged. Paul spells it out in Romans 8:22–23:

> *For we know that the whole creation has been groaning together in the pains of childbirth until now.* [23] *And not only the creation, but we ourselves, who have the firstfruits of the Spirit, groan inwardly as we wait eagerly for adoption as sons, the redemption of our bodies.*

Every person can perceive how this world has been scarred by human sin. Throughout history, the unredeemed have tried to recreate the world in their own image, to make it what they believe it should be. But these promises always tragically fail to deliver, as the unredeemed bounce from one broken promise to another.

For the redeemed, our hope is in the promise that Jesus will set this world right when He returns. In Matthew 5, Jesus tells us the inheritors of the kingdom of God are the poor in spirit, mourners, righteous, merciful, pure-hearted, peacemakers, persecuted, and meek. They're comforted, given mercy, and called sons of God!

The redeemed know only Jesus has the power to fulfill the promise of creating the world every human heart longs for. On that day, we, the new Jerusalem, enter a new heaven and earth, where we will revel in God's full beauty and majesty for eternity, with no chance of evil ever ruining it again.

CHAPTER FORTY-EIGHT

The Perfect Church

Revelation 21:9–27:

> [9] Then came one of the seven angels who had the seven bowls full of the seven last plagues and spoke to me, saying, "Come, I will show you the Bride, the wife of the Lamb." [10] And he carried me away in the Spirit to a great, high mountain, and showed me the holy city Jerusalem coming down out of heaven from God, [11] having the glory of God, its radiance like a most rare jewel, like a jasper, clear as crystal. [12] It had a great, high wall, with twelve gates, and at the gates twelve angels, and on the gates the names of the twelve tribes of the sons of Israel were inscribed—[13] on the east three gates, on the north three gates, on the south three gates, and on the west three gates. [14] And the wall of the city had twelve foundations, and on them were the twelve names of the twelve apostles of the Lamb.
>
> [15] And the one who spoke with me had a measuring rod of gold to measure the city and its gates and walls. [16] The city lies foursquare, its length the same as its width. And he measured the city with his rod, 12,000 stadia. Its length and width and height are equal. [17] He also measured its wall, 144 cubits by human measurement, which is also an angel's measurement. [18] The wall was built of jasper, while the city was pure gold, like clear glass. [19] The foundations

> *of the wall of the city were adorned with every kind of jewel. The first was jasper, the second sapphire, the third agate, the fourth emerald,* [20] *the fifth onyx, the sixth carnelian, the seventh chrysolite, the eighth beryl, the ninth topaz, the tenth chrysoprase, the eleventh jacinth, the twelfth amethyst.* [21] *And the twelve gates were twelve pearls, each of the gates made of a single pearl, and the street of the city was pure gold, like transparent glass.*
>
> [22] *And I saw no temple in the city, for its temple is the Lord God the Almighty and the Lamb.* [23] *And the city has no need of sun or moon to shine on it, for the glory of God gives it light, and its lamp is the Lamb.* [24] *By its light will the nations walk, and the kings of the earth will bring their glory into it,* [25] *and its gates will never be shut by day—and there will be no night there.* [26] *They will bring into it the glory and the honor of the nations.* [27] *But nothing unclean will ever enter it, nor anyone who does what is detestable or false, but only those who are written in the Lamb's book of life.*

Imagine being part of a perfect church that fully meets every expectation of Jesus. What would it look like? Do we start with Scripture-centric theology and teaching or do we start with the ability to be loving and accepting? How much emphasis would that church place on righteous and holy living, or on a strong evangelistic focus? Would we see massive diversity, filled with different kinds of people, or would it prioritize sacrificial generosity?

There is no perfect church today, but this next passage in Revelation describes exactly what one would look like—what God sees, what God is building, and what we will ultimately become.

What Would John's Readers Have Noticed?

Familiar Symbolism

John's readers would have noticed several significant numbers from the Old Testament and from earlier in Revelation itself. First, they'd spot the number 12. It appears frequently on its own and as a factor or multiple of other prominent numbers. Throughout the Old Testament, the number 12 symbolizes the completeness of God's people. Examples include the twelve tribes of Israel, Jesus' chosen twelve apostles, and even the twelve stars on the woman's crown in Revelation 12. Another significant number is 3, which often represents God's perfection. It's been used to describe the three persons of His being, the Holy Trinity: the Father with His perfect judgment, the Son with His perfect righteousness, and the Spirit with His perfect presence.

John wanted to help his readers imagine the unimaginable, so he used symbols and objects his Jewish audience would have recognized as beautiful—like pure gold, pearls, and precious stones—to describe the indescribable. But even these images fall short of the perfect beauty he sees. He describes the city's shape and its composition, its massive walls, and even clear glass. The new Jerusalem is stunning, perfect in all its beauty.

The twelve precious gemstones embedded in the four foundations of the city would immediately raise eyebrows among John's readers, because they'd remember that those same stones were embedded in the high priest's ephod or breastplate of judgment in the Old Testament. The ephod was symbolic of the spiritual authority God vested to the high priest to serve as the mediator for His people.

Not an Actual City

From the twelve foundations adorned in precious stones, which call back to the arrangement of precious stones in four separate rows of three stones each on Aaron's breastpiece, to the cube shape of the city and the intentional placement of the gates, everything was laid out and arranged in ways John's readers would have recognized. These arrangements were similar to descriptions of the original temple in Jerusalem, where the presence of God dwelled. They would have known right away that the new Jerusalem was a metaphor for God's complete, chosen, protected people, and not a literal brick-and-mortar city.

WHAT WAS JESUS TELLING THE CHURCHES?

This description of the new Jerusalem is so full of familiar symbols that John's readers would have known this description went much deeper than stunning architecture. Much like the design of the American flag, where the stars, stripes, and colors each have special meanings, everything in this description represents something.

Here's a guide to decipher what John's readers recognized:

Cube-Shaped City
The Holy of Holies Within Solomon's Temple

The dimensions of the Holy City are given as 12,000 stadia (or 1,380 miles) long, wide, and high. The original holy of holies Moses built in the Old Testament was also shaped like a cube. The holy of holies housed the inner room in the temple where God's presence dwelled, as we see in 1 Kings 6:19–20: "The inner sanctuary [holy of holies] he prepared in the innermost part of the house, to set there the ark of the covenant of the LORD. The inner sanctuary was twenty cubits long, twenty cubits wide, and twenty cubits high."

Notice the number 12,000, which is 12 x 1,000. *Twelve* was the number representing God's people, and *one thousand* is often used as a literary metaphor for multiplied growth.

Walls
A Symbol of God's Sovereign Protection of His People

The thickness of the walls was given as 144 cubits, or about 216 feet. This number (12 x 12), which is symbolic of God's people, here indicates the strong and secure nature of the city's protection. The walls represent God's unbreakable promise of salvation and protection for His people. These walls can also symbolize the promise Jesus made that He will never leave us, even to the end of the age!

Twelve Gates Around Four Walls
Accessibility for Every People, Tribe, and Nation

The twelve gates are arranged in groups of three on each wall, which face the four corners of the earth for easy access to all people, everywhere. You see, these walls aren't designed to keep people out—they're always left open as an eternal monument to the fact that evil has been defeated! These gates are each named after one of the twelve tribes of Israel, connecting the Old and New Testament faithful as one family of God.

Twelve Foundations with Precious Stones
Apostolic Doctrinal Authority

Ephesians 2:20 notes the church is "built on the foundation of the apostles and prophets, Christ Jesus himself being the cornerstone." John says the foundations of the new Jerusalem are a symbol of apostolic doctrine that was taught first by Jesus. They are the foundation for the church.

Street of Pure Gold Like Glass
One Pure Path to God Through Jesus

The single glassy street in the Holy City is a metaphor for Jesus and the gospel being the one way to the Father—the way, truth, and the life. No one comes into the presence of the Father except through Him (John 14:6).

No Temple
God Lives in His People, Not a Building

Jerusalem and the temple meant everything to the first-century Jewish people. Even though the Second Temple had been destroyed by AD 90, both still would have been special in the hearts of John's readers. Before Jesus came, these places were the only portals between heaven and earth! But now that the Lamb has come, there is no more need for either. The new Jerusalem and the people of God have taken their place, and there is no more need for sacrifices or intercessors or intermediaries. We are fully with Jesus, and He is fully with us! Lastly, observe that all these measurements are multiples of 12, which is no coincidence. The number 12 symbolizes God's people, embodying New Jerusalem as a metaphor for the unity and perfection of all of God's people in His presence.

WHAT IS JESUS TELLING US TODAY?

I've sorted through hundreds of paintings, looking for one that might capture the majesty of the new Jerusalem, but none of them seem to do it justice. That's because it is a perfectly constructed theological expression of God's sovereign plan of redemption. John's breathtaking description of the city descending from heaven reveals the culmination of God's mercy and love. The new Jerusalem represents every person God has ever chosen to redeem, living together as one family with Him in the new heaven and earth.

What a beautiful picture of the day we, the people of God, will all be united in the full presence of our Savior, Jesus! But how can this impact us right now, today? How can this be more than just some future hope? Peter tells us in 1 Peter 2:5, "You yourselves like living stones are being built up as a spiritual house, to be a holy priesthood."

Here's the amazing part: the new Jerusalem isn't just a future dream. It's under full construction right now! We the redeemed are those same precious living stones God is using to build the new Jerusalem. And even though we are still a work in progress, God already sees us as the new Jerusalem—the perfect, complete church. Even in the process of building it, He has promised He is with us always, even till the end of the age. Paul describes this comfort in Ephesians 2:19–22 (emphasis mine):

> *You are no longer strangers and aliens, but you are **fellow citizens** with the saints and members of the household of God, [20] built on the foundation of the apostles and prophets, Christ Jesus himself being the cornerstone, [21] in whom the whole structure, being joined together, grows into a holy temple in the Lord. [22] In him you also are being built together into a dwelling place for God by the Spirit.*

As followers of Jesus, we have a deep understanding of the feeling of being strangers and aliens in this world, don't we? We have this deep supernatural yearning to live as the church is described as living in the new Jerusalem. We want to experience complete unity with all our brothers and sisters from throughout redemptive history. We want to enjoy, together with them, the unfettered access to Jesus and our Father.

We followers of Jesus can live with gratitude and eternal inspiration that the rest of the world just can't understand because, even though we know we aren't home yet, we're striving to live as though we are. Let's rejoice in what God is building, as we anticipate the day He reveals the final product in all its perfect beauty. Until then, we should live like citizens of the new Jerusalem now by loving and serving one another and preaching the gospel to all the nations, just as our Jesus commanded.

CHAPTER FORTY-NINE

You Will Be Satisfied

Revelation 22:1–5:

> *¹ Then the angel showed me the river of the water of life, bright as crystal, flowing from the throne of God and of the Lamb ² through the middle of the street of the city; also, on either side of the river, the tree of life with its twelve kinds of fruit, yielding its fruit each month. The leaves of the tree were for the healing of the nations. ³ No longer will there be anything accursed, but the throne of God and of the Lamb will be in it, and his servants will worship him. ⁴ They will see his face, and his name will be on their foreheads. ⁵ And night will be no more. They will need no light of lamp or sun, for the Lord God will be their light, and they will reign forever and ever.*

In John 7:37, Jesus was in Jerusalem for Sukkot, the Feast of Booths, and addressed the crowd: "If anyone thirsts, let him come to me and drink."

Millennials have coined a modern term for a person's relentless pursuit or desire for something or someone: *thirsty*. To be labeled as thirsty implies you will go to great lengths, even if it's risky or embarrassing, to satisfy your craving for the things of this world.

But isn't it hypocritical to single out individuals when, in fact, every one of us is thirsty and hungry? The world doesn't realize it, but this universal human thirst and hunger stem from a spiritual craving. Our profound desire for personal fulfillment drives us to explore every corner, leaving no stone unturned in our pursuit. It is not wrong or sinful to yearn for satisfaction; after all, we were created this way by God. But this world is filled with enticing propositions and false promises that will never satisfy but only leave us hungrier and thirstier. Followers of Jesus know something the rest of the world doesn't—only Jesus can satisfy.

WHAT WOULD JOHN'S READERS HAVE NOTICED?

Paradise Spoiled

Doesn't the fruit on the tree in this passage sound delicious? Can you imagine how good the water in that river will be? When John's first-century Jewish Christian readers got to his vision in Revelation 22:1–5, they would have been transported back to Genesis 2:8–14:

> The LORD God planted a garden in Eden, in the east, and there he put the man whom he had formed. ⁹ And out of the ground the LORD God made to spring up every tree that is pleasant to the sight and good for food. The tree of life was in the midst of the garden, and the tree of the knowledge

of good and evil. ¹⁰ A river flowed out of Eden to water the garden, and there it divided and became four rivers. ¹¹ The name of the first is the Pishon. It is the one that flowed around the whole land of Havilah, where there is gold. ¹² And the gold of that land is good; bdellium and onyx stone are there. ¹³ The name of the second river is the Gihon. It is the one that flowed around the whole land of Cush. ¹⁴ And the name of the third river is the Tigris, which flows east of Assyria. And the fourth river is the Euphrates.

Eden was a paradise designed to completely satisfy humanity by letting Adam and Eve enjoy all of God's creation and to live in perfect harmony with each other, and with God Himself. The two life-giving elements in Eden were the Tree of Life and the river flowing through the garden to the rest of the world. God entrusted Adam and Eve with caring for His creation, but, above all, He wanted them to revel in it, to enjoy it to its fullest!

Adam and Eve did face a daily choice, though, between the Tree of Life and the Tree of Knowledge of Good and Evil. The choice was between being satisfied in their relationship with God and His creation or believing the serpent's lies. Genesis 2:15–17 shows us this:

> The LORD God took the man and put him in the garden of Eden to work it and keep it. ¹⁶ And the LORD God commanded the man, saying, "You may surely eat of every tree of the garden, ¹⁷ but of the tree of the knowledge of good and evil you shall not eat, for in the day that you eat of it you shall surely die."

By remaining faithful to their Creator, Adam and Eve could live eternally, in harmony with God and creation. But

Satan promised they could be like God if they ate the forbidden fruit. Adam and Eve became so *thirsty*, so fearful they were missing out on something more, that they chose to try to quench that thirst by betraying their Creator.

WHAT WAS JESUS TELLING THE CHURCHES?

Paradise Restored

The three elements featured in Genesis—two trees and the rivers of life—are powerful metaphors that help us interpret Revelation 22:1–5. The Tree of Knowledge of Good and Evil is notably absent from Revelation 22, and rightly so. It doesn't belong. This tree symbolizes human depravity, temptation, and the origins of our fallen nature. It also represents our continuous struggle between human desire and our need for redemption through God's grace.

Despite bearing the sole forbidden fruit in Eden, its presence may seem like a cruel test, but it was an act of love. God granted Adam and Eve the free will we all desire. And just as we often do, they used that autonomy for unfaithfulness and selfishness, as we see in Genesis 3:22–23:

> The LORD God said, "Behold, the man has become like one of us in knowing good and evil. Now, lest he reach out his hand and take also of the tree of life and eat, and live forever—" [23] therefore the LORD God sent him out from the garden of Eden."

Because of their thirst to be like God, the serpent's lies seemed like choice morsels they hoped would satisfy. Consequently, they lost access to the two vital life-giving components of paradise—the Tree of Life and their relationship with God Himself. This may seem punitive, but it was also an act of love, because it would have been horrifying for them to become immortal in their sinful condition like Satan and His angels are. But God wouldn't let Adam and Eve be forever separated from Him. This set in motion His plan for Jesus, the Last Adam, to restore our connection to the Tree of Life and the river that nourishes it.

We see the Tree of Life both at the beginning of the Bible in Genesis and here in Revelation 22. In Genesis, fruit from the Tree of Life was the daily source of power and sustenance, allowing Adam and Eve to live without fear of death. In Revelation, fruit from the Tree of Life is again the source of nourishment, and its leaves are a source for the healing of the nations. Remember how Adam and Eve tried to use fig leaves to conceal their sin (Genesis 3:7)? These new leaves don't just conceal, they heal!

Jesus often says—especially in John's gospel—that He provides life and healing for us. We hear Him say in John 14:6, "I am the way, and the truth, and the life." And in John 15:5, He reminds us, "I am the vine; you are the branches. Whoever abides in me and I in him, he it is that bears *much fruit*" (emphasis mine). Of course, most believers are very familiar with His declaration in John 6:35: "I am the bread of life; whoever comes to me shall not hunger, and whoever believes in me shall never thirst." Jesus, as the Tree of Life, provided the fruit for eternal life by defeating death through his own death and resurrection.

The trees could not provide such healing on their own. In Genesis, the river nourished every plant in the garden of Eden, including the Tree of Life. Revelation 22:1–5 describes the Tree of Life growing all around the river of the water of life, flowing from the throne of God. To the Jews, *living water* was water that flowed naturally, such as in a river or spring. In John 4:10, Jesus said He is the source of living water. Here, we see that this Tree of Life and the living water are the power of God to redeem creation to be even better than it was before!

Together, the Tree and the Water will satisfy every hunger and every thirst without fail, forever. They are the heart of new Eden, right in the center of the great city of God! Both represent Jesus, who conquered sin and death.

What Is Jesus Telling Us Today?

Satisfied in Paradise

Whether they admit it or not, everyone in this world is hungry and thirsty for something only Jesus can satisfy. This world says it has satisfying water, but it's a lie—we'll always be thirsty, no matter how often we drink. And the world claims its fruit will fill us up, but the truth is, the world's fruit comes from a poisonous tree that ultimately brings death.

Just like Adam and Eve, every human has chosen and been disappointed by the world's water and the world's fruit. We experience an appetite and a thirst that's only ever temporarily satisfied, and even then, it's only satisfying to a degree. It doesn't satisfy our whole being. Don't you get tired of drinking the same water every day, water that never quenches your thirst? Don't you get tired of eating the world's poisonous fruit that not only never satisfies but also makes you sick and ends in death?

The familiar story of Jesus and the Samaritan woman at a well in the midday heat in John 4:13–14 is a powerful example of this endless dissatisfaction:

> *Jesus said to her, "Everyone who drinks of this water will be thirsty again, 14 but whoever drinks of the water that I will give him will never be thirsty again. The water that I will give him will become in him a spring of water welling up to eternal life."*

Most of the community would have drawn their water in the cooler morning or evening hours. But this woman was shunned and shamed by her community for her lifestyle, so she'd come to draw water during the worst heat of the day. She wanted to avoid her neighbors, but she needed water to survive. She had no choice.

Jesus taught her she also had a spiritual thirst, and if she drank the water He provided, she would never thirst again. That day, the woman at the well had her thirst quenched—her desires satisfied—by the Living Water, and so can you! This is the same river of living water flowing from the throne of God into the River of Life in Revelation 22.

The woman responds in John 4:15, "Sir, give me this water, so that I will not be thirsty or have to come here to draw water." For some of you, her plea is your prayer. It should be so for all of us: "Jesus, please give me living water. I don't want to drink the world's water anymore. It never quenches my thirst. I am weary of going to the well of the world to drink water that never satisfies!" Jesus was clear in Matthew 5:6: "Blessed are those who hunger and thirst for righteousness, for they shall be satisfied."

Are you like the woman at the well, ready to be satisfied by the living water and the Tree of Life? Or are you like Adam and Eve, discontent with what God has provided, hoping to be satisfied by the world's fruit? Our resurrected Jesus is the Tree of Life. He is the river of living water. Let Jesus satisfy your hungry, thirsty soul!

CHAPTER FIFTY

The Last Prophecy

Revelation 22:6–11:

> ⁶ And he said to me, "These words are trustworthy and true. And the Lord, the God of the spirits of the prophets, has sent his angel to show his servants what must soon take place."
>
> ⁷ "And behold, I am coming soon. Blessed is the one who keeps the words of the prophecy of this book."
>
> ⁸ I, John, am the one who heard and saw these things. And when I heard and saw them, I fell down to worship at the feet of the angel who showed them to me, ⁹ but he said to me, "You must not do that! I am a fellow servant with you and your brothers the prophets, and with those who keep the words of this book. Worship God."
>
> ¹⁰ And he said to me, "Do not seal up the words of the prophecy of this book, for the time is near. ¹¹ Let the evildoer still do evil, and the filthy still be filthy, and the righteous still do right, and the holy still be holy."

The allure of biblical prophecy has long captivated the hearts and minds of followers of Jesus, for better or for worse.

Since the first century, many have claimed to be prophets with new information from God known only to them. But what if that's all wrong? What if God has delivered one final prophecy to humanity and has nothing else to say to us?

Well, there is a final prophecy from God. He is done speaking. Everything He needs to reveal to us has been revealed. He has, in fact, given that prophecy that promises grace for His people and judgment for everyone else. It's the gospel.

What Would John's Readers Have Noticed?

"The Spirits of the Prophets"

John's use of the phrase "God of the spirits of the prophets" was a bold, immediate signal to his readers that Revelation carries all the attributes of every prophecy that came before it. Those attributes include four critical elements: urgency, credibility, authority, and a call to action and accountability.

Urgency

Every prophecy carries a sense of urgency, calling for an immediate response from those who've heard it. A prophecy was the ultimate authority from the very moment it was given until it was superseded by a new one. God's people were required to proclaim and follow whichever prophecy was the most recent.

The phrase "I am coming soon" declares the duration of this prophecy's authority to its readers—until Jesus returns. It signals the importance of readiness, anticipation, and prompt obedience to its commands. It encourages those who hear it to remain faithful and obedient to it until God's plan of redemption is completed.

Credibility

To be taken seriously, though, each prophecy needed credibility. Prophets, as representatives of God's words, were held to high standards of moral and spiritual accountability. John was affectionately known as "John the Elder" because he was the last surviving apostle. His six decades of faithful, sacrificial service to the church further solidified his standing. He was also known as the "disciple whom Jesus loved" because of his special connection with Jesus (John 13:23). Together, these factors made John, by far, the most credible, beloved, and trusted person in the late first-century church.

Authority

A prophecy had to be given with authority too. For every Jew, including John's first-century Christian readers, the Old Testament was their Bible, the authoritative Word of God. Isaiah reinforces this idea when he says, "The grass withers, the flower fades, but the word of our God will stand forever" (Isaiah 40:8).

By invoking the spirits of the prophets, John asserted that the prophecy in Revelation possesses the same spiritual authority as those delivered by Isaiah, Ezekiel, Jeremiah, and Elijah. In fact, he's declaring the same authority Peter and the other apostles declared about their teachings to the church that we see in 2 Peter 1:20–21: "No prophecy of Scripture comes from someone's own interpretation. For no prophecy was ever produced by the will of man, but men spoke from God as they were carried along by the Holy Spirit."

Call to Action and Accountability

Accountability played a critical role in every prophecy, as each one called upon God's people to take specific action. We see an example of this in Deuteronomy 30:19–20: "Therefore choose life, that you and your offspring may live, loving the LORD your God, obeying his voice and holding fast to him, for he is your life and length of days." Prophetic ministry did not allow for a neutral position; it placed everyone on the side of either obedience or rebellion. Obedience to a prophecy's call to action resulted in promise and blessing, while rebellion resulted in accountability and judgment.

What Was Jesus Telling the Churches?

John's Revelation of Jesus stands as God's final prophecy, His ultimate revelation of the plan of redemption. As the last prophecy, it contains the fulfillment of all things. Its authority supersedes all others in scope, impact, and significance. While its promises are the most beautiful and merciful, its judgments are the most dire and severe. They're not just for Jews, either, because they apply to every tribe and nation throughout history. The promises are beautiful and precious, but the judgments hold inescapable and terrifying eternal consequences.

But unlike all previous prophecies with commands that seemed humanly impossible to keep, its commands are simple: believe in Jesus' work for salvation, and proclaim this prophecy to the world. It's a beautiful display of God's grace. In return, those who believe will receive promises far greater than those offered by any previous prophecy. They will be transformed into God's faithful redeemed for all eternity.

Since this is the final prophecy, the angel told John's readers "do not seal up" any of it, but proclaim it to the entire word (the Great Commission, Matthew 28:16–20). He also warned this gospel prophecy isn't a unifying message. It will divide everyone into two groups: the wicked and the righteous, the condemned and the saved, unbelievers and believers (the Great White Throne of Judgment, Revelation 20:11–15).

The divisive nature of the gospel prophecy was predicted in Daniel 12:10: "Many shall purify themselves and make themselves white and be refined, but the wicked shall act wickedly. And none of the wicked shall understand, but those who are wise shall understand." In fact, Jesus Himself said the same thing in Luke 12:51–53:

> *"Do you think that I have come to give peace on earth? No, I tell you, but rather division.* ⁵² *For from now on in one house there will be five divided, three against two and two against three.* ⁵³ *They will be divided, father against son and son against father, mother against daughter and daughter against mother."*

The gospel prophecy leaves no room for ambiguity. Those who don't follow the Lamb will continue in their wickedness and face the eternal judgment reserved for them, while those who believe and proclaim will be made righteous and live with God forever. This forces everyone to determine how they see Jesus. Is He your King, or isn't He?

WHAT IS JESUS TELLING US TODAY?

Time for an experiment. Try reciting John 3:16 from memory . . . go! All right, now what about the five verses following 3:16? Can you recite verses 17 through 21?

That wasn't as easy, was it? Here's the whole text from John 3:17–21:

> *"For God did not send his Son into the world to condemn the world, but in order that the world might be saved through him.* ¹⁸ *Whoever believes in him is not condemned, but whoever does not believe is condemned already, because he has not believed in the name of the only Son of God.* ¹⁹ *And this is the judgment: the light has come into the world, and people loved the darkness rather than the light because their works were evil.* ²⁰ *For everyone who does wicked things hates the light and does not come to the light, lest his works should be exposed.* ²¹ *But whoever does what is true comes to the light, so that it may be clearly seen that his works have been carried out in God."*

Why is it that almost everyone can quote John 3:16, but very few can even summarize the next five verses? Is it because verse 16 emphasizes mercy, but verses 17 to 21 lean toward judgment? Even unbelievers can look at John 3:16 and say, "Oh, that's a nice sentiment. I don't believe it, but it's a nice message."

Our obedience to this prophecy means we proclaim not only John 3:16 but also verses 17 to 21. The gospel has the authority to save all who believe, but it also has the authority to condemn and judge those who don't. There is no third option. No middle ground.

The New Testament is all about this last prophecy from God, the proclamation of both the gospel's promises and its judgments! It's Jesus equipping and commanding us to proclaim the comfort of verse 16 to those who believe and the judgment of verses 17 to 21 to those who don't. Paul tells us in Galatians 1:6, 8–9, "I am astonished that you are so quickly deserting him who called you in the grace of Christ and are turning to a different gospel. . . . But even if we or an angel from heaven should preach to you a gospel contrary to the one we preached to you, let him be accursed. As we have said before, so now I say again: If anyone is preaching to you a gospel contrary to the one you received, let him be accursed."

It's tempting to "seal up" the judgmental aspects of the gospel prophecy to make it more palatable. However, altering the gospel prophecy takes away its urgency, its authority, its credibility, and its call to action and accountability. What we get when we do that is a false gospel, one that comes from evil, with only one outcome: judgment for those who are led astray.

How do you feel about the gospel prophecy? Are you ashamed of any part of it? From a human perspective, it's understandable why we would be torn, and why we can be hesitant to fully proclaim both sides. But that's why God gave John the previous twenty-one chapters—to reveal the big-picture battle between good and evil.

John says reading this prophecy blesses us, strengthens our faith, renews our confidence in its divine authority, heightens our desire for its promises, and empowers us to remain faithful until Jesus returns. It teaches us that evil in this world, as powerful as it may be, will not win and that we can, with great confidence, follow the Lamb wherever He goes. We should proclaim it to the world outside, and we should proclaim it to ourselves and to each other at every opportunity, reminding one another how important it is!

CHAPTER FIFTY-ONE

Cherished Words

Revelation 22:12–21:

¹² "Behold, I am coming soon, bringing my recompense with me, to repay each one for what he has done. ¹³ I am the Alpha and the Omega, the first and the last, the beginning and the end."

¹⁴ Blessed are those who wash their robes, so that they may have the right to the tree of life and that they may enter the city by the gates. ¹⁵ Outside are the dogs and sorcerers and the sexually immoral and murderers and idolaters, and everyone who loves and practices falsehood.

¹⁶ "I, Jesus, have sent my angel to testify to you about these things for the churches. I am the root and the descendant of David, the bright morning star."

¹⁷ The Spirit and the Bride say, "Come." And let the one who hears say, "Come." And let the one who is thirsty come; let the one who desires take the water of life without price.

¹⁸ I warn everyone who hears the words of the prophecy of this book: if anyone adds to them, God will add to him the plagues described in this book, ¹⁹ and if anyone takes away from the words of the book of this prophecy, God will take

> *away his share in the tree of life and in the holy city, which are described in this book.*
>
> [20] *He who testifies to these things says, "Surely I am coming soon." Amen. Come, Lord Jesus!*
>
> [21] *The grace of the Lord Jesus be with all. Amen.*

Let's say you received important parting words from someone you love or admire, maybe someone you've relied upon, who was about to move away and whom you wouldn't see for a long time—if ever again. Perhaps these parting words were critical instructions for an important task you would face alone and for which the person wanted you to be prepared.

How would you treat those words? Would you be on your phone, distracted while they were being imparted? Would you take notes to preserve and cherish them? And after the moment had passed, would you disregard the advice, or would you revisit its importance often?

That's what we have here in Revelation 22—Jesus' final words to His followers until the day He returns. Compared to any other, you would think Jesus' farewell message would be more important than any other, correct? It's ironic, then, that the parting instructions from the most important person in history might be among the most overlooked in Scripture.

WHAT WOULD JOHN'S READERS HAVE NOTICED?

Revelation's Likely Impact on the Early Church

Imagine what John's readers were thinking as they gathered to read and study Revelation in community. The faithful among the seven churches were living under intense persecution by Romans and Jews due to their loyalty to Jesus and the teachings of the apostles. They were in desperate need of encouragement. Others within those seven churches varied in their devotion, from those who had become completely cold and apostate to well-intentioned followers of Jesus with misaligned priorities. Those individuals needed revival.

From the moment Revelation was circulated among the churches, early Christians would have read the book in community, dissecting its meaning together and exploring its beautiful connections with the Old Testament. I imagine they discovered a profound new spiritual understanding of how the world functions. They understood how God's plan of redemption was unfolding. They saw the futility and ineffectiveness of earthly empires. They wouldn't be as easily deceived or distracted as the rest of the world. They perceived the dark forces behind this world, including this world's methods and motivations.

Repentance and Revival

I have no doubt a revival took place. The faithful were given renewed inspiration to remain loyal to the Lamb. Those whose priorities were out of line were confronted, and they made the necessary adjustments to their lives. Those who had grown complacent toward Jesus were convicted of sin and repented. The believers now had everything they needed to faithfully proclaim the gospel prophecy as they waited for Jesus to return.

WHAT WAS JESUS TELLING THE CHURCHES?

And here, at the very end of those visions, John's readers received one more message from the Lord, but not through an angel. This message came directly from our Jesus! They're the very last words anyone will hear from Jesus until the day He returns. Let's take a few minutes to reflect on the final words spoken to us by our Jesus until the day He comes back.

What did He tell us? "*I Am* coming soon . . ." (v. 12). And when He does, He will reward the faithful and judge the wicked. "*I Am* the Alpha and Omega . . ." (v. 13). He was identifying Himself as both the Creator (in Genesis) and the Judge (at Armageddon). As the Creator, Jesus was the beginning of all things. He was declaring ownership of His creation, as is affirmed by John 1:3: "All things were made through him, and without him was not any thing made that was made."

As the Judge, Jesus has the authority to examine the living and the dead and determine the ultimate destiny of humanity. John 5:22 tells us, "For the Father judges no one, but has given all judgment to the Son." And Paul described Him in 2 Timothy 4:1 as "Christ Jesus, who is to judge the living and the dead."

His authority to judge the wicked means that Jesus alone decides who can eat from the Tree of Life and who can't. Jesus sorts out those who will dwell in the new Jerusalem with Him from those who will be banished outside the city. The authority of Jesus to judge who is in each group is a constant reminder to us, the righteous, that we are no longer slaves to unrighteousness!

Jesus said He was the one who sent the angel to tell John these things. And what did the angel tell John? That *Revelation is for all the Churches* (v. 16), because He is the one who wants ALL the churches to know ALL that is revealed within. Jesus also said *the Spirit and the Church will proclaim* (v. 17), because it's the Holy Spirit through the bride (the church) who will proclaim the gospel prophecy and invite those with ears to hear to drink freely from the river of living water. How beautiful is that? Jesus was saying that we the church are now His chosen voice in this world. We proclaim these parting words.

Everyone who hears has been directly and specifically warned about how to handle these words. Over the years, many have polluted or denied Scripture so that it would serve their purposes instead of God's purpose. Those who add to the prophecy or create a new one will face judgment reserved for the wicked in this book. Those who neglect or ignore anything in it will be among the wicked banished outside the city.

Finally, Jesus reminded everyone that He is coming soon. John's readers desperately needed this assurance, because every day they were tempted to choose between survival and faithfulness to Jesus. That's why Jesus appeared to John—to remind the early Christians, and us, that remaining faithful to Jesus will be worth it.

What Is Jesus Telling Us Today?

These last words from Jesus should receive our full attention much more often than they do. I mean, why wouldn't we want to take sixty seconds at least once a week to go back and read them over again? They provide the inspiration to follow Jesus with urgency, anticipation, and confidence, because He's coming again! They provide motivation to constantly evaluate our passions and priorities, making necessary adjustments early on when we begin to stray, so that we can remain in full, faithful devotion to our Jesus and the rest of His church.

These last words from Jesus can immunize us from anxiety over the latest news headlines, political drama, or painful trials that come from living in this world. They retrain our focus on the good news of Jesus Christ. They remind us to keep the proclamation of the gospel prophecy a high priority. And let's be honest: when life gets hard, it's easy to get distracted by this world and let our proclamation fade.

John writes to us at the very beginning of Revelation 1:3, "Blessed is the one who reads aloud the words of this prophecy, and blessed are those who hear, and who keep what is written in it, for the time is near." Many Christians avoid Revelation because they are intimidated by its content. But if we have learned anything throughout this book, it's that we don't need to feel intimidated. In fact, Revelation is quite simple.

Revelation isn't about decoding hidden messages to predict future events, including Jesus' return. It isn't about identifying whether a vaccine or a microchip is the mark of the beast or which politician might be the Antichrist. It's about overcoming our own tendency to stray. It's about overcoming in a world that seems hell-bent on marginalizing, persecuting, and actually killing God's people. It's about having a steely resolve to follow the Lord at all costs. And it's about exposing the foolishness of placing hope in any human wisdom or worldly systems. No matter how promising they may appear, none of them will ever deliver lasting prosperity and peace.

We see Jesus actively marking and drawing His chosen into His kingdom, despite the chaos of the nations around us. Revelation proclaims Christ's victory over evil, His imminent return, and how the forces of evil know they are doomed! And we now know that once His kingdom is full, Jesus will return and eradicate evil, healing creation from the carnage of human history. Throughout Revelation, Jesus is saying, "Pay attention and stay faithful, because I am coming back!"

So, how should reading and studying Revelation have impacted us? How should we be different now than before? How can we be like the first-century church, which was, no doubt, transformed by it? Paul sums the answer up in Hebrews 10:24–25 when he writes, "Let us consider how to stir up one another to love and good works, not neglecting to meet together, as is the habit of some, but encouraging one another, and all the more as you see the Day drawing near."

For me, this journey has diminished my affection for this world and amplified my loyalty to Jesus and my church family. It has made me more committed and excited than ever for the work God is doing. It has taught me how important it is that, if we are truly followers of the Lamb, we shouldn't neglect gathering together. Instead, we will want to meet as often as possible and to love one another tenaciously. John speaks of this unity in Revelation 14:4 when he writes, "It is these who follow the Lamb wherever he goes."

I don't know about you, but I don't ever want to go back to seeing the world how I used to see it before I read Revelation. From that perspective, this last section, and *every* word of Revelation, should be cherished words until Jesus returns.

Waiting for Jesus to return won't be easy. Until then, His final words in Revelation 22:21 can inspire and encourage us every time we read them:

"The grace of the Lord Jesus be with all. Amen."

About the Author

Joe is the founding pastor of GraceLife Church (www.gracelifesrq.com) in Sarasota, Florida. He holds a Doctor of Divinity, a master's degree in theology, a bachelor's degree in biblical studies, and another in pastoral studies.

After beginning vocational ministry at age 18, Joe spent his first twenty-two years of ministry as a youth pastor and an outreach pastor in three different churches. He coached high school football and basketball for nearly twenty years.

In 2008, Joe founded Mobilepreacher.org (www.mobilepreacher.org), an organization designed to help seasoned ministers create ministries that might not fit inside traditional church walls. He is also the founder and executive director of the Nightlife Center in Sarasota (www.nightlifecenter.org).

Joe's books include *The GraceLife: What Philippians Teaches Us About Loving One Another Relentlessly; Growing to Love God's Word: An In-Depth Study of Psalm 119; Surviving in Egypt: The Life of Joseph;* and *Swimming Lessons: The Story of Jonah.*

Joe is husband to Laura and father to Ben. You can find him on Twitter (@mobilepreacher), Instagram (Mobilepreacher), and Facebook (facebook.com/Mobilepreacher).

About Renown Publishing

Renown Publishing is the proud publishing imprint of Speak It To Book, an elite team of publishing professionals devoted to helping you shape, write, and share your book. Renown has written, edited, and worked on hundreds of books (including New York Times, Wall Street Journal, and USA Today best-sellers, and the #1 book on all of Amazon).

We believe authentic stories are the torch of change-makers, and our mission is to collaborate with purpose-driven authors to create societal impact and redeem culture.

If you're the founder of a purpose-driven company, visit RenownPublishing.com.

If you're an aspiring author, visit SpeakItToBook.com.

REFERENCES

Notes

1. Bachmann, E. Theodore, ed. *Luther's Works: Word and Sacrament.* Vol. 35. Muhlenberg, 1960.

2. Strong, James. "G602 – apokalypsis." *The New Strong's Expanded Exhaustive Concordance of the Bible.* Red letter ed. Thomas Nelson, 2010.

3. Strong, "G602."

4. Perrotte, Ken. "'Leaveth All Hopes Behind' – Visiting Florida's Remote Fort Jefferson and the Story of Dr. Mudd." Outdoors Rambler. July 7, 2023 https://www.outdoorsrambler.com/post/leaveth-all-hopes-behind-visiting-florida-s-remote-fort-jefferson-and-the-story-of-dr-mudd.

5. Strong, James. "G3531 – nikolaitēs." *The New Strong's Expanded Exhaustive Concordance of the Bible.* Red letter ed. Thomas Nelson, 2010.

6. Thayer, Joseph Henry, Carl Ludwig Wilibald Grim, and Christian Gottlob Wilke. "G3531 – nikolaitēs." *Thayer's Greek-English Lexicon of the New Testament: Coded with Strong's Concordance Numbers.* Hendrickson, 1996.

7. Strong, James. "G3528 – nikaō." *The New Strong's Expanded Exhaustive Concordance of the Bible.* Red letter ed. Thomas Nelson, 2010.

8. For more information, see:

Fishwick, Duncan. *The Roman Imperial Cult in the Latin West: Studies in the Ruler Cult of the Western Provinces of the Roman Empire.* Vol. 1–4. Brill Academic, 1987–2005.

Wilken, Robert Louis. *The Christians as the Romans Saw Them.* Yale University Press, 2003.

9. *International Standard Bible Encyclopedia Online,* "Perga." Edited by James Orr. 1939. https://www.internationalstandardbible.com/P/perga.html.

10. *International Standard Bible Encyclopedia Online,* "Perga."

11. *Smith's Bible Dictionary,* "stones."

12. Strong, James. "G3528 – nikaō." *The New Strong's Expanded Exhaustive Concordance of the Bible.* Red letter ed. Thomas Nelson, 2010.

13. Fant, Clyde E., and Mitchell G. Reddish. "Philadelphia." *A Guide to Biblical Sites in Greece and Turkey.* Online ed. Oxford Academic, 2020. https://doi.org/10.1093/oso/9780195139174.003.0043.

14. Strawn, Brent E., "Moses' Shining or Horned Face?" The Torah.com. https://www.thetorah.com/article/moses-shining-or-horned-face.

15. *Oxford English Dictionary*, "myriad, n. & adj."

16. "The 4th Seal: The Pale or Green Horse." Bibleview. https://bibleview.org/en/bible/revelationoneone/4thseal/.

17. Fowler, Megan. "Christian Martyr Numbers Down by Half in a Decade. Or Are They?" *Christianity Today*. February 17, 2020. https://www.christianitytoday.com/ct/2020/march/christian-martyrs-numbers-down-by-half-in-decade-or-are-the.html.

18. "Christianity in China." BillionBibles.com. https://www.billionbibles.com/china/how-many-christians-in-china.html.

19. Chase, Mitchell L. "What Are the Seventy Weeks of Daniel? (Daniel 9)." Crossway. October 13, 2018. Adapted from *ESV Expository Commentary*. Vol. 7, *Daniel–Malachi*. Edited by Iain M. Duguid, James M. Hamilton Jr., and Jay Sklar. https://www.crossway.org/articles/what-are-the-seventy-weeks-of-daniel-daniel-9/.

20. Strong, James. "G1228 – diabolos." *The New Strong's Expanded Exhaustive Concordance of the Bible*. Red letter ed. Thomas Nelson, 2010.

21. Strong, James. "H7854 – śāṭān." *The New Strong's Expanded Exhaustive Concordance of the Bible*. Red letter ed. Thomas Nelson, 2010.

22. "Finding Nero: Third Roman Temple in Silchester May Have Been Part of Emperor's Vanity Project." University of Reading:

News Archive. November 22, 2017. https://archive.reading.ac.uk/news-events/2017/November/pr749147.html.

23. Draper, Rober. "Rethinking Nero." *National Geographic.* September 2014. https://www.nationalgeographic.com/magazine/article/emperor-nero.

24. Draper, "Rethinking Nero."

25. Tertullian. *Apologeticum* (lost text). Quoted in Eusebius, *Ecclesiastical History*, II.25.4. Translated by Arthur Cushman McGiffert.

26. Gopen, Nathan. "Pergamos: The Seat of Emperor Worship," Bible World Now. December 29, 2018. https://bibleworldnow.org/tour-sites/item/43-pergamos-the-seat-of-emperor-worship

27. Klauck, Hans-Josef. "Do They Never Come Back? 'Neo Redivivus' and the Apocalypse of John." *The Catholic Biblical Quarterly* 63, no. 4 (2001): p. 683–698. https://www.jstor.org/stable/43727253.

28. Strong, James. "G717 – *armagedōn*." *The New Strong's Expanded Exhaustive Concordance of the Bible.* Red letter ed. Thomas Nelson, 2010.

29. Strong, James. "G602 – apokalypsis." *The New Strong's Expanded Exhaustive Concordance of the Bible.* Red letter ed. Thomas Nelson, 2010.

30. Strong, James. "G717 – *armagedōn*." *The New Strong's Expanded Exhaustive Concordance of the Bible*. Red letter ed. Thomas Nelson, 2010.

31. Strong, James. "H894 – *bābel*." *The New Strong's Expanded Exhaustive Concordance of the Bible*. Red letter ed. Thomas Nelson, 2010.

32. Strong, James. "G4203 – *porneuō*." *The New Strong's Expanded Exhaustive Concordance of the Bible*. Red letter ed. Thomas Nelson, 2010.

33. Bradshaw, Robert I. "The City of Tyre in History and Prophecy." Biblical Studies.org.uk. 1999. https://biblicalstudies.org.uk/article_tyre.html.

34. Strong, James. "G315 – *anagkazō*." *The New Strong's Expanded Exhaustive Concordance of the Bible*. Red letter ed. Thomas Nelson, 2010.

35. Strong, James. "G2532 – kai." *The New Strong's Expanded Exhaustive Concordance of the Bible*. Red letter ed. Thomas Nelson, 2010.

www.ingramcontent.com/pod-product-compliance
Lightning Source LLC
Chambersburg PA
CBHW071732150426
43191CB00010B/1549